A Concise History
of Hong Kong

A Concise History of Hong Kong

John M. Carroll

ROWMAN & LITTLEFIELD PUBLISHERS, INC.
Lanham • Boulder • New York • Toronto • Plymouth, UK

ROWMAN & LITTLEFIELD PUBLISHERS, INC.

Published in the United States of America
by Rowman & Littlefield Publishers, Inc.
A wholly owned subsidiary of The Rowman & Littlefield Publishing Group, Inc.
4501 Forbes Boulevard, Suite 200, Lanham, Maryland 20706
www.rowmanlittlefield.com

Estover Road, Plymouth PL6 7PY, United Kingdom

British Library Cataloguing in Publication Information Available

Library of Congress Cataloging-in-Publication Data

Carroll, John M. (John Mark), 1961–
  A concise history of Hong Kong / John M. Carroll.
      p. cm.—(Critical issues in history)
  Includes bibliographical references.
  ISBN-13: 978-0-7425-3421-6 (cloth : alk. paper)
  ISBN-10: 0-7425-3421-9 (cloth : alk. paper)
  ISBN-13: 978-0-7425-3422-3 (pbk. : alk. paper)
  ISBN-10: 0-7425-3422-7 (pbk. : alk. paper)
  1. Hong Kong (China)—History. I. Title. DS796.H757C37 2007
  951.25'04—dc22

Printed in the United States of America

∞™ The paper used in this publication meets the minimum requirements of
American National Standard for Information Sciences—Permanence of Paper
for Printed Library Materials, ANSI/NISO Z39.48-1992.

Contents

Acknowledgments

Completing this book took approximately as long as the Sino-British negotiations of 1982–1984, which established the terms for Hong Kong's reversion to Chinese sovereignty in 1997. I am particularly grateful to the other scholars whose work I have referred to throughout the book. Consulting editor Donald Critchlow encouraged me to contribute to the Critical Issues in History series, and I would like to thank the editorial staff at Rowman and Littlefield, especially Susan McEachern and Sarah Wood, for their assistance and patience. A Faculty Research Initiative Grant from Saint Louis University enabled me to complete the early chapters of the book. Alan Smart of the University of Calgary, Michael Houf of Texas A&M University at Kingsville, Colin Day of Hong Kong University Press, and Christopher Munn all offered invaluable comments on earlier drafts, and Charles Parker of Saint Louis University and Steven Miles of Washington University provided encouragement and moral support. Tim Ko kindly supplied three photographs from his personal collection. Space prevents me from listing all the many friends and family members who have helped along the way, but I would be remiss if I did not express my sincere thanks to my wife and daughter, Katie Monteil and Emma Carroll-Monteil.

Note on Romanization and Sources

Chinese is written with characters (sometimes called ideographs) rather than with an alphabet, which means that personal and place names must be romanized (transliterated into Roman letters corresponding to the sounds that their characters represent) for non-Chinese readers. Until the 1970s, however, there was no single accepted standard of romanization for Mandarin, or Putonghua, the standard dialect of mainland China, let alone for the many nonstandard dialects spoken across China. Thus, for example, until recently the cities known today as Beijing and Guangzhou were generally known in the English-speaking world as Peking and Canton, respectively; the Muslim admiral and explorer Zheng He who sailed the seas in the early 1400s was Cheng Ho; and the Communist leader Mao Zedong was Mao Tse-tung.

Most people in Hong Kong have historically spoken not Mandarin but rather Cantonese, which lacks a standard romanization system. Rather than convert Cantonese personal and place names to the Hanyu pinyin system of romanization used today in China, I have retained contemporary usage (for example, Ho Kai rather than He Qi and Tung Wah Hospital instead of Donghua Hospital); whenever appropriate, pinyin equivalents are provided in the index. Names of people in mainland China generally follow the pinyin system, except for figures such as Sun Yat-sen and Chiang Kai-shek, who are already known to many readers by other romanizations. The names of treaties, which are especially significant for Hong Kong's history, are listed according to contemporary standards (for example, the Treaty of Nanking), with pinyin (Nanjing) in the index. With the exception of Canton as it was written in colonial documents and the Hong Kong press and until very recently would have been known to English-speaking Chinese, place names in mainland China are in pinyin (Beijing rather than Peking).

The research for this history of Hong Kong is based primarily on colonial records, local newspapers and journals, and a wide range of English- and Chinese-language secondary sources. Because the book is aimed primarily at students and general readers, however, notes have been kept to a minimum. Thus, only quotes from widely available English-language secondary sources or edited documentary collections are cited in the notes that follow each chapter. A more extensive bibliography, including recent Chinese-language sources from Hong Kong and mainland China, follows the epilogue.

Hong Kong and Vicinity

Map of Hong Kong

Introduction

Hong Kong in History

On January 25, 1841, a British naval party landed and raised the British flag on the northern shore of Hong Kong, a small island located in the Pearl River Delta in southern China. The next day, the commander of the British expeditionary force took formal possession of the island in the name of the British Crown. Except for three and a half years during World War II when Hong Kong was part of the short-lived Japanese Empire, the British occupation would last until midnight on July 1, 1997, whereupon Hong Kong became a Special Administrative Region of the People's Republic of China. As newspapers throughout China proudly declared, Hong Kong was "home at last."

Technically speaking, the name "Hong Kong" (which means "Fragrant Harbor" in Chinese) refers to Hong Kong Island, ceded by the Qing dynasty to Great Britain "in perpetuity" in 1842 under the Treaty of Nanking. Located about 80 miles southeast of the city of Canton (known today as Guangzhou), this tiny island is only 11 miles from east to west and 2 to 5 miles from north to south. The name "Hong Kong," however, is generally used to cover a larger area with three main parts: Hong Kong Island; Kowloon Peninsula, consisting of 8 square miles and ceded to Britain in 1860 under the Convention of Peking; and the New Territories, an area of 365 square miles leased to Britain for ninety-nine years in 1898 that includes approximately 230 outlying islands. Although Hong Kong has no natural resources to speak of, its harbor, deep and sheltered by steep granite hills, is one of the best in the world. With a population of around seven million and very little good land for building, Hong Kong is one of the most densely populated places on earth. Hot and humid for much of the year, it is hardly surprising that some early British colonists wondered why their government ever took Hong Kong Island in the first place.

Over time, Hong Kong would become a booming port and thriving metropolis. Until recently, however, historians paid little attention to Hong Kong. Scholars of British colonialism concentrated mainly on Africa and India, while a handful of locally based British historians focused primarily on Hong Kong's colonial administration—especially the roles played by various British governors and civil servants—practically overlooking the Chinese who comprised around 98 percent of the colony's population. And until the years leading up to the transfer to Chinese sovereignty in 1997, mainland Chinese historians all but ignored Hong Kong. Only one university in China had a research institute dedicated to studying Hong Kong. Even for the few scholars on the mainland who studied Hong Kong, the colony had little intrinsic importance beyond its significance as the fruit of British imperialism and colonialism and as a base for the Western imperialists' invasion of China in the 1800s.

In the past twenty years, scholars—mostly based in Hong Kong—have reconstructed a much more complex and nuanced history that considers both Hong Kong's colonial features and the contributions of local Chinese to its historical development. Why have historians outside of Hong Kong taken so long to take Hong Kong seriously? The answer says less about Hong Kong than about the way historians approach their subjects. In the United States, the call for a China-centered history of China has led to a tendency to downplay the international aspects of China's history. In China, one reason for this neglect is the bias against acknowledging foreign influences, except for negative ones. Another reason is the shame of colonization and Hong Kong's commercial success: like Taiwan, capitalist Hong Kong until recently served as an embarrassing counterpoint to Communist China. The traditional Chinese disdain for emigrants, who were often seen as either criminals or unfilial scoundrels for leaving the motherland and abandoning their families, is another reason. Finally, people in northern China, where political power has traditionally been centered, have often looked down on southern China and its inhabitants.

Compared to cities such as Beijing, China's capital, Hong Kong may seem politically peripheral. Compared to cities such as Shanghai, the bustling metropolis once considered the "Paris of the Orient," Hong Kong may seem commercially peripheral. Hong Kong was arguably the most important place in China for more than 150 years, however, precisely because it was not politically part of China. Sun Yat-sen, the man who led the revolution that toppled the last Chinese dynasty in 1911, was educated in colonial Hong Kong. The father of modern Chinese law, Wu Tingfang, was raised and educated in Hong Kong, where he was better known as Ng Choy. From its early colonial days, Hong Kong served as a haven for Chinese refugees: during the Taiping Rebellion (1851–1864), after the republican revolution of 1911 and throughout the turbulent 1920s, after the outbreak of the Sino-Japanese War in 1937, and after the Communist revolution of 1949.

Hong Kong has been China's most critical link to the rest of the world since the Silk Road and the Mongols. Until recent decades, about 90 percent of all Chinese emigrants went through Hong Kong. From the 1960s until the 1980s, Hong Kong exported goods throughout the world. More recently, it has attained worldwide acclaim for its innovative cinema. To people in China, Hong Kong is even more significant for its imports. The Chinese who returned to China from North America or Southeast Asia almost always came through Hong Kong. Money from overseas Chinese was remitted through Hong Kong. After the Communist revolution of 1949, capitalist Hong Kong played an important and ironic role in building China's Socialist economy: as a window to the outside world, as a center for remittances from overseas Chinese that provided valuable foreign exchange, and as a base for importing goods that China could not produce. Hong Kong was of particular use to the Chinese during the Korean War, as scarce goods such as gas, kerosene, and penicillin were smuggled in during the American and United Nations embargoes. Hong Kong investors were also partly responsible for China's dramatic economic transformation that began in the late 1970s and continues to this day.

Especially because Hong Kong has reverted recently to Chinese sovereignty, scholars today usually emphasize the Chineseness of Hong Kong. To be sure, Hong Kong's geographical location meant that its history was affected primarily by events in China, especially in Guangdong province just across the border. Hong Kong's population was always overwhelmingly Chinese, while the proximity to China meant that Chinese affairs mattered more than British affairs to most residents. But Hong Kong had a particularly complex relationship with mainland China. As a popular Chinese saying went, "when there's trouble in Hong Kong, go to China; when there's trouble in China, go back to Hong Kong." For most of Hong Kong's colonial history, however, the trouble was almost always in China, which meant that Hong Kong was often at the receiving end of a massive wave of immigrants from China. Hong Kong depended on these immigrants for their labor and capital, yet colonial Hong Kong contributed so much to China's nation-building that many observers in the early 1990s predicted that Hong Kong would continue to change China after the handover in 1997, rather than vice versa.

Not only is Hong Kong an important part of modern Chinese history, it is also part of British colonial history. Despite Hong Kong's Chinese influences, we should not underestimate the effect of British colonial rule. Colonialism transformed Hong Kong's historical development, shaped the form of the encounters between the Chinese and British, and determined power relations between them. Simply put, Hong Kong would not have become the place it did had it not been a British colony for over 150 years. Chinese criminals were often transported to other British colonies, such as the Straits Settlements in

Malaya and the island of Labuan off the coast of Borneo. British colonists always kept abreast of affairs in other colonies, particularly in India where many had family ties or business relations. Especially in the mid-1800s, Hong Kong was tightly connected to India—through trade, primarily cotton and opium, and by a regular passenger ship service between the two colonies. In the early days, troops in the British garrison were paid in rupees, which were widely used in the colony until the 1860s. Until the establishment of the Hong Kong and Shanghai Bank in 1864, most of the Western banks in Hong Kong and China were branch offices of Anglo-Indian banks. Indigenous Chinese architecture was the norm in rural areas of the region until the twentieth century, but the ubiquitous "Chinese" architectural style that characterized early urban Hong Kong—the shop with living quarters upstairs and a verandah—was imported to Hong Kong from another British colony, Singapore, which in turn was affected by older colonial cities in India, such as Bombay, Calcutta, and Madras.

Hong Kong's history was also greatly influenced by it colonial administrators. Until the early 1970s, governors were selected from the British colonial service and had served in other colonies before coming to Hong Kong. Alexander Grantham, governor from 1947 to 1957, had worked for the Hong Kong government in the 1920s and 1930s and had served in Bermuda, Jamaica, Nigeria, Fiji, and the South Pacific before returning to Hong Kong. These governors' experiences in other colonies often shaped their attitudes toward Hong Kong. In the 1950s and 1960s, Hong Kong received a group of colonial "retreads," second-generation colonial servants transferred from the recently independent British colonies and dependencies in Africa, South Asia, and the Middle East. From top to bottom, Hong Kong's government was a colonial one. For example, as late as the 1960s, the Hong Kong police force was organized along traditional colonial lines. Most of its senior officers were expatriate veterans from Africa, Malaya, and Palestine, while junior officers were generally Chinese.

Hong Kong is also important for understanding comparative colonial history. Many scholars argue that much of the world is still colonial, or neocolonial, in that the Euro-American nations have historically derived much of their wealth and power at the expense of the less fortunate African, Asian, and Latin American nations. Much of Africa, carved up by the European powers in the late 1800s, remains impoverished and torn by ethnic violence. India, once Britain's "Jewel in the Crown" and now second in population only to China, is also plagued by poverty and by religious and ethnic violence. But any generalizations about colonialism must consider how Australia, Canada, New Zealand, and the United States—all formerly British settler colonies—enjoy a higher standard of living than Britain (although living standards for much of these nations' indigenous populations remain very low). Living standards in Hong Kong and Singapore, also once a British colony, are also generally higher than in Britain, just as living conditions in Taiwan and South Korea, both formerly Japanese colonies, are also very high. Indian, Pakistani, and West Indian teams frequently beat the British at cricket, a sport bequeathed to them by the British, while Australians, New Zealanders, and South Africans often defeat them in rugby, another British legacy.

Whereas historians used to focus mainly on either the beneficial or the damaging aspects of colonialism, today they offer a much more nuanced view. We realize, for example, that precolonial societies were not always the peaceful and harmonious societies that anticolonial nationalists have often made them out to be. We understand that colonialism was made possible with collaboration from local peoples, as it was throughout Hong Kong's colonial history. Whereas colonialism was once seen as a traumatic experience for native peoples, it is now understood more as a layer of encounters, some based on bewilderment but others based on mutual understanding. Repressive and racist as it was, colonialism in Hong Kong was not always confusing or disruptive for the local Chinese population. Mutual fear of the chaos that engulfed China for much of the nineteenth and twentieth centuries as well as shared commitment to economic freedom and political stability often provided an idiom that both the British colonialists and their Chinese subjects could understand. Colonialism in Hong Kong was thus based as much on similarities and affinities as on otherness and difference.

Historians rarely pay much attention to this aspect of either Hong Kong history or American history, but America has also had a special interest in Hong Kong since the early 1800s. American opium traders had a significant presence in early colonial Hong Kong, and the colony was a major terminus for America's transpacific trade in the nineteenth and twentieth centuries, importing goods such as ginseng, flour, lumber, and kerosene and exporting commodities such as silk, tea, rattan, and human labor. Although many Americans, especially during and after World War II, viewed the idea of empire with distaste, they became less critical during the Cold War, when colonialism appeared preferable to the spread of Communism. Hong Kong thus became of great use to the United States as a listening post on China, a base for anti-Communist propaganda, and a popular destination for rest and recreation for American servicemen during the Korean War and the Vietnam War. After the Korean War, Hong Kong supplied the American consumer market with manufactured goods such as clothing, plastic flowers, and wigs, many produced in factories funded by American capital. The establishment of the U.S. Chamber of Commerce in 1969 demonstrated America's increasing involvement in Hong Kong's economy, and by the late 1970s the number of Americans in Hong Kong had begun to surpass the number of British expatriates. Even though the economic reforms in mainland China have enabled American firms to expand their operations there, many of these firms still have a large presence in Hong Kong, while the American government is determined to ensure that the Chinese government keeps its promise to abide by the one country, two systems model that has governed Hong Kong since its reversion to Chinese sovereignty in 1997. Hong Kong's reputation as a free port with low taxes and minimal government intervention in its economy has also drawn the praise of free-market economists and conservatives such as noted economist Milton Friedman.

Lying at the strategic intersection of Chinese and British imperial history, Hong Kong also has its own history and identity, replete with contradictions, problems, and idiosyncrasies that have shaped its present. Some of the contradictions and problems are endemic to any capitalist society. For example, although Hong Kong has some extraordinarily rich people, they make up a tiny percentage of the population. Other contradictions are legacies of colonialism. Despite a relatively high degree of personal freedom, for example, until the late 1980s and early 1990s Hong Kong had no political representation or political parties. Some of the idiosyncrasies result from Hong Kong as an encounter between China and Britain, creating what is arguably the most cosmopolitan city in Asia. (Some would say that the honor goes to Shanghai, as it would have in the 1920s and 1930s.) Small Chinese shops sit comfortably on streets named after British royalty and colonial administrators, while British law, Christianity, and modern Western medicine coexist happily with traditional Chinese medicine, several hundred Chinese temples, a plethora of religious festivals and ceremonies, and a fervent belief in feng shui (geomancy, or the balance between humans and nature) applied in even the most modern Western-style buildings and in the new Disneyland that opened in 2005. Especially noticeable in a region with so little open space is another British legacy and Hong Kong's most popular pastime: horse racing in Happy Valley on Hong Kong Island and Sha Tin in the New Territories, eagerly embraced by the local population and protected under the one country, two systems model.

Hong Kong's historical relationship with China and Britain also has its human legacies. This relationship produced a community of Chinese residents who have often distinguished themselves as a special group of Chinese and as different from their counterparts on the mainland. Although many scholars have seen this sense of Hong Kong identity as a relatively recent phenomenon, it took root in the late 1800s when the Chinese in Hong Kong contrasted the order and prosperity there against the political chaos and economic backwardness of China. The Chinese and expatriate communities of Hong Kong still live largely separate lives as they have for more than 150 years, with most expatriates rarely bothering to learn how to speak Chinese. All expatriates come into frequent contact with Chinese people at work, but it is still not uncommon for Chinese to have never met any Westerners, to whom they frequently refer as "foreign devils."

Just as Hong Kong's history between China and Britain had its own unique characteristics, so did its decolonization in 1997. Hardly a colonial embarrassment, the region had become more economically advanced than most independent countries. Apart from being a major financial center, by the end of British rule Hong Kong held the world's seventh-largest foreign reserves and was the world's third-largest exporter of clothing—no mean feat given the region's small size. It had the second-highest per capita gross domestic product in Asia (after Japan), having passed that of Australia, Britain, and Canada. Rather than being granted independence, Hong Kong was turned over to a considerably more authoritarian government than the colonial one that had ruled for so long, a point that became glaringly obvious after the brutal crackdown in Beijing's Tiananmen Square in June 1989. Nor did the Communist government of China, dedicated though it was to ending imperialism around the globe, ever try to liberate Hong Kong. The main cause for the termination of colonial rule was also very different than in most colonies. The impetus was neither internal demand (far from it, for most Hong Kong residents preferred British colonial rule to Chinese rule) nor international pressure. Rather, the decision came from the Chinese government, which in 1972 had declared Hong Kong's future a purely internal Chinese matter to be resolved when the government decided the time was right. By the time the Sino-British Joint Declaration on Hong Kong's future was signed in 1984, the British Empire, over which the sun never set, had long faded into the imperial sunset. China, however, was on its way to becoming a world power.

1

Early Colonial Hong Kong

The Chinese government's official position toward Hong Kong's history is spelled out succinctly in The Basic Law of the Hong Kong Special Administrative Region of the People's Republic of China, the miniconstitution that has governed Hong Kong since its reversion to Chinese sovereignty in July 1997: "Hong Kong has been part of the territory of China since ancient times; it was occupied by Britain after the Opium War in 1840." Whereas Chinese historians often stress how Hong Kong has played a vital role in Chinese history since time memorial, until recently British sources generally dismissed the idea of Hong Kong as having any real history until the British arrived. A guidebook written in 1893 by a local British resident insisted that until 1841 Hong Kong "existed only as a plutonic island of uninviting sterility, apparently capable only of supporting the lowest form of organisms."[1] Many years later, journalist Richard Hughes, who popularized the idea of Hong Kong as a "borrowed place living on borrowed time," wrote that "Hong Kong did not exist, so it was necessary to invent it."[2]

Precolonial Hong Kong was not the "barren island" or "barren rock" that British historians, colonial officials, and journalists have often described. Archaeological findings from the Hong Kong region date back almost six thousand years, to the Neolithic period. According to Chinese historical records, southern China was settled by the Hundred Yue tribes, who were more closely related to Malays, Vietnamese, or Polynesians than to Han Chinese, the ethnic majority of China, and who are believed to have made the rock carvings still preserved in several local sites. The Southern Yue Kingdom ruled Hong Kong until 111 BCE, when it fell to the army of Wu Di, emperor of the Han dynasty. A tomb uncovered at Lei Cheng Uk, Kowloon, in 1955 is believed to be from the Han period. Over the next millennium, partly because of the warfare and disunity that characterized much of that period and partly because of the economic opportunities in southern China, Chinese increasingly moved from north to south, including to Kowloon, the peninsula across the harbor from Hong Kong Island. Chinese historical records frequently mention Kowloon as the place where the emperor of the Southern Song dynasty sought refuge after China fell to the Mongols.

During the Mongol Yuan dynasty (1276–1368), Hong Kong was inhabited mainly by farmers, fisherfolk, and pirates, some of them Song loyalists. By the end of the Yuan dynasty, the Hong Kong region had been settled mainly by seven large families who owned much of the land. Throughout the Ming dynasty (1368–1644), settlers from Guangdong and Fujian, the two prominent coastal provinces of southeastern China, migrated to Kowloon. Some of these settlers moved across the harbor to Hong Kong Island, but the island remained lightly populated, with only a few villages scattered along its southern coast. During the Qing dynasty (1644–1911), when China was ruled by the Manchus, Hong Kong became more closely integrated with the rest of China. Fishing boats from other parts of southern China used the local harbors. The island was part of Xin'an county, and an assistant magistrate from Kowloon visited the island occasionally to collect land taxes and register fishing vessels, leaving local headmen or village elders in charge of local government. In the early 1800s, the island was the stronghold of the infamous pirate Zhang Baozai, who used the island's peak as a lookout for his buccaneering exploits.

Not only was Hong Kong hardly a "barren island" when the British arrived in the late 1830s, but Hong Kong's people were far from the "handful of fishermen and pirates" they have often been described as. As historian and former colonial official James Hayes explains, farming was the "principle occupation." The island had "several villages of some size, as well as hamlets, and a few larger coastal villages which served as market towns for the villages and as home ports for a permanent boat population and visiting craft." Hayes concludes that "long before 1841," the inhabitants of Hong Kong Island had "settled into the routine of a settled life. Tied to their fields and houses, and to their businesses and daily occupations, they had established institutions of the kind that is usual in Chinese communities, including the shrines and temples that were the object of periodic and special rites through the calendar year." Hong Kong's temples alone, argues Hayes, prove that "the island was certainly well-established in settled communities long before 1841."[3]

THE WEST RETURNS TO CHINA

The rise of the British presence in China, which led to the colonization of Hong Kong, is part of the longer story of European expansion that began in the late 1400s and lasted until after World War I. Merchants came to China from Europe during the Tang (618–907) and Yuan dynasties via the Silk Road, the overland trade routes connecting the northwest frontiers of China with the Middle East. Under the Pax Mongolica, when China and much of Asia were ruled by the Mongols, many Europeans visited China to trade, some even working for the Yuan government. After the collapse of the Yuan in the mid-1300s, however, China had little contact with Europe.

Western merchants reentered the Chinese scene in the early 1500s when the Portuguese began trading along the southern China coast, a commercial region with a long tradition of overseas and intra-Chinese trade. Partly as a reward for their help in suppressing piracy and partly as a way to confine them to a specific locale, the Ming government allowed the Portuguese in 1557 to establish a permanent settlement at Macau (now written Macao), a small peninsula to the southwest of Hong Kong. Although the Qing banned overseas trade, Macau soon became the center of a "hemispheric exchange of commodities."[4] Chinese goods such as silk, tea, and porcelain made their way from Macau to Europe in Portuguese galleons in exchange for silver from mines in Japan and the Americas. Through the efforts of European missionaries such as Matteo Ricci, Macau also became a base for the introduction of Christianity and Western learning to China.

By the 1600s, Britain was challenging Portugal and the Netherlands as the major European trading power in Asia. As British ships eventually made their way into Chinese waters, in 1654 the Portuguese allowed the British East India Company (EIC) to land in Macau. After the Qing ban on overseas trade was lifted in 1684, British merchants used Macau as their headquarters to trade in the harbor at Huangpu, a riverine island known to Europeans as Whampoa and located some ten miles from Canton, the most important seaport in southern China. In 1771 the EIC was allowed to open a post in Canton, which in 1759 the Qing government had declared the only legal Chinese port for overseas trade.

Under what became known as the Canton System, or the Cohong System, China's international trade was conducted through a group of Chinese hongs, or merchant houses, specially authorized and licensed by the Qing government. (The word "cohong" comes from *gonghang*, meaning "officially authorized firms.") Western merchants traded in Canton from October to March, confined to factories, or manufactories, rented from the Chinese hongs. Named after similar centers in British India where the EIC's agents or factors operated, these were the warehouses and residences along the riverfront outside Canton. During the off-season, from April to September, the merchants returned to trade in Macau. Although the foreigners frequently complained about the restrictions and conditions in Canton, these inconveniences were minor compared to the fortunes that could be made in silk, porcelain, tea, and, later, opium. Even though several British diplomatic missions in the late 1700s and early 1800s failed to secure greater trading concessions and diplomatic rights from the Qing government, by the early 1840s almost one hundred foreign trading firms were trading on the southern China coast.

British historians have often stressed how the acquisition of Hong Kong, like much of the expansion of the British Empire, was almost an accident. Britain, so the standard argument goes, took Hong Kong not to obtain more territory but rather to promote and protect its commercial interests in China. Hong Kong, explained Secretary for the Colonies Lord Stanley in 1843, was "occupied not with a view to colonization, but for diplomatic, commercial and military purposes."[5] G. B. Endacott, until the 1970s the foremost historian of Hong Kong, wrote, "A healthy trade demanded settled conditions, suppression of robbery, guarantee of contract and of impartial justice. Since the Chinese were thought to be unable to provide these conditions, the British had to provide them. This is fundamental to understanding any history of Hong Kong."[6]

Hong Kong was indeed founded primarily as an imperial outpost rather than to civilize or Christianize its Chinese residents. After the British first occupied Hong Kong in 1839 during the First Opium War with China, few British officials considered seriously the idea of Hong Kong as a permanent colony. (It would not formally become a colony until June 26, 1843.) Even after the British took formal control of Hong Kong in 1841 under the short-lived Convention of Chuenpi (which both sides considered so unsatisfactory that some scholars wonder if the treaty was even signed), British officials held differing and often conflicting views about Hong Kong's potential. Foreign Secretary Lord Palmerston did not think the island worthwhile, while his successor, Lord Aberdeen, believed that keeping Hong Kong would be too expensive and would harm Britain's relations with China and other European countries. However, Charles Elliot, British superintendent of trade in China and first administrator of colonial Hong Kong, was convinced that Hong Kong would be the perfect base for British commercial, military, and political operations in China. Henry Pottinger, Elliot's successor and the first governor of Hong Kong, was also convinced that Britain needed a base on the China coast. Although he was initially skeptical, Pottinger eventually agreed with Elliot on Hong Kong's commercial and military value. In general, officials in London were much less enthusiastic about Hong Kong's worth than were those based in Hong Kong and southern China.

The British acquisition of Hong Kong, however, was no accident; it was "the outcome of a long crusade by British free traders to promote trade with China."[7] British interest in a reliable trading base on the China coast dated back almost as far as the British presence in Asia. Unlike the other European maritime empires of Holland, Portugal, and Spain that had bases in Batavia (today's Jakarta), Macau, and Manila, respectively, Britain had no significant territory in Asia outside of India. In 1815 an EIC official in Canton called for Britain to establish a base as close as possible to the capital at Beijing. After 1821, when Canton authorities drove the illegal opium trade from Whampoa, British traders set up shop on several coastal islands, including Hong Kong. In August 1834, Lord Napier, British superintendent of trade in China, suggested that a small British force should take possession of Hong Kong Island to secure European trading rights in China. James Matheson, head of Jardine and Matheson, the largest British firm operating in the region, urged the British government to establish a base for protecting British trading interests in southern China.

Although several other islands, including Taiwan (known to most foreigners as Formosa), were generally considered more attractive choices, British traders in Canton preferred the deep-water harbor of Hong Kong, sheltered from typhoons and easily accessible from both China and the open sea. Robert Fortune, an English botanist and adventurer who visited Hong Kong in 1843 and 1845, summarized the virtues of Hong Kong's harbor: "Hong-kong bay is one of the finest which I have ever seen: it is eight or ten miles in length, and irregular in breadth; in some places two, and in other six miles wide, having excellent anchorage all over it, and perfectly free from hidden dangers. It is completely sheltered by the mountains of Hong-kong on the south, and by those of the main land of China on the opposite shore; land-locked, in fact, on all sides; so that the shipping can ride out the heaviest gales with perfect safety."[8]

"FOREIGN MUD": OPIUM AND WAR

Britain acquired Hong Kong during the First Opium War (1839–1842). Ostensibly a conflict over the contraband trade in opium, the war was as much about trading rights and diplomatic representation. By the late 1700s, the volume of trade between China and Britain was tilted in China's favor; the British had little more than silver to offer the Chinese for their silk and tea. The British responded by importing opium, grown and prepared in British India. Although opium had been introduced to China by Arab traders almost one thousand years earlier and was also cultivated in southern China, it was used primarily for medicinal purposes. By the 1700s, however, it was being smoked mainly as a narcotic. When the Qing reaffirmed its ban on importing opium in 1796, the EIC responded by selling its opium to country traders—British, Indian, Parsee, and Armenian traders—who then imported the drug to China in small, private "country ships." Although importing opium was prohibited again by Qing imperial edict in 1800, the trade thrived. In small, fast launches known to foreigners as smug boats and to Chinese as scrambling dragons or fast crabs, the drug could be transported quickly beyond the Chinese coast. William Hunter, an American trader, recalled that the opium trade was "an easy and agreeable business for the foreign *exile* who shared in it at Canton. His sales were pleasantness and his remittances were peace. Transactions seemed to partake of the nature of the drug; they imparted a soothing frame of mind with three per cent. commission, one per cent. on returns, and no bad debts!"[9]

As the demand for opium increased, British merchants became frustrated with both the constraints of the Canton System and the Qing ban on opium. When the EIC's monopoly over British trade with China ended in 1834, the British government dispatched Lord Napier to supervise British trade with China. Whereas the EIC traders had dealt with the superintendent of the Guangdong maritime customs, Napier was determined to deal directly with Qing officials as diplomatic equals. Instead, Napier was held hostage in the Canton factories until he agreed to leave China, an incident that might have led to confrontation between Britain and China had Napier not died shortly after from malaria.

The problem from the British perspective was both commercial and political: increasing trade with China, retaining some semblance of diplomatic equality, and preserving prestige. The problem from the Chinese side was both more immediate and more complex. Because taxes were paid in silver, the outflow of silver used to pay for opium had the potential to create a vicious cycle of weakened livelihoods, decreased state revenues, and domestic unrest. Acknowledging Britain as a diplomatic equal would tarnish the Qing emperor's reputation as the Son of Heaven, not just in China but throughout Asia. As the number of Chinese opium addicts soared, already scarce land was being wasted on poppy cultivation. How could the emperor allow this trade to continue without jeopardizing his moral claims to the throne and to being "the mother and father of the people"? Some Qing officials argued that the worst of the problems (including the corruption encouraged by the high price of opium as contraband) could be ended by legalizing the opium trade, but in 1838 the Daoguang emperor decreed that the trade in this "foreign mud" must end.

Many British officials agreed that the Qing government had every right to prohibit the opium trade. But some Europeans were convinced that the Chinese themselves had caused the demand for opium. An early European historian of Hong Kong later insisted how "the taste for opium" was "a congenital disease of the Chinese race."[10] And very few Westerners in China took the Qing emperor's edicts seriously. The opium trade had been tolerated for so long, and the Qing government simply appeared too weak to restrict it. William Hunter, the American trader, recalled how "the immunity so long enjoyed with the inherent weakness of the Chinese Government, caused foreigners to believe that any serious attempt to put a stop to the

European engraving of the First Opium War. Courtesy of the Prints and Photographs Division, Library of Congress, Washington, D.C.

trade was simply impracticable. The Imperial edicts were considered as so much waste paper. Opium was imported and sold, while the 'oozing out of fine silver' went on as usual."[11] However, in March 1839 Lin Zexu, an official recently appointed by the Qing to end the opium trade, launched an antiopium campaign in Guangdong province. Lin subsequently took hostage some 350 foreigners—among them British Superintendent of Trade Charles Elliot—in Canton and confiscated their opium stocks.

When war broke out between Britain and China in autumn 1839, the Royal Navy quickly blockaded Canton. Although he would go down in history for later dismissing Hong Kong as little more than "a barren island with hardly a house upon it," Foreign Secretary Lord Palmerston declared his intention to seize Hong Kong. On January 25, 1841, Captain Edward Belcher landed with a small group on the northern shore of the island and raised the British flag at what would become known as Possession Point. The next day the naval commander of the British expeditionary force, Gordon Bremer, took formal possession in the name of the British Crown. In February 1841, Elliot tried to attract Chinese and foreign traders to Hong Kong with guarantees of free trade and protection under the British flag for Europeans and Chinese and the right to practice Chinese customs and religions. One year later, the British Superintendency of Trade was moved from Macau to Hong Kong, prompting British firms to do the same.

The First Opium War ended officially with the Treaty of Nanking, signed on August 29, 1842. Apart from imposing on China a huge indemnity, ending the cohong monopoly, fixing rates for customs duties, and opening five Chinese ports to foreign trade and residence, this treaty ceded the island of Hong Kong to Britain "in perpetuity." It also granted the British the right of "extraterritoriality" (meaning that British subjects in China would be tried by British judges), and the "most-favored-nation" clause guaranteed that Britain would receive the same concessions subsequently granted to any other nation. This treaty is known in China as the first of the many so-called unequal treaties forced on a weak China after military defeats by Western powers in the nineteenth century. Treaties ending wars are invariably unequal, but these treaties are particularly notorious in Chinese history as markers of the Century of Shame that lasted until the establishment of the People's Republic of China in 1949.

COLLABORATION

The military victory that gave the British the upper hand in the Treaty of Nanking was made possible not just by British military superiority but also by Chinese collaborators. The British received help from the Chinese before and during the First Opium War and in the building of their new colony. Even though authorities in Canton ordered the Chinese in Hong Kong to resist the "barbarians," the British encountered practically no resistance when they first occupied Hong Kong Island. A British military surgeon wrote that the inhabitants of Hong Kong "appear to be industrious and obliging. . . . From all accounts they seem in general to have been very peaceably disposed; nor did they exhibit any marked approbation or disapprobation, on their transfer to the British sway."[12] In the early 1900s, Chow Shouson, a wealthy businessman and the first Chinese member of the colonial Executive Council, used to boast how his ancestors, who had lived on the island before the British arrived, had helped the British post Elliot's proclamation that Hong Kong would be a free port.

No single reason adequately explains why some Chinese were so eager to help the British. Nor did the British find Chinese collaborators everywhere during the First Opium War. For example, the British had great difficulty obtaining supplies in the early part of the war, especially during their unsuccessful and short-lived occupation of Zhoushan (known to foreigners as Chusan), a small island near Shanghai on the China coast where the local Chinese refused to cooperate. Some collaborators justified their actions through their resentment of the Manchus. Others were from subethnic groups who had long cooperated with Europeans in the waters off the southern China coast. For most of these collaborators, however, working with the British was primarily a matter of wealth and power.

One colorful collaborator was Loo Aqui, who rose to prominence through piracy and provisioning foreign vessels. Loo was a Tanka, one of the minority ethnic groups that lived along the southern China coast. Ostracized by other Chinese, these so-called egg families lived in communities of small boats, making their livelihood from fishing, shipping, and provisioning. Like many other fishing communities, they often resorted to piracy, especially when economic conditions were rough. From the earliest days of the foreign presence in Canton, Tankas had traded with foreign merchants and served as middlemen, even though the Qing government prohibited this on pain of death. During the war, some Tankas provided British naval and merchant vessels with supplies. Loo was later rewarded for provisioning the British forces with a large plot of valuable land in the Lower Bazaar, where much of the Chinese population of Hong Kong would eventually settle. He soon became one of the colony's wealthiest and most powerful Chinese residents.

Kwok Acheong was another Tanka boatman who supplied provisions to the British forces during the First Opium War. After the British takeover of Hong Kong, Kwok settled in the colony. He joined the Peninsular and Oriental (P&O) Steam Navigation Company in 1845 and soon became its comprador. (Named after the Portuguese word for "buyer," the comprador system originated in the late Ming dynasty but came to prominence after the Canton System was abolished in 1842 and compradors replaced the hong merchants as the main intermediaries between Chinese and Western traders.) In the 1860s Kwok started a fleet of steamships that competed with the European-owned Hong Kong, Canton and Macao Steamboat Company. In 1876 he was the third-largest taxpayer in the colony. By 1877 he owned thirteen steamships, making him not just a successful local Chinese businessman but also a regional shipping magnate. Although he spoke only pidgin English, Kwok was known for getting along well with foreigners and was a frequent advisor to the colonial government.

Hong Kong's physical development was also made possible by Chinese builders, contractors, merchants, and laborers. European colonialism was not only an encounter between different cultures, it was also a process of physical construction that ranged from government, residential, and commercial buildings to entire cities and towns. As in many other Asian colonies, in Hong Kong this construction was completed by Chinese workers and contractors, many of whom had prior experience working for Europeans. Tam Achoy, the most successful of these contractors, was one of the most prominent members of the Chinese community in early colonial Hong Kong. Originally from Kaiping, a county in Guangdong province known for sending emigrants to Southeast Asia and, later, to California, Tam came to Hong Kong in 1841 from the British colony of Singapore, where he had been a foreman in the colonial government dockyards. He built some of the most important buildings in the colony, including the P&O Building and a building that the government later purchased for use as the colony's first Supreme Court. For his services to the British in Hong Kong and Singapore, Tam was granted land in the Lower Bazaar.

The British offered another powerful reward for collaboration: lucrative monopolies. Historians have often stressed the role of free trade in Hong Kong's economic development. In the early years, however, this economy was neither impressive nor free. An elaborate system of monopolies, usually offered for sale by public auction, regulated commodities such as opium, salt, liquor, and tobacco. Ironically, it was from these same types of regulations and monopolies that the British had insisted the First Opium War and the "imperialism of free trade" would liberate China. These monopolies, which accounted for 10–25 percent of the government's annual revenue, were almost always held by local Chinese merchants or contractors. The largest and longest-lasting of the monopolies was the opium monopoly, which in the nineteenth century could make up almost one-quarter of the government's annual revenue.

Although it does not explain why these Chinese helped the British during the First Opium War, colonial Hong Kong also enabled men such as Loo, Kwok, and Tam to achieve a level of social prominence that they could not achieve in China. As Tanka outcasts, both Loo and Kwok were barred from assuming any gentry functions in China. By working for the British in Singapore, Tam had violated Qing prohibitions against overseas emigration. In British Hong Kong, however, such prohibitions meant nothing. Tam became a trustee at three local Chinese temples and was a well-known philanthropist. In 1847 a local British newspaper described him as "probably as respectable and intelligent as any man of his class in the Colony." In 1856 he helped form a Chinese fire brigade, equipped with an American-made engine. In this new colonial environment, Loo, who hailed from a dubious background, also became a prominent member of the Chinese community. He was widely believed to be involved with triad groups and pirates and to encourage corruption among the police force. But he also had a reputation about town for helping "those who were in distress, in debt or discontented."[13]

HONG KONG'S TROUBLES

The British occupation made Hong Kong into a boomtown. Hong Kong in the early 1840s had all the rugged excitement of a frontier town, not unlike the gold rush towns in the American West or in Australia and New Zealand.

When the British took control of Hong Kong in January 1841, the northern shore of the island was for the most part unoccupied, and the rest of the island consisted mainly of small farming and fishing villages. The island's total population was probably between five thousand and seven thousand. However, Hong Kong soon drew Chinese of all walks of life from Guangdong and European merchants and missionaries from Macau. By early 1842, Hong Kong was a bustling town with between fifteen thousand and twenty thousand inhabitants, complete with official buildings such as a magistrate's office, post office, land and record office, and jail. A few rough roads linked these buildings with commercial facilities such as wharves, piers, warehouses, shops, brothels, gambling houses, tailors' shops, and a marketplace. By 1845, European visitors frequently commented on Hong Kong's palatial government buildings and opulent merchants' residences.

Scholars who celebrate Hong Kong's political stability and economic success as a capitalist paradise often forget that the colony's early history was a rocky one. Colonialism created tremendous opportunities for wealth, but it also meant crime, tension, and confusion. The new wealth in Hong Kong (especially compared with the poverty in the surrounding areas on the mainland), the easy access from China, and the large number of European adventurers all led to crime on land and piracy in the surrounding waters. The large and sudden influx of both Chinese and European newcomers meant land shortages and the end of traditional land rights. Some villagers found themselves paying rent not only to the colonial government but also to the Tang family, which had owned most of the land in Hong Kong, or to the Chinese authorities in Guangdong. Unresolved issues about jurisdiction over Hong Kong's Chinese residents meant that officials in Guangdong often refused to recognize British jurisdiction in Hong Kong, leading to constant tensions between Britain and China that affected relations between the Chinese and European residents of Hong Kong.

Despite Hong Kong's promise, it did not immediately become "the Great Emporium of the East" envisioned by its colonial founders. The entrepôt trade developed slowly, leaving Hong Kong little more than a colonial outpost and an opium center. In July 1842 the *Canton Press* lamented that the early land sales and poor trade conditions had left the Chinese buyers "as poor as rats, the dollars they had being laid out to erect houses, and the same may be said of the few European residents here; they are all sellers, none buyers."[14] Disease was endemic. In May 1843, almost 25 percent of the British garrison died of malaria. Piracy was rampant, and crime—especially theft and burglary—was equally bad on land. Even Government House, the governor's office and residence, was burgled on April 26, 1843, while two large British firms were burgled two nights later.

In July 1844 Robert Montgomery Martin, the colonial treasurer, reported that the climate, landscape, and trade conditions of Hong Kong were so bad that the British government should abandon the island. The island's commercial prospects were extremely bleak: "There does not appear to be the slightest probability that, under any circumstances, Hong Kong will ever become a place of trade." Even the colony's famously deep harbor was not worth the expense and trouble: "I can see no justification for the British Government spending one shilling on Hong Kong."[15] History would prove Martin wrong, but many contemporary observers shared similar sentiments. The botanist Robert Fortune predicted that "viewed as a place of trade, I fear Hong-kong will be a failure."[16] Alexander Matheson, head of Jardine and Matheson, told the British House of Commons in May 1847 that had they not already invested so much money in land and buildings, most English firms would have already withdrawn from Hong Kong years earlier. After a plague in the fall of 1850 exacerbated already bad health and sanitary conditions, a popular song in London music halls rang "You may go to Hong Kong for me."

British officials had hoped that the colony would attract Chinese merchants from Macau and Canton, transforming it into the trading center of southern China, but this did not happen. Part of the problem lay in the Treaty of Nanking, which ceded Hong Kong to Britain but also opened five Chinese ports, thereby diverting trade from Hong Kong. Because trading at the treaty ports was cheaper, British merchants preferred to buy directly from China. Chinese merchants preferred to use British ships for importing and exporting goods to and from Southeast Asia because they were faster, safer, and cheaper than their own junks. Although this benefited British shipping companies, their ships bypassed Hong Kong. Martin lamented how "after three years and a half's uninterrupted settlement there is not one respectable Chinese inhabitant on the island." One wealthy opium trader had built a house and freighted a ship in Hong Kong, but he soon returned to Canton, where he died of a fever and cold contracted in the colony.[17]

One reason that Hong Kong was unable to attract large Chinese merchants was that Chinese authorities in Canton used various restrictions to discourage wealthy Chinese traders from coming to the colony. Some colonial officials were convinced that Chinese authorities in Guangdong deliberately deported vagabonds, vagrants, and thieves to Hong Kong, both as a way to get rid of criminals and to undermine the stability of the colony. But the European population had more than its own share of unsavory characters. In Britain, the island had become known as a haven for European outlaws, deserters, reckless adventurers, and speculators. The *Economist* noted in August 1846 how "Hong Kong is nothing now but a depot for a few opium smugglers, soldiers, officers and men-of-war's men." Oswald Tiffany, an American visitor, recalled how "scapegoats and scoundrels from the purlieus of London, creatures that only missed Botany Bay by good fortune, were to be found in the town of Victoria, lording it over the natives, many of whom were more respectable and respected than they had ever been or ever could be."[18]

The main reason that Chinese merchants were reluctant to come to Hong Kong was that the colonial government could not provide a safe business environment. In June 1844 a force of 150 pirates plundered a waterfront warehouse. Governor John Davis reported in 1845 that Hong Kong's trade with China had been "comparatively paralysed" by pirate vessels blocking both the eastern and western channels to the harbor. Threats of a giant pirate attack put the entire island on emergency alert during the summer of 1854. In October of that year, a group of Chinese boat masters trading in Hong Kong petitioned the colonial government to dispatch a steamer to end piracy, which they claimed had greatly harmed their business. The same month, a wealthy Chinese merchant had hired armed boats to escort his vessel as he moved his family and valuables to Hong Kong. His vessel had survived most of the trip only to be attacked by pirates as it entered Hong Kong waters. In September 1855, Governor John Bowring concluded that the piracy plaguing the colony was "interfering ruinously with its comforts and its prosperity."

The colonial government could not suppress piracy without help from the Chinese government. However, the colonial government could do little to control crime within Hong Kong itself. Robert Fortune claimed that the "town swarms with thieves and robbers."[19] The colonial government was also unable to assure Chinese merchants that it was committed to retaining the island. Like some Europeans in Hong Kong, many Chinese feared that the colony might be returned to China. With good reason, these concerns persisted even after Imperial Commissioner Qiying issued a proclamation in 1843 that Chinese who had served the British forces would be pardoned. In July 1844 a Chinese merchant working for the British commissariat in Zhoushan was abducted and beheaded by the local authorities. In November an anti-British placard summoned all Chinese residents to leave the colony, wishing that China would drive out the British barbarians. Although in April 1845 Qiying forbade the Chinese in Canton and Hong Kong to molest foreigners, anti-British placards continued to appear.

THE SECOND OPIUM WAR

In the midst of this uncertainty and insecurity, Hong Kong became embroiled in another war between Britain and China. Most historians have focused on the Second Opium War primarily as yet another Sino-British conflict or on the war's effects on Hong Kong. However, both the war and its local repercussions were shaped not only by developments in Hong Kong and China but also by global events that affected the British Empire.

The underlying cause of the war was that the Treaty of Nanking had not given the British all that they wanted, whereas from the Qing point of view it had conceded too much. Britain hoped the treaty would lead to more treaties that would eventually open China to foreign trade, primarily for the benefit of Britain but also for China and the world. For the Qing, the treaty was simply a way to keep the foreigners at bay. The treaty had not produced the boom in trade that the British had expected and had left too many issues unresolved. Throughout the 1850s, Sino-British relations were plagued by the Canton question: the English text of the treaty gave the British the right to enter the city of Canton, but the Chinese text restricted them to its port. Not only did the treaty not grant the British diplomatic residence in the capital at Beijing, but British officials did not have direct access to Chinese officials in Canton.

Although it is not true, as it is often claimed, that the treaty did not even mention opium—Article 4 stipulated that the "Emperor of China agrees to pay the sum of Six Million Dollars as the value of Opium which was delivered up at Canton in the month of March 1839"—the treaty did not discuss the opium trade or its legality. Furthermore, the treaty made no provision for future revisions. Because the Treaty of Wanghia signed between the United States and China in 1844 included provision for revisions in twelve years, the British hoped that they might use the most-favored-nation clause in the Treaty of Nanking to push for revisions. Most important, Britain's global position depended on opium: Britain used the revenue from the opium trade to buy tea and silk from China and to support the occupation of India, Chinese merchants used the profits from tea and silk to buy opium from British traders, Indian producers used revenues from opium to buy British goods, and British merchants used the profits from selling British goods to buy cotton from the United States. The sale of Indian opium to China, writes historian J. Y. Wong, "was a great link in the chain of commerce with which Britain had surrounded the world."[20] Thus, in 1854 the British requested more concessions, including the legalization of the opium trade, the freedom to sail and trade on the Yangzi River, and the right to diplomatic representation in Beijing.

Hong Kong was intricately linked to this second war between Britain and China. Governor Bowring, who was also British plenipotentiary and superintendent of trade in China, requested an official meeting with Governor-General Ye Mingchen in Canton, but the two could not agree on a suitable meeting place. Bowring had come to Hong Kong in 1854 convinced that another conflict with China was on the horizon. With his interest in Chinese culture, Bowring was determined to patch up Anglo-Chinese relations even though his predecessors had failed. But Bowring's four years in Canton as British consul left him convinced that Britain needed a more vigorous policy toward China and that only through force could China be brought to its senses. A Unitarian and a friend and admirer of liberal philosophers Jeremy Bentham and John Stuart Mill, Bowring was an ardent believer in free trade. Convinced that no nation could resist this "great tide of tendency" that would eventually change the world, he once said that "Jesus Christ is Free Trade and Free Trade is Jesus Christ."[21] Bowring had earlier been president of the Peace Society, which advocated the abolition of war and the peaceful resolution of international disputes through conciliation (in 1855 he became the first Westerner to make a treaty with Siam), and he wanted more humane policies for the Chinese in Hong Kong (in 1846, as a member of Parliament, he had condemned the routine use of flogging in Hong Kong for minor offenses). Nonetheless, he helped cause another war between China and Britain.

Hoping to foster a sense of colonial loyalty, in 1855 Bowring allowed Chinese who leased land in Hong Kong to register their vessels under the British flag, which many did to protect themselves from piracy in the surrounding waters and from rapacious officials in Chinese ports. On October 8, 1856, Chinese police in Canton boarded the *Arrow*, a Chinese-owned vessel registered in Hong Kong, and arrested a dozen Chinese crewmen suspected of being involved in piracy and smuggling. Although details of the incident were murky, the boat's registration had expired, and its British captain claimed that the British flag had been torn down during the scuffle. (Both Canton authorities and the boat's crew later denied that the flag had been flying at all when the Chinese police boarded.) Harry Parkes, British consul at Canton, demanded that Chinese authorities both release the crew and apologize for defacing the British flag. When the Chinese released the crew but refused to apologize, Parkes asked the Royal Navy to bombard Ye's residence in Canton. The Qing responded by burning the European factories in Canton.

Although many British officials did not want another war over such a minor incident, the issue became a matter of national honor. When the Chinese refused to apologize to Parkes, Bowring assembled forces to attack Canton. For Bowring, the *Arrow* incident was the perfect pretext to solve the remaining problems from the First Opium War and to revise the Treaty of Nanking on more favorable terms. Britain sent a punitive expedition, while France sent its own expedition, supposedly to punish the Chinese for the murder of a Catholic missionary in Guangxi province. With help from American naval forces, the Anglo-French forces eventually took Canton in December 1857, captured Governor-General Ye (who was exiled to Calcutta), and established an interim government under Parkes.

The Treaty of Tientsin, signed in June 1858 by China, Britain, France, Russia, and the United States, meant more indemnities, diplomatic residence in Beijing, the opening of ten more Chinese ports to foreign trade, and access to China's hinterland for Western missionaries and traders. A supplementary treaty in October imposed a tariff on the importation of opium, effectively legalizing the opium trade. The war continued, however, with the Anglo-French forces occupying Beijing, burning the Summer Palace, and forcing the Xianfeng emperor into exile. The Convention of Peking, accepted in 1860 by the emperor's younger brother, Prince Gong, raised the indemnities, reaffirmed the British right to diplomatic residence in Beijing, and ceded to Britain the Kowloon Peninsula along with Stonecutters Island, a small island to the west of Hong Kong Island.

Bowring was widely criticized in Britain for causing another war with China, but he enjoyed great support from Lord Palmerston, who by now was prime minister. Bowring had even more encouragement from the Europeans of Hong Kong. When he arrived in Hong Kong in 1854, the European community was already in a state of anxiety. A general sense of disappointment in how Hong Kong had turned out was pervasive. Tensions between Chinese and Europeans were especially high in the late 1840s, especially when Governor Davis sent a punitive expedition in 1847 to bombard Canton after foreigners there had been assaulted. In July 1848, some local Chinese tried to poison members of the Royal Artillery. In December, an arsonist tried to burn down the Central Market. In February 1849, a group of Chinese pirates killed two British military officers after the officers made sexual advances toward a village girl. After the Portuguese governor of Macau was assassinated in August 1849, rumors in Hong Kong claimed that the authorities in Guangdong had put a price on the head of Governor George Bonham. Although it would eventually help transform Hong Kong, the Taiping Rebellion in China often threatened to overflow into Hong Kong. In autumn 1854, Taiping rebels struggled with Qing forces for control of Kowloon City, just across the harbor from Hong Kong Island. Taiping troops periodically marched through the streets of Hong Kong, where some of their leaders had ties with British missionaries such as James Legge of the London Missionary Society.

These concerns and fears among Hong Kong's European community reflected how the mid-1850s to mid-1860s was a period of crisis and anxiety for the British Empire. From late 1853 to early 1856, Britain, France, and the Ottoman Turks had been at war with Russia on the Crimean Peninsula in the Black Sea. Although the British and their allies emerged victorious, the war had been waged extremely poorly by both sides and had cost some five hundred thousand lives in total. Particularly tragic for the British had been the Battle of Balaklava in October 1854. Written into legend by the English poet Lord Alfred Tennyson in "The Charge of the Light Brigade," the battle wiped out almost one half of the Light Brigade. The Crimean War, which revived concern about defense of British India, was followed by a war in Persia from 1856 to 1857. In Southeast Asia, riots by the Chinese in Singapore in 1854 were followed by yearly riots from 1857 to 1867 by the Chinese in Penang. Sarawak saw similar riots by the Chinese in 1857 and an uprising by the native Iban people from 1859 to 1860. In 1857 a massive millenarian protest by the Xhosa people of South Africa aimed at driving whites out of the region. Many British politicians and military officials feared the rising power of the United States. (Concerned, albeit unnecessarily, about threats from American warships during the American Civil War, the colonial treasurer of Hong Kong called for a larger garrison to protect the colony.) And one historian has argued that Britain's failure to open the China and Latin America markets even fueled the brutal suppression of the Morant Bay Rebellion in Jamaica in 1865, an event that confirmed British planters' age-old fear of black uprisings.[22]

No event during this decade would shake the British Empire more than the Indian Rebellion (or the Great Mutiny as it was known to Britons). Although the rebellion was eventually suppressed with help from loyal Indian troops, it rattled the very foundations of British imperialism. Newspapers throughout the empire had a field day with a rebel massacre in July 1857 at Cawnpore (also written as Kanpur), with reports of sexually violated white women and English babies thrown by the rebels onto bayonets. The British punished the rebels in Cawnpore by making them clean up the blood of the murdered Europeans (with their tongues, if they refused) before hanging them. Rebel leaders were strapped in front of cannons and blown apart, a practice that the British inherited from the former Mughal rulers of India.

While there had been much enthusiasm in Britain for the Crimean War, the reaction toward the Indian uprising was one of shock and terror. Some Britons denounced the barbaric execution of the rebels, but the rebellion seemed to disprove the naive yet widely held notion that British rule would keep imperial subjects content and obedient. "To the British," writes historian Ronald Hyam, "it seemed that Satan had rebelled and the mark of a black skin was the mark of Cain. . . . There had been one universal belief that no danger could ever approach the British in India, and that God was on the side of the empire and that everybody loved the British."[23] That Indian civilians had also been involved made things even worse. A mutiny had expanded into a general rebellion, convincing many Britons that the Indians were no longer harmless and docile heathens but rather were treacherous and sinister savages. Formerly loyal Indian friends and servants had suddenly—and seemingly inexplicably—become spies and murderers.

Understanding these events elsewhere in the world and the British Empire helps explain the tension and insecurity in Hong Kong throughout the 1850s and 1860s, especially during the Second Opium War and in late 1857 and early 1858 in particular. Governor-General Ye ordered the Chinese of Hong Kong and Canton not to cooperate, offering rewards in silver for each English head delivered to him. Placards on street corners throughout Canton and Hong Kong called on all loyal Chinese to rise up against the English barbarians by poisoning or stabbing them or by burning their property. European factories in Canton were burned down; several European steamships were captured in Chinese waters, their passengers murdered; and in Hong Kong the buildings of several European firms were attacked, and a government official was strangled by one of his servants.

In such an atmosphere, many Europeans in Hong Kong saw the bread-poisoning incident of January 15, 1857, as a direct response to Ye's calls for Chinese in Hong Kong to attack their British colonizers. That morning, several hundred Europeans, including the governor's wife, Lady Bowring, had eaten bread baked by the E Sing Bakery and had become violently ill. The offending ingredient was quickly determined to be arsenic. As the amount of arsenic was so large, most of the Europeans had vomited it before digesting much of the poison. But because the bakery was the only Western-style one remaining in the colony, Europeans saw the incident as a plot to wipe out their entire community. Their fears appeared to be confirmed as the owner of the bakery, a comprador named Cheong Ah Lum, had left for Macau that morning with his family just before the Europeans had their breakfast. Arrested and brought back for trial to Hong Kong, Cheong claimed that he and his family had also been poisoned after eating the same bread.

Although the bread-poisoning case is often held up as a shining example of impartial British justice, it was more of a test of British justice. Some Europeans believed that there was not enough evidence to convict Cheong, but others wanted to lynch him and his employees. Even the attorney general insisted that it would be "better to hang the wrong man than confess that British sagacity and activity have failed to discover the real criminals," although Chief Justice John Walter Hulme, who had also been poisoned, warned that "hanging the wrong man will not further the ends of justice." Represented by a British lawyer, Cheong was acquitted on lack of sufficient evidence, but 52 of his employees were imprisoned for four days in a small room, nicknamed the "Black Hole of Hong Kong" (after the "Black Hole of Calcutta," a dungeon where 123 European prisoners had allegedly died in 1756). Although 10 of the employees were tried, the remaining 42 were detained in the room for more than twenty days. Only after protests from the European and Chinese communities were they released, on the condition that they leave Hong Kong. Hundreds more Chinese were subsequently arrested and deported.

Insufficient evidence exists of how this incident played out among the Chinese community of Hong Kong. But all sorts of conflicting theories and questions arose among the European community. Although a local English newspaper later suggested that the flour in the bread might have been contaminated on board a ship carrying arsenopyrite, there was good reason to believe that the poisoning had been deliberate, for some Chinese servants had warned their European employers about the plan. Regardless, the case had revealed the tensions and suspicions in Hong Kong not just between the Chinese and Europeans but within the European community as well. William Tarrant, a newspaper editor and former colonial official whose frequent attacks on the colonial government led to libel, fines, and even his imprisonment, sued Cheong for damages. Although Tarrant was successful, Cheong left town again without paying up. When Tarrant then accused the acting colonial secretary of letting Cheong escape, the acting colonial secretary in turn sued Tarrant for libel. Tarrant lost, but his sympathizers came up with the compensation. Small wonder, then, that the *Times* complained in March 1859 how "Hongkong is always connected with some fatal pestilence, some doubtful war, or some discreditable internal squabble, so much so that, in popular language, the name of this noisy, bustling, quarrelsome, disconnected little Island may not inaptly be used as a euphemous synonym for a place not mentionable to ears polite."[24]

This "doubtful war" achieved what the British had wanted: diplomatic recognition in Beijing, the opening of ten additional Chinese ports to international trade, and the legalization of opium. The war also had several important effects on Hong Kong. The colonial government issued a mass of emergency measures that practically put the colony's Chinese residents under martial law, including curfews, deportations, and rewards for informants. The government also granted the European community self-defense measures, such as erecting barricades, locking up Chinese servants at night, and allowing night sentries or patrolmen to shoot on sight any suspicious-looking Chinese. Although many of these measures were later rescinded, some stayed on the books long after the war had ended. For example, the night curfew for Chinese was not suspended until 1897, after protests in 1895 from some Chinese and Eurasian leaders, as a gesture of goodwill in honor of Queen Victoria's Diamond Jubilee. Even then, the governor retained the right to reinstate the curfew.

The war and the local tensions it provoked or exacerbated drew the European community together by making all Chinese in Hong Kong potential enemies. As in many colonies, Europeans in Hong Kong had always worried about some sort of mass treachery through poisoning or uprising, although in Hong Kong they often convinced themselves that the number of Chinese who came to Hong Kong proved that colonial rule there was different than in other colonies. Wang Tao, a Chinese scholar and journalist who came to Hong Kong during the Taiping Rebellion, noted with surprise how the colony's reservoir was guarded by sentries to prevent its water supply from being poisoned.

Although they must have reinforced the Chinese community's resentment of colonial rule, the effects of the Second Opium War and the emergency measures taken during the war on Hong Kong's Chinese community are somewhat harder to characterize. Partly in response to Governor-General

Ye's order to leave the colony, in early 1857 some five thousand Chinese left Hong Kong. After Anglo-French forces occupied Canton in December 1857, many Chinese left Hong Kong from January 1858 through October 1861. In July 1858 alone, some twenty thousand artisans, builders, laborers, and tailors left Hong Kong. As historian Jung-fang Tsai has argued, however, antiforeignism "did not necessarily entail Chinese national consciousness."[25] Any attempts to attribute these mass departures to a sense of Chinese patriotism or loyalty to the Qing government are also complicated by the fact that the departures were not always voluntary. For example, the exodus in July 1858 appears to have been partly a response to threats by magistrates in nearby Chinese villages who declared that if the Chinese in Hong Kong did not leave, their relatives in China would be punished as rebels. Even in China, Ye's prohibitions against food being exported to Hong Kong were rarely obeyed. And the British encountered no significant resistance when they took over Kowloon Peninsula in January 1861.

Many Chinese in fact collaborated actively with the British during the war. For example, the wealthy brothers Li Sing and Li Leong, only recently arrived in Hong Kong, quickly sided with the British and French by providing money and porters. For their efforts, the Li family received part of the war indemnity, including some pieces from the Imperial Summer Palace in Beijing. Finally, Bowring, who was partly responsible for the war, enjoyed great popularity among some parts of the Chinese community. When he left the colony in May 1859, the Western community ignored his departure. The Chinese community, however, sent two deputations to see him off and showered him with praise and gifts.

THE TAIPING REBELLION AND CHINESE EMIGRATION

Not only did many Chinese show their affiliation with Hong Kong by disobeying orders from Canton to return to China during the Second Opium War, but the local Chinese population also greatly expanded during this period. And even though racial antagonisms and mutual suspicions between the Chinese and European populations increased during the war, the expansion of the Chinese community would eventually help make Hong Kong a major trading center. This expansion occurred not because of the colonial government's attempt to attract wealthier Chinese to Hong Kong but because of the combination of Chinese domestic turmoil and the worldwide rise of Western capitalism and imperialism, which encouraged Chinese emigration in two ways.

The opening of Canton and other treaty ports by the Treaty of Nanking disrupted local economies. Imports such as British cotton now competed with Chinese products in the markets of Canton, while Chinese junks lost out to larger, faster foreign vessels. By the late 1840s and early 1850s, Canton had lost its hold on both tea and silk trades, causing unemployment throughout Guangdong. Almost simultaneously, the abandonment of slavery by England, France, and some parts of the United States encouraged a demand for cheap, forced labor in Canada, the United States, Australia, New Zealand, and the West and East Indies. In 1849 after gold was discovered in California, the first shipload of Chinese laborers came through Hong Kong, en route to the United States. By December 1850, two thousand Chinese had left China for California. Between January and June 1850, some ten thousand tons of shipping were loaded or partly loaded in Hong Kong and shipped to the western coast of the United States. With this growth of overseas trade also came new Chinese labor and talent. In 1850, Governor Bonham reported an increase in the Chinese population, mainly artisans from Canton working in the California trade. Three years later he noted that the colony's "commercial prospects are slowly but certainly extending and assuming a character of greater permanency."

Hong Kong's economic recovery began in the early 1850s, when many Chinese merchants came to Hong Kong to escape the Taiping Rebellion. In 1837, Hong Xiuquan, a Chinese from Guangdong who had failed the civil service examination, had a nervous breakdown. Years later, after failing the examination a fourth time and reading Christian tracts produced by Protestant missionaries, he became convinced that he was the second son of Jehovah and the younger brother of Jesus Christ. He had been ordered to oust the Manchu "imps and demons" from China and to establish the Taiping Kingdom, or "Heavenly Kingdom of Great Peace." When Hong and his Society of God Worshippers started proselytizing in Guangxi province, an area outside of government control and teeming with secret societies that claimed their loyalty to the Ming dynasty, their crusade gained a political edge. Armed with an ideology based on quasi-Christian beliefs, the abolition of private property and the institution of a communal land system, the segregation of men and women, and strict prohibitions against liquor, tobacco, and opium, Hong's rebels moved northeast from Guangxi and through the middle Yangzi Valley. In 1853 they captured Nanjing, renaming the city the "Heavenly Capital" and making it their capital for more than ten years. The rebellion might have ended the Qing dynasty were it not eventually suppressed in 1864 by provincial armies led by Chinese commanders, along with help from Western munitions and mercenaries.

The Taiping Rebellion and its suppression cost at least twenty million lives, devastated parts of the Chinese countryside, and wiped out entire cities. Those who could afford to do so fled to the safety of the treaty ports, especially to Shanghai, protected by its large Western settlement. Although the rebellion fueled tensions in Hong Kong, it also helped pull the colony out of its economic slump. From 1853 to 1859 the Chinese population of

Hong Kong rose from approximately forty thousand to around eighty-five thousand, even with the mass departures during the Second Opium War. Officials and visitors often commented on how the turbulent conditions in China had brought new traders to the colony and improved living standards. When journalist Wang Tao first arrived in Hong Kong, "merchants generally wore short jackets and put on a cotton overcoat when the weather got cold. The women paid little attention to their dress." But he later observed that "drastic changes are now taking place in the way of life in Hong Kong. People are beginning to pursue luxury. . . . Bright lamps burn through the night, and loud music is heard until the small hours. Hong Kong's prosperity now exceeds that of Canton, and it is all the result of fate and chance."[26]

The combination of the Taiping Rebellion, Chinese emigration, and the growth of overseas Chinese communities had three important effects on Hong Kong's economy. It transformed Hong Kong from a colonial outpost into the center of a transnational overseas Chinese trade network stretching from the China coast to Southeast Asia and all the way to Australia and the Americas. The rebellion and the rise of overseas Chinese communities also created a new class of wealthy Chinese in Hong Kong, where they became settlers rather than sojourners. Among these new immigrants were wealthy Chinese who brought their families, capital, entrepreneurial skills, and business connections. Examples include the Li brothers, who came from Guangdong during the early 1850s. In 1857 the brothers became the largest brokers of immigrant labor and charterers of immigrant ships. By the mid-1860s, their family holdings included insurance, real estate, and interests in the opium monopoly. As head of this successful family, Li Sing became one of the colony's most prominent merchants. With the arrival of such men, a new Chinese business elite had emerged in Hong Kong colony by the late 1850s.

Finally, Hong Kong's economic growth benefited local European merchants and attracted new foreign investment. Several new European banks were opened in the late 1850s and early 1860s. American and Portuguese firms moved from Canton and Macau. In 1857 Douglas Lapraik, a Scot who had begun his Hong Kong career as a watchmaker's apprentice, cofounded Hong Kong's first dry dock. By the time of his death in 1869, he owned a fleet of seven steamships. Shipping between Hong Kong and Canton and the United States and Australia also increased. The clearest indicator of foreign investors' new confidence in the colony's economy can be seen in the founding of the Hong Kong and Shanghai Bank in July 1864. Until then, local banking services for foreign merchants had been provided by larger European hongs. Most of the Western banks in Hong Kong and China were branch offices of Anglo-Indian banks such as the Oriental Bank and the Chartered Bank of India, Australia and China—exchange banks controlled from India or England. The founding of the new bank was heralded as a sign of the colony's prosperity. Chinese capital was important from the start, and the bank would become the leading bank on the China coast. In the absence of any formal central bank, the Hong Kong and Shanghai Bank would act as Hong Kong's central bank until the last years of the colonial era. By the late twentieth century, it had become one of the largest financial institutions in the world.

NOTES

1. *A Hand-Book to Hong Kong: Being A Popular Guide to the Various Places of Interest in the Colony, for the Use of Tourists* (Hong Kong: Kelly and Walsh, 1893), reprinted as *The Hong Kong Guide, 1893*, with an introduction by H. J. Lethbridge (Hong Kong: Oxford University Press, 1982), i.

2. Richard Hughes, *Borrowed Place—Borrowed Time: Hong Kong and Its Many Faces*, 2nd rev. ed. (London: André Deutsch, 1976), 97.

3. James Hayes, "Hong Kong Island before 1841," *Journal of the Hong Kong Branch of the Royal Asiatic Society* 24 (1984): 106, 114, 128. This article is also reprinted in David Faure, ed., *Hong Kong: A Reader in Social History* (Hong Kong: Oxford University Press, 2003), 3–37.

4. Jonathan Porter, *Macau: The Imaginary City* (Boulder: Westview, 1996), 3.

5. Great Britain, Colonial Office, Original Correspondence: Hong Kong, 1841–1951, Series 129 (CO129), Public Record Office, London, CO 129/1843/8, June 3, 1843, reprinted in Steve Tsang, ed., *Government and Politics. A Documentary History of Hong Kong* (Hong Kong: Hong Kong University Press, 1995), 17.

6. G. B. Endacott, *A History of Hong Kong,* rev. ed. (Hong Kong: Oxford University Press, 1973), vii–viii.

7. Chan Wai Kwan, *The Making of Hong Kong Society: Three Studies of Class Formation in Early Hong Kong* (Oxford, UK: Clarendon, 1991), 9.

8. Robert Fortune, *Three Years' Wanderings in the Northern Provinces of China, Including a Visit to the Tea, Silk, and Cotton Countries: With an Account of Agriculture and Horticulture of the Chinese, New Plants, Etc.* (London: J. Murray, 1847), 13.

9. William C. Hunter, *The "Fan Kwae" at Canton before Treaty Days, 1825–1844* (London: Kegan Paul, Trench, and Co., 1882), 72–73.

10. E. J. Eitel, *Europe in China: The History of Hong Kong from the Beginning to the Year 1882* (1895; reprint, Hong Kong: Oxford University Press, 1983), 75.

11. Hunter, *The "Fan Kwae" at Canton,* 106.

12. K. S. McKenzie, *Narrative of the Second Campaign in China* (London: R. Bentley, 1842), 160, quoted in Hayes, "Hong Kong Island before 1841," 115.

13. *China Review* 1 (1872): 333, quoted in Carl T. Smith, *Chinese Christians: Elites, Middlemen, and the Church in Hong Kong* (Hong Kong: Oxford University Press, 1985), 203.

14. Quoted in John M. Carroll, *Edge of Empires: Chinese Elites and British Colonials in Hong Kong* (Cambridge: Harvard University Press, 2005), 37.

15. "Report on the Island of Hong Kong," reprinted in G. B. Endacott, *An Eastern Entrepot: A Collection of Documents Illustrating the History of Hong Kong* (London: Her Majesty's Stationery Office, 1964), 99.

16. Fortune, *Three Years' Wanderings,* 28.

17. "Report on the Island of Hong Kong," 99.

18. Oswald Tiffany Jr., *The Canton Chinese; or, The American's Sojourn in the Celestial Empire* (Boston: James Monroe and Company, 1849), reprinted in Barbara-Sue White, ed., *Hong Kong: Somewhere between Heaven and Earth* (Hong Kong: Oxford University Press, 1996), 38–39.

19. Fortune, *Three Years' Wanderings,* 27.

20. J. Y. Wong, *Deadly Dreams: Opium, Imperialism, and the Arrow War (1856–1860) in China* (Cambridge: Cambridge University Press, 1998), 409.

21. Quoted in Ronald Hyam, *Britain's Imperial Century, 1815–1914* (Basingstoke, UK: Palgrave Macmillan, 2002), 113.

22. Denis Judd, *Empire: The British Imperial Experience, from 1765 to the Present* (New York: Basic Books, 1996), 87.

23. Hyam, *Britain's Imperial Century,* 137–38.

24. Quoted in Eitel, *Europe in China,* 325.

25. Jung-fang Tsai, *Hong Kong in Chinese History: Community and Social Unrest in the British Colony, 1842–1913* (New York: Columbia University Press, 1993), 55.

26. Wang Tao, "My Sojourn in Hong Kong," translated by Yang Qinghua, in *Renditions* (Hong Kong: Chinese University Press, 1988), reprinted in White, *Hong Kong,* 64.

2

State and Society

As in other colonies, colonialism in Hong Kong could be repressive and yet offer opportunities. Until the 1860s, when the British presence in China shifted to Shanghai, Hong Kong provided several economic and diplomatic functions for Britain. It was from Hong Kong, which was the British head-quarters for the China trade, that the British plenipotentiary and superin-tendent of trade administered all British subjects in China. (After John Bowring retired in 1859, the office of Hong Kong governor was separated from that of plenipotentiary and superintendent of trade in China.) The colony was a naval station and the first port of call after Singapore for Eu-ropean travelers. Hong Kong also provided the security and the freedom of movement and residence that the treaty ports did not. These functions all meant that Hong Kong offered a variety of opportunities for Chinese to serve as contractors, laborers, servants, clerks, and interpreters.

ECONOMY: OPIUM AND EMIGRATION

Hong Kong was founded primarily for trade, which indelibly shaped its his-torical development. Although the colonial government initially had a hard time attracting large Chinese merchants to Hong Kong, its promise of free trade, along with easy access to markets in China, attracted a wide range of foreign merchants involved mainly in the China trade in silk, tea, and opium; in the international trade; and in insurance and shipping. The British firm most closely tied to Hong Kong's economic history was Jardine and Mathe-son, but other prominent British firms included Dent (Jardine and Mathe-son's main rival) and Butterfield and Swire, which did not arrive until 1870

33

but quickly developed interests in trading, shipping, and sugar refining. Among the American trading companies was Russell, a Boston firm whose partners included Warren Delano, grandfather of future American president Franklin Delano Roosevelt. German traders did not arrive until the 1850s, but firms such as Siemssen soon became active in the China trade. Several important Portuguese firms, such as J. J. dos Remedios, moved to Hong Kong from Macau. In the mid-1840s, approximately one-quarter of the foreign businesses in Hong Kong were Indian, either Parsee or Muslim. An ethnic and religious minority who had come to Bombay from Persia, the Parsees played a large role in the early China trade, especially in opium. Large Parsee firms included D. Ruttonjee. Indian Muslim firms, which had been in Canton since the late 1700s, also settled in Hong Kong after the cession. Among these was Abdoolally Ebrahim. Sephardic Jewish firms such as D. Sassoon, established in Canton in the early 1840s, had a prominent position in the opium trade.

Although the opening of the Chinese treaty ports after the opium wars also benefited British firms, Hong Kong remained a more reliable commercial base because Britain enjoyed full political control over the colony. Hong Kong soon became the Asian headquarters for many British firms that had powerful economic and political connections with London. Similarly, local Chinese merchants' connections with the overseas Chinese trade made Hong Kong a commercial base for trade with Southeast Asia. Hong Kong's economic development moreover benefited from a steady supply of cheap labor from China and from the numerous services that arose to support the colony's trade: banking, insurance, shipping, shipbuilding, and ship repairing.

More important for Hong Kong's economic prosperity than any of these factors, however, were opium and Chinese emigration. With the exception of two American companies run by Quakers, all major foreign firms in early Hong Kong dealt in opium. Between 1845 and 1849, three-quarters of India's opium crop passed through Victoria Harbour, and an average of forty thousand chests of opium were stored in Hong Kong warehouses. Although the British government had initially considered banning opium ships from mooring in the harbor, colonial officials insisted that this would only divert the trade elsewhere. Not only was the opium trade highly lucrative, but colonists also often contrasted the calming effects of opium on Chinese laborers with the violent effects of alcohol on the local European working class. And even colonial officials who later considered curbing the opium trade realized that any attempt to control the influx of opium would be blocked by the government of British India.

Opium was so lucrative that from 1845 to 1941 the Hong Kong government derived much of its revenue from the trade. Indeed, writes historian Christopher Munn, "the opium trade and Hong Kong are so obviously intertwined that it is hardly possible to consider the early history of the colony without some reference to the drug: the colony was founded because of opium; it survived its difficult early years because of opium; its principal merchants grew rich on opium; and its government subsisted on the high land rent and other revenue made possible by the opium trade."[1] In the nineteenth century, most of this revenue came from taxes on the processing and retail of opium, granted to the highest bidder. When the Hong Kong government, under orders from the British government in 1908, reluctantly closed opium divans, the British government had to reimburse the colony for its losses. Wealthy Chinese businessmen argued that although banning the sale of opium would be good for the Chinese public, it would hurt both government and merchant revenues. Even after the export of opium to China was ended in 1913, the monopoly on opium consumed within Hong Kong provided a substantial source of government revenue. Although the League of Nations urged the British government after World War I to end the monopoly on opium and to criminalize smoking opium, the Hong Kong government still derived considerable revenues from the sale of opium. The government monopolies were not abolished until after World War II, when opium smoking was also banned.

Apart from opium, the main source of early Hong Kong's prosperity was Chinese emigration. Chinese historians have often argued that the emigrant trade, along with its often deplorable conditions, was the product of Western colonialism and that colonial governments and foreign merchants were the main beneficiaries. Like opium, however, this was a trade from which foreign and Chinese merchants alike benefited. Although emigration was illegal under Qing law, Chinese authorities neither tried nor could do much to stop it. The border between Hong Kong and China was simply too porous. Apart from generating trade, emigration helped relieve population pressures along China's coast. Most emigrants never reaped the riches they dreamt of, but many sent remittances via Hong Kong to their families in China. With money to be made at all levels, the emigration trade involved an extensive network of Chinese collaborators: labor recruiters in mainland villages, contractors and other middlemen in Hong Kong and other ports, interpreters and overseers on board the ships, and large labor brokers, ship owners, and brokers in Hong Kong. Two of the largest brokerage companies in Hong Kong that sent workers to California were owned by local Chinese merchants. Primarily through opium and Chinese emigration, Hong Kong became a nexus of five overlapping trade networks with China, Southeast Asia, India, Britain (and thus Europe), and the Americas.

SOCIETY

Although Hong Kong was a British colony and a predominantly Chinese city, like the treaty ports that dotted the coast and waterways of China and like most cities in the British Empire it was multiethnic from the start. In addition to the British and the Chinese, there were Eurasians, Indians, Portuguese from Macau, Jews from Bombay, other Europeans, Armenians, and Americans. As in most colonial dual cities, these communities lived in two main areas from the earliest days, with European businesses and residences claiming the better land and Chinese settling mainly in small huts along the beach and on the overlooking hillsides. Governor Bowring lamented in September 1858 that "the separation of the native population from the European is nearly absolute; social intercourse between the races is wholly unknown."[2]

This does not mean that the Chinese and European communities had no contact with each other. All Europeans in Hong Kong, writes Christopher Munn, had "a range of daily contacts with Chinese inhabitants, and a substantial population of Chinese existed in the colony to serve European or colonial needs."[3] Rather, a mixed society evolved that was from the beginning determined by the political dominance of the British and the economic importance of the Chinese. Colonialism brought Chinese and Europeans into both collaboration and conflict. Even more so than in other colonies, given the island's small size and limited land for building, space in Hong Kong could be highly contested. Sources do not reveal much about how the Chinese viewed the Europeans, but Europeans often complained about the smells and sounds from the Chinese community: open-air markets and incense, musical instruments and firecrackers from religious ceremonies, and the cries of hawkers and peddlers. European residents also frequently criticized the government for allowing Chinese residents to run "houses of disreputable women" in or near European neighborhoods and to profane the Christian Sabbath by holding theatrical performances on Sunday. Both European residents and colonial officials often complained that the Chinese built flimsy wood structures that were too close together, increasing the risk of fire and the spread of disease. This contact between Chinese and British led to racism on both sides, but it particularly made many Europeans think of themselves as members of a special community.

Chinese

Because so much of our knowledge of working- and middle-class Chinese comes from colonial records, even the most thoughtful studies of early Hong Kong society have been unable to reveal much, for example, about family life or material culture. Most of the Chinese who came to Hong Kong in the early years were from the lower classes, such as laborers, artisans, Tanka outcasts, prostitutes, wanderers, and smugglers. That these people violated orders from authorities in Canton against working with foreigners suggests both the dismal conditions in China and the opportunities that British colonial rule offered. Even after the influx of wealthy Chinese families during the Taiping Rebellion, most Chinese in Hong Kong were men who left their families in China. In the mid-1850s, only one-fourth to one-third of Hong Kong's population was female. Given the colonial government's concerns about maintaining order among its Chinese subjects, we have a better idea of how Chinese society in early Hong Kong was organized, and these organizations in turn shed light on the opportunities and problems facing the Chinese population. One important feature of the Chinese social structure in early Hong Kong was temples such as the Man Mo Temple, which was dedicated to the worship of the gods of literature and war. Another early temple, the Kwong Fook Yee Chee, was a place where Chinese could worship their ancestors.

Hong Kong's early history is replete with examples of how working-class Chinese learned to organize to protect their interests. Workers, artisans, and shopkeepers often went on strike to protest ordinances to regulate or license their trades. Although these strikes rarely achieved their goals, they are evidence of a growing sense of collective action. In 1891, for example, carpenters went on strike for better wages, while rattan chair makers struck for shorter work hours. The coopers' guild went on strike four times from 1894 to 1895 after some of its members were dismissed and replaced by outsiders. Whether these examples of collective action were motivated by hatred for the British or by economic concern is hard to determine. Some historians have tried to demonstrate that these actions were either examples of a nascent Chinese patriotism or acts of economic self-interest, but realities are never so neat. While some strikes had anti-British overtones, others were based primarily on protecting livelihoods, and still others were mainly resistance to British efforts to control and regulate the Chinese population.

Consider the anti-French strike of 1884. In the late 1850s and early 1860s, France sent forces to Vietnam supposedly to protect Catholic missionaries and their converts. After France forced Vietnam to sign a treaty in 1874, Vietnam (historically a Chinese dependency) asked China for help in resisting French incursions. By the early 1880s, Chinese and French troops were fighting sporadic battles along the border between China and Vietnam. When French forces attacked Taiwan and the coastal city of Fuzhou in August 1884, Chinese in southern China attacked Europeans and burned down their churches. In Hong Kong, the Chinese press helped foster national awareness by publishing news about the conflict with France and about the attacks on Taiwan and Fuzhou. Tensions escalated in mid-September 1884 when the colonial government, ignoring a petition from Chinese merchants not to do so, permitted French naval vessels to use Hong Kong's harbor for supplies and repairs.

Whereas the strikers avoided reckless looting and restricted their attention mainly to foreigners and Chinese who appeared to help the French, the colonial government made the situation worse by fining workers who refused to

Dockworkers, late 1800s. Courtesy of the Prints and Photographs Division, Library of Congress, Washington, D.C.

work for the French and prosecuting editors of local Chinese newspapers for publishing the anti-French proclamations from Chinese authorities. When the colonial magistrate fined Chinese cargo workers for refusing to load French ships, the target of the strike expanded to include the colonial government. After Indian policemen opened fire on crowds that were attacking British officers and other foreigners, strikes and riots lasted until October.

Although the anti-French strike was partly based on Chinese nationalism, it was considerably more complex. Officials in Beijing were anxious that the situation not get out of control. They relied on loans from Hong Kong banks to finance the war and depended on weapons and munitions imported through the colony, and they did not want to risk Britain teaming up with France. But authorities in Canton had issued proclamations forbidding Chinese to work for the French, offering rewards of official titles to anyone who killed French troops or destroyed French munitions and threatening to execute traitors and to punish their relatives. The strike shows that although the Chinese workforce was often divided, it could come together when threatened by outsiders. However, the strike also shows that labor solidarity and nationalism were limited, for activists often had to use force to coerce reluctant workers to participate in the strike. When Chinese authorities tried to get triads and secret societies involved by offering them monetary rewards, these groups helped lead the riots and intimidated workers who did not strike. Striking workers, many of whom were afraid of recrimination against their relatives in Guangdong, coerced others into joining the strike.

We know considerably more about the Chinese elites of Hong Kong than about the middle and working classes, mainly because they appear more often in government records and because they formed various organizations that have left written records. Barred from the colonial political machinery, these elites used a wide range of resources to enhance their status and power. Starting with neighborhood committees, Chinese merchants in Hong Kong soon developed an extensive network of voluntary associations that established them as the leaders of the local Chinese community.

Although these organizations were similar to those found in China and among overseas Chinese communities, they were also particular to Hong Kong's geographical and political situation. With a government determined to run its colony as cheaply as possible and taking so little interest in its Chinese subjects, these people had to rely on themselves and personal networks and to foster their own leadership to represent their needs and interests. Whereas in China the avenue to social success was through the civil service examination, no such system existed in Hong Kong. Chinese businessmen thus had to find other ways of transferring their wealth and prestige among the local Chinese community. This they did by assuming the role traditionally played by the local gentry in China, where historically people had preferred to rely on extralegal authorities such as village elders or local elites to resolve disputes. Finally, Hong Kong's close proximity to China meant that the turbulent conditions in China could benefit merchants in Hong Kong.

The earliest of these Chinese voluntary organizations was the Man Mo Temple, founded in 1847 by Loo Aqui and Tam Achoy (whom we met in chapter 1). Although its ostensible purpose was to worship the gods of literature and war and to observe religious festivals, the temple served other important functions. It soon became the main social center for Hong Kong's Chinese population, regardless of their regional or occupational affiliations. The temple also evolved into the self-managed, informal government of the Chinese community, with the merchants electing a committee to deliberate disputes. Thus, between the Man Mo Temple and the smaller neighborhood committees, the Chinese community soon developed mechanisms for managing its own affairs. Although the European community often eyed the temple suspiciously for clandestinely controlling "native affairs," the colonial government was happy with the arrangement since it fit with the government's policy of ruling the Chinese on the cheap.

The establishment of the District Watch Force in 1866 enabled the leaders of the Chinese business community to deal with the colonial government's inability to control crime. One of the defining themes of colonial rhetoric was that colonialism ensured peace and order, but early Hong Kong was riddled with crime and piracy. Chinese and European merchants frequently complained about the inefficiency and corruption of the police force, composed mainly of Indians and discharged European sailors. Both the European and Chinese business communities learned to rely on Chinese guards, watchmen, and street detectives for security. In early 1866, amid rumors that Chinese in Canton planned to burn and loot Hong Kong, several neighborhood committee leaders, including Tam and prominent merchant and landowner Ho Asik, asked Governor Richard MacDonnell for permission to form a group of guards and watchmen to protect their property. As the group was to be funded completely by the Chinese community, the government saw the establishment of the District Watch Force as evidence of the growth of civic duty among the wealthier Chinese.

Another important Chinese organization was the Nam Pak Hong Kung So, established in 1868. Originally founded as a mutual assistance association for the Nam Pak Hong (the various Chinese import-export firms), this became the largest commercial and occupational group in the colony. Apart from managing guild activities and providing banking and insurance services, this organization ran a uniformed neighborhood watch force and a fire brigade. As in other Chinese communities inside and outside of China, these efforts were both neighborhood services and concerns for the safety of corporate holdings. They represented an expansion of Chinese participation in the local public sphere, showing the community spirit, urban consciousness, and commitment to collective civic betterment that colonial officials hoped to draw from their Chinese subjects.

The most important Chinese voluntary organization in Hong Kong was the Tung Wah Hospital, established in 1869. The founding of the hospital says much about the abilities and resources of the Chinese elite, the history of medicine in Hong Kong, and the government's and European community's attitudes toward the local Chinese population. Although disease had plagued Hong Kong from its early days, the colonial government was concerned primarily about the health of Hong Kong's European population and of the European and Indian troops in the colonial garrison. The Chinese population's prejudice against Western medicine meant that very few Chinese sought treatment from the government's limited medical facilities. In April 1869, an investigation revealed corpses and dying patients lying next to each other in the Kwong Fook Yee Chee ancestral hall. Both the colonial government and Chinese leaders were embarrassed and eager to control the situation. Less than two months after a group of Chinese merchants offered to build a Chinese hospital, a hospital committee composed of about twenty of the more prominent Chinese residents had been formed. The committee chairman was Ho Asik; Leung On, another comprador, also played an active role.

Officially opened in 1872, the Tung Wah Hospital was founded mainly to administer Chinese medicine. As historian Elizabeth Sinn writes, however, "its work pervaded so many aspects of society that it became inevitably caught up in the most mundane as well as the most sensational matters": caring for the destitute, sending corpses and remains back to China for proper burial, repatriating kidnapped laborers and women, and running an insane asylum.[4] Equally important as the hospital's medical, social, and charitable services were its community services. The hospital became the cultural and social center of the Chinese community, a place where Chinese gathered to observe religious occasions. Eager to avoid unfamiliar British law, with its courts and corrupt clerks, many Chinese preferred to have civil disputes settled by the hospital committee. The hospital also provided invaluable services to the colonial government by managing the Chinese population, especially as emigration from Guangdong increased in the mid-nineteenth century.

Europeans

Europeans in early Hong Kong fell into five main groups: colonial officials, merchants, professionals, those in supervisory or low-status jobs, and missionaries for groups such as the London Missionary Society. Working for a firm such as the Hong Kong and Shanghai Bank provided a much better lifestyle than British clerks were used to back home. Many Portuguese from old families in Macau, often educated by Catholic missions there and in Hong Kong, worked for the colonial government and for British firms as clerks and interpreters. The European working class consisted mainly of policemen, government inspectors, supervisors and overseers, soldiers, naval and merchant sailors, mechanics, artisans, and prostitutes who came to Hong Kong mainly because the pay was better than in Britain. Although he preferred the Mediterranean feel of Portuguese Macau, George Chinnery, the best known of the China trade painters, spent some time in Hong Kong. The early European population also included a small group of beachcombers, wanderers, and outcasts—usually discharged seamen, deserters, or criminals. Like the Chinese community, the European community in early Hong Kong was overwhelmingly male. Some European women worked as maids or nursemaids, while a few owned their own dress and millinery shops.

Visitors to Hong Kong were frequently struck by the aloofness of the local Europeans, their lack of interest in Chinese culture, and their scorn and disdain for the local Chinese, and noted how they would beat Chinese workers with sticks and umbrellas. In 1877 a visiting Englishman complained that British military officers abused Chinese "as if they were a very

inferior kind of animal to themselves."[5] Europeans often treated Chinese
rickshaw pullers very poorly and rudely, throwing their coins on the ground
instead of handing them to the puller and often even beating them. Yet
there was never one single European or British attitude toward the Chinese
of Hong Kong any more than there was one type of European. Europeans
in Hong Kong could be more accepting of wealthier Chinese, especially
those who spoke English and engaged in philanthropic activities. As historian G. B. Endacott writes, the European population of early Hong Kong
had its share of both "greedy self-seeking adventurers" and "men of high
principle devoted to the public welfare."[6] And although European women
could be as racist as men, they often took a great interest in the problems
facing the Chinese community.

It would also be unfair to ignore the many problems facing Europeans in
early Hong Kong, not the least of which was the high mortality rate mainly
from tropical diseases such as malaria. The mortality rate for European
women was especially high, particularly for missionaries. One of the first
Western women in Hong Kong, Henrietta Shuck, was an American missionary who died from complications after childbirth in November 1844. Mary
Legge, wife of the missionary James Legge, died at the age of thirty-six in October 1852. Governor Bowring's daughter, Emily, who became a Cannosian
Sister and helped open several mission schools, died at the age of thirty-seven.

While most Europeans in Hong Kong saw themselves as members of a special community distinct from the Chinese, Indian, and Eurasian communities, visiting Europeans frequently noticed the many divisions within Hong
Kong's European community. The Portuguese, who were more likely than the
British to marry Chinese and to speak Cantonese, appear to have ranked in-
termediate between other Europeans and Eurasians. They generally lived in
Kowloon after it was ceded in 1860, their identity strengthened by their residential separateness. The British were more obsessed than the other communities with social status. Living on Victoria Peak, the highest point on Hong
Kong Island and overlooking the main business district, was the pinnacle of
social status. The Peak, explained an anonymous writer for a local English-
language newspaper, "looks down on everything and everybody."[7] Perched
high above the rest of the colony, the Peak resembled Simla, the Indian hill
station north of Delhi. Geographically and socially isolated, the Peak had all
the features of a self-sufficient, quaint English town: English-style homes and
villas, clubs, a hotel, a private hospital, an Anglican church, and the Peak
Tram, opened in May 1888. Apart from residence, British social status was
represented primarily though membership in such elite clubs as the Hong
Kong Club, the Cricket Club, the Jockey Club, and the Ladies Recreation Club.
None of the major European clubs in Hong Kong admitted Chinese. Founded
in 1846, the Hong Kong Club originally excluded "shopkeepers, Chinese, Indians, women and other undesirables."

Sedan carriers transporting European residents from the Peak, 1902. Courtesy of the Prints and Photographs Division, Library of Congress, Washington, D.C.

Sociologists have attributed this obsession with social status mainly to how, whatever their claims and pretensions to the contrary, most Britons in Hong Kong actually came from the British middle class. There was no real aristocracy, and unlike in British colonies such as India, British officials and traders in Hong Kong were relatively equal in social status. Even working-class whites generally were foremen or supervisors, so they always had Chinese below them. This obsession with social status within the European community caused the creation of social clubs and interest groups, which strengthened the European community by providing recognized patterns of behavior and determining the means and rules for leadership. Rather than weaken the cohesiveness of the European community, the many social divisions helped that community maintain a sense of unity in an alien and confusing culture.

Eurasians

Early Hong Kong also had a sizable Eurasian population, usually the progeny of relations between European men and Chinese women. Eurasians had a complex and often confusing position in Hong Kong society that defies any rigid categorization. "Neither fish nor fowl," explains author May Holdsworth, Eurasians "hovered between Caucasians for whom they symbolized shameful liaisons with native women, and the Chinese community which, holding strict ideas about kinship and lineage, scorned anyone who couldn't emblazon his father's name on an ancestral tablet."[8]

Given that colonialism was based primarily on racial and class divisions, Eurasians posed a threat to Europeans because of their precarious racial and social status. They were, according to Vicky Lee, "liable to a double distrust, for having a different identity in the first place, but also for not really having an identity at all, being neither one thing nor the other, and consequently sneaky and opportunistic."[9] Unlike the Portuguese in Macau, the British in Hong Kong never saw miscegenation as a positive practice that would promote racial harmony and stability. On the contrary, many Europeans considered Eurasians to resemble the "mean whites of the Southern States of America," while colonial officials frequently worried that colonial mixing produced a new category of "wavering classes." John Bowring once expressed concern that the "children of native mothers by foreigners of *all* classes" were "beginning to ripen into a dangerous element out of the dunghill of neglect."[10]

As in other European colonies, the growth of the Eurasian population produced all sorts of fears among the local European community about miscegenation, disease, and biological and moral contamination. Yet many Eurasians prospered in Hong Kong. Because Eurasians were locally born residents who usually spoke both English and Chinese, Europeans often considered them more trustworthy, loyal, and reliable than the pure Chinese. As in other Asian colonies, Eurasians in Hong Kong often filled commercial and government clerical posts. Some Eurasians, such as the Ho brothers—Robert Ho Tung, Ho Kam Tong, and Ho Fook—became fabulously wealthy businessmen and leaders of the Chinese business community. Still, they often remained socially ostracized by both Europeans and Chinese. Many thus married into other Eurasian families, creating a distinct Eurasian community with its own cemetery.

*The Parsee Cemetery. Courtesy of the Prints and Photographs Division,
Library of Congress, Washington, D.C.*

Indians

Hong Kong's non-Chinese population also included many Indians. Among
them were Parsee traders, who were some of the first landowners in colonial Hong Kong. As in Bombay, the Parsees became known in Hong Kong
for their business acumen, honesty, and philanthropy. Although the Parsee
community was small, some members became very prosperous through the
opium trade. Despite their wealth, loyalty to the British Crown, and generosity, the Parsees were excluded from the European social world. For the
most part they formed their own community and were granted their own

cemetery in 1854. The majority of Hong Kong's Indians, however, were Muslims and Sikhs who came to Hong Kong as traders, soldiers, and policemen. Indians were often employed as police and prison warders since they would be less likely to help Chinese prisoners escape. From the beginning, the Indian population was overwhelmingly male. In 1845, for example, 346 of the 362 Indians (excluding the Indian troops in the garrison) were adult males, the rest being women and children. Excluded by both Europeans and Chinese, these Indians remained their own community.

GOVERNMENT, LAW, AND THE ADMINISTRATION OF JUSTICE

Many interrelated factors shaped Hong Kong's early governmental system. Because organizing the early colony went hand in hand with developing the China trade, until 1860 the governor had three distinct jobs: negotiating with Chinese authorities, protecting British trade in China, and regulating Hong Kong's economy. After the British won diplomatic privileges in the Treaty of Tientsin and the Convention of Peking, the Foreign Office took over the China side, leaving the governor to concentrate on Hong Kong. Because the British government was determined to keep the colony running as cheaply as possible, this meant very little money for social welfare or education. In addition, any concern for the colony's Chinese residents was limited mainly to keeping them under control and preventing them from harming the interests of the local European community.

Constitutional Frameworks

According to Hong Kong's constitution, laid out in the Letters Patent of April 5, 1843, Hong Kong would be run by a governor appointed by the British Crown. The governor would administer the colony with help from a lieutenant governor, a colonial secretary, an Executive Council, and a Legislative Council. The two councils were each to have both official and nonofficial members appointed by the governor. Often described as the governor's cabinet, the Executive Council was mainly an advisory body with members drawn primarily from the British business elite. Its members, however, sometimes disagreed with the governor and served to restrain his power. Until the 1880s, members of the Legislative Council were almost all non-Chinese. Although this basic constitutional framework saw minor modifications over the years, it experienced no significant changes until the early 1980s.

The issue of political representation arose early in Hong Kong's history. In August 1845, British merchants petitioned Governor John Davis for less taxation and more representation. The Colonial Office, however, agreed with Davis that this would give the British merchants too much power over the majority Chinese. In 1856, Bowring suggested that taxpayers (including Chinese) who owned land worth more than ten British pounds should be given the right to elect one member of the Legislative Council. The Colonial Office rejected Bowring's proposal on the grounds that representation would enable Chinese interests to dominate and that the Chinese were not ready for representation. Colonial Secretary Henry Labouchere explained that with "perhaps a few honourable exceptions," the Chinese of Hong Kong, like most members of "the Chinese race," were "very deficient in the most essential elements of morality."[11]

After this there were few calls for representation. Although local European merchants wanted some form of municipal government, they were determined that their Chinese counterparts should not be included. These Europeans feared that any such proposals for representation would involve giving too much power to the Chinese of Hong Kong, which not only might harm British interests but might also help the Qing take control of Hong Kong. Nor were there ever any serious demands from the Chinese community. Rather, most calls for constitutional reform came from European merchants who felt that the government needed to protect the interests of the European community and be more like the colonial governments in Canada, Australia, and New Zealand.

Law and the Administration of Justice

The first legal concern for the British was whether the Chinese in Hong Kong should be governed according to British or Chinese law. This consideration was grounded both in legal theory and practice throughout the empire and in the specific local conditions of Hong Kong. Because the British selectively incorporated the legal traditions of the people they conquered, as more territories were incorporated the empire inherited a web of legal systems that combined English common law, British statutory law, and local customary law. Part of the reason for incorporating local law was practical: the British realized that they could not impose radical changes on areas as large and diverse, for example, as India. But another reason was the belief that non-British peoples could be ruled only through their own native systems. Also, during the negotiations for the Treaty of Nanking, Qing officials had demanded that Chinese in Hong Kong be subject to Chinese legal jurisdiction. The result was some allowance for Chinese law and custom as long as they did not violate British prohibitions against slavery.

Until recently, historians have generally assumed that this arrangement left the Chinese population of Hong Kong mainly to its own devices. The early British vision of colonial Hong Kong was frequently called "Anglo-China," which in the words of Christopher Munn meant "a model of British good government, a living exhibition of European civilization, a meeting point between east and west, where the manners, institutions and technologies of both cultures would engage each other in a productive and beneficial way." Because the colonial government failed to help Hong Kong fulfill this vision and was unable to obtain reliable help from the local Chinese leadership, until the late 1800s both the government and European residents increasingly viewed the majority of Hong Kong's Chinese population as criminals. Hong Kong had one of the largest police forces in the British Empire, a huge military presence, an elaborate system of monopolies and taxes, and oppressive curfews and registration programs for controlling the majority Chinese population. With a criminal justice system that created new offenses and punishments applicable only to them, the Chinese in Hong Kong "lived under a constantly changing, labyrinthine system of intrusive regulatory laws and policing practices, which increasingly criminalized many daily activities and brought thousands of people into direct contact with the police and the courts."[12]

Hong Kong's early criminal justice system was supposed to blend the best of the Chinese and English systems. In practice, argues Munn, "the Chinese in the colony got the worst of both worlds. Heavy policing and a mesh of mystifying legislation designed to regulate behaviour that would have been regulated by other means in China brought them into more frequent contact with the authorities than they would have experienced at home."[13] Nor was the administration of justice in Hong Kong in accordance with legal practices in England. Because the chief magistrate was part of the executive branch rather than an independent judiciary, he was often more concerned with fighting crime than administering justice. Early magistrates were very poorly qualified or even unqualified. Instead, the government relied on so-called China experts such as Chief Magistrate William Caine, who was often implicated in corruption and was so well known for his harsh punishments that the British House of Commons expressed concerns. The Hong Kong Supreme Court had no grand jury to determine if prosecutions should go to trial. The attorney general served as the public prosecutor. Juries were small, consisting of six men who were almost all European.

Colonial officials' frequent declarations to the contrary, the administration of justice in early Hong Kong law was not impartial. Courts often presumed that Chinese defendants were guilty, and judges such as John Walter Hulme were known for being especially tough on non-European defendants. Unfamiliar with British law, Chinese were less able to appeal unfavorable verdicts. They were often charged and convicted for very minor offenses. Because many Europeans believed that Chinese were undeterred by "easy" British justice, Chinese were usually punished more severely than Europeans. Public flogging was routinely applied to Chinese because many colonists believed that poor Chinese preferred the colonial jail to life on the street. Punishments such as caning and wearing the cangue were applied only to Chinese. In March 1859, after two British nationals were hanged for killing a Chinese boy, Colonial Secretary William Mercer offered the executions as an example of how "under the authority of British law, equal justice is dealt to all persons without regard to nation, to blood, or to any accidental circumstances whatsoever." Although this execution is said to have impressed Chinese authorities in Kowloon with the quality of British justice, crimes committed by Europeans against Chinese were generally treated more lightly than those committed by Chinese against Europeans.

The colonial legislature also passed various ordinances applying only to the Chinese population. In October 1842, after a rash of gang robberies, Caine issued a proclamation prohibiting all Chinese, except for watchmen, from walking in the streets after 11:00 p.m. After 1845, the registrar general had the right to enter any house inhabited by Chinese; all Chinese households had to be registered with the government, as did Chinese servants working for Europeans. An ordinance passed in 1857 during the Second Opium War required Chinese to carry night passes issued by the superintendent of police. It also allowed any European "acting as a Sentry or Patrol at any time between the hour of Eight in the Evening and Sunrise" to "fire upon, with intent or effect to kill, any Chinaman whom he shall meet with or discover abroad and whom he shall have reasonable ground to suspect of being so abroad for an improper purpose, and who being challenged by him shall neglect or refuse to make proper answer to his challenge."[14]

Although most of the discriminatory measures of the 1857 ordinances were removed in 1858, a wave of other ordinances followed. The Victoria Registration Ordinance of 1866 required Chinese households and Chinese servants working for Europeans to register. Ordinance 14 of 1870 required all Chinese in Victoria to carry lanterns after dark. The Regulation of Chinese Ordinance of 1888 forbade Chinese to hold public meetings, except for religious ceremonies and festivals, without a permit from the governor. The European District Preservation Ordinance of 1888 reserved part of the main town for European-style houses. Although Governor John Hennessy once called these ordinances "a monstrous piece of class legislation," many colonial officials justified these measures on the grounds that most Chinese in Hong Kong had come there on their own accord and could leave if they wanted to. Yet even this justification was flawed, for the colonial government made no attempt to differentiate between the Chinese who had lived in Hong Kong before the British occupation and the newcomers or between the Chinese who indicated their desire to stay in Hong Kong for the long-term and the sojourners who left their families in China.

Managing the Chinese

Although much of the colonial government's legal apparatus was dedicated to controlling the Chinese community, the government made little effort to understand its Chinese subjects, their society, or their customs. Whereas in India learning local languages and cultures was considered essential for controlling Britain's "Jewel in the Crown," most British officials in China and Hong Kong did not share this concern. There were, of course, exceptions. Before coming to Hong Kong as governor, Davis had been one of the few East India Company officials to study Chinese. Thomas Wade, a linguist and diplomat who served in Hong Kong as assistant "Chinese" secretary to the superintendent of trade, later became professor of Chinese at the University of Cambridge. Samuel Fearon, the colony's first registrar general, became professor of Chinese at King's College, London. But such people were rare in early Hong Kong. Shortly after his arrival in Hong Kong in 1859, some twenty years after the British first occupied the island, Governor Hercules Robinson complained that not a single senior colonial officer in his new administration could read or write Chinese.

Nor did the early Hong Kong government make any serious attempt to incorporate Chinese opinion. Until the first Chinese was appointed to the Legislative Council in 1880, the only person in charge of the Chinese community's welfare was the registrar general, a Chinese-speaking European originally appointed by Governor Davis in 1844. Instead, until the 1880s the colonial government relied on a tiny handful of European linguists, often with very poor results. One particularly intriguing and colorful of these so-called China experts was Registrar General Daniel Caldwell, who was married to a Chinese woman. Another was Karl Gutzlaff, a Lutheran missionary who also served as an interpreter for opium traders in exchange for using their boats to spread Christian scriptures. But the colonial government's narrow reliance on these China experts and on interpreters and intermediaries in general often created a barrier between the government and its subjects that could cause serious problems. Caldwell, who accepted bribes and was suspected of running brothels and associating with pirates, did not speak the Hakka dialect spoken by many of Hong Kong's Chinese residents. Gutzlaff's weak command of Chinese led him to mistranslate government proclamations, sometimes resulting in violent, even fatal, altercations between the colonial government and the Chinese community.

Although some colonial officials believed that the Chinese were best governed by their own "natural leaders," the colonial government had to avoid incurring the resentment of the European community by giving too much power to the Chinese elite. In 1844, Governor Davis introduced an ordinance giving the governor the power to appoint "native Chinese Peace Officers." When in 1853 Governor George Bonham expanded the system by giving the peace officers the right to settle civil disputes and by making the Chinese community pay for the peace officers, a group of British residents argued that such attempts had failed in India and were even less likely to succeed in Hong Kong: "There are no more corrupt people upon earth than the Chinese, and from the Emperor on the throne to the beggar on the dung-hill, there is not a Chinese who is not prepared to lie and support his lie with an oath." When Bowring proposed a bill in 1856 allowing Chinese to practice law, a European member of the Legislative Council objected, arguing that the Chinese "are a peculiar race of people, and . . . are generally crafty, corrupt, mendacious, and deficient in those qualifications which are needed in a trustworthy legal adviser."[15] Nevertheless, in 1857 the British government allowed Chinese to qualify as lawyers, and in 1858 Bowring introduced an ordinance allowing Chinese to serve on juries and for Chinese-style wills to be valid in court. Partly because of opposition from the European community and partly because the government decided to improve its relationship with the emerging Chinese merchant class, the peace officer schemes were abolished in 1861.

A larger obstacle to giving the Chinese a greater role in managing themselves was the colonial government's contradictory policy. To ensure that the local Chinese understood government policy, Robinson, Bowring's successor, ordered a Chinese edition of the *Government Gazette*. Yet Robinson made practically no effort to enlist the help of the Chinese elite. Although he frequently talked about the importance of the Chinese in making Hong Kong a successful port, he was also convinced that the Chinese community consisted mainly of criminals. He devised registration plans for Chinese who would be more likely to come into contact with Europeans and their property. To protect European property transported in Chinese cargo boats, in 1860 he introduced an ordinance requiring boat owners and their crews to purchase licenses and giving the police wide powers to search cargo boats without warrants. In 1863 he introduced measures for regulating sedan chairs and carriers. Robinson was the first governor not to receive a formal farewell from the Chinese community when he left in 1865.

No governor tried to control the Chinese population as vigorously as Robinson's successor, MacDonnell, who came to Hong Kong with almost twenty years' experience as colonial governor in the British Empire. Although he claimed to have lowered the crime rate and reduced the number of prisoners in Hong Kong, he did so by expanding the power of the police, strengthening curfews, and increasing the use of flogging, hanging, and deportation—not only for convicted criminals, but also for beggars, lepers, and "dangerous" or "suspicious" characters. In 1866, MacDonnell introduced a solution for relieving Hong Kong's overcrowded jails: prisoners would volunteer to be branded or tattooed and deported, on the condition that they would be flogged and reimprisoned if they ever returned to Hong Kong.

Even more convinced than Robinson that Europeans and Chinese should not be treated equally under the law, MacDonnell introduced a wider registration program for managing the Chinese population. In 1866, he tried to control all Chinese boats entering and leaving the harbor. MacDonnell's most controversial reform was his short-lived plan to end police corruption by regulating gambling through licensing. Almost all of MacDonnell's measures led to opposition from the Chinese community of Hong Kong, with mixed results. Some Chinese simply left Hong Kong after the 1866 registration ordinance, while others resisted other ordinances by not paying for the new licenses, but this opposition generally had little effect on government policy. Chinese elites did, however, succeed in forcing MacDonnell to end his scheme for regulating gambling. In 1871 they argued in a petition that the system had increased corruption, bankruptcy, robbery, suicide, and the selling of children into slavery.

Like his predecessors, Hennessy, MacDonnell's successor, used a broad definition of crime and high rates of prosecution to control the Chinese population. However, convinced that MacDonnell's programs had been inhumane and a violation of British justice, Hennessy tried to abolish flogging as well as branding and tattooing. Trying to modernize the penal system along contemporary British lines, he introduced longer prison terms instead of branding and deportation. While some Chinese elites also opposed Hennessy's reforms, the Chinese community generally supported them. Hennessy eventually had his way, and both branding and flogging practices were abolished by the Colonial Office in 1880 (although Hennessy's successor, George Bowen, approved the flogging of prisoners as young as twelve and for very minor offenses).

Having been favorably impressed by the Chinese in Labuan when he was governor there, Hennessy was also the first governor to make a serious effort to enlist the help and opinion of Chinese in Hong Kong. It was Hennessy who in 1880 appointed the first Chinese, Ng Choy, to the Legislative Council. Although Ng's appointment was only temporary, it reflected the increasing influence of the Chinese merchant community, which in 1879 had asked for more representation. The only British-educated Chinese barrister in the colony, Ng was born in Singapore (making him a British subject) and in 1877 became the first Chinese called to the British bar. After his short term expired Ng went to China, where, better known as Wu Tingfang, he became a legal advisor to the Qing government and then the first Chinese minister to the United States. Only after 1883, when Governor Bowen convinced the Colonial Office to let him nominate three unofficial Legislative Council members, one of whom would be Chinese, was there always a Chinese member on the Legislative Council. Bowen nominated Wong Shing, a journalist and businessman educated at the Morrison Education Society School and in the United States, where he later served in the Chinese legation in Washington. According to Bowen, Wong was "fully qualified to look at Chinese affairs with English eyes and at English affairs with Chinese eyes."[16]

Hennessy also tried to reduce racial discrimination and segregation. In 1877 and 1880 he allowed Chinese to buy land in areas previously reserved for Europeans. In 1880 he helped local Chinese leaders end the discriminatory policy of the City Hall museum and library, where Chinese were allowed only at certain times. Hennessy's liberal ideas about racial equality had already alienated the British community of Barbados, where he had been governor. In Hong Kong, the European community blamed his "pro-Chinese" policies for increased crime and even for the alleged lack of discipline and respect for Europeans among the Chinese population. He was so disliked by the European community that when he left the colony in early 1882, no members of the British business community went to the pier for the traditional farewell ceremony. Leading members of the Chinese community, however, came to bid the governor farewell, presenting him with gifts and embroidered silk banners.

TECHNIQUES OF CONTROL?

Scholars who study how colonial governments managed their subjects generally focus nowadays more on the cultural aspects of colonialism than on its political or economic aspects. For example, they often see colonial education as a potent tool for making students useful in the new colonial hierarchy, producing subordinate citizens, and separating colonizers from colonized while creating a proper colonial elite. Similarly, enforcing Western ideals of gender relations helped European colonialists control their subjects. In India, for example, the British introduced a minimum age for marriage and, against Hindu custom, urged widows to remarry. In 1829 they outlawed suttee, the custom whereby a Hindu widow is willingly cremated on the funeral pyre with her deceased husband as an act of devotion. Although many Indians supported the attempts to end the practice, some scholars have seen outlawing suttee as a way for the British to show their own moral superiority and to justify colonialism. In China, efforts by European women to end the traditional practice of foot binding helped legitimize the semicolonial Western presence there.

Colonial Education

As in other colonies, in Hong Kong neither the intent nor the result of these cultural projects was ever so clear-cut. For example, although colonial education was designed to train compliant subjects and to help further Sino-British commercial and diplomatic relations, it was shaped by several factors: political conditions and educational developments in China and Britain, Britain's changing relations with China, and conditions in Hong Kong, including the "social composition and attitude of the local Chinese community."[17]

The first schools in colonial Hong Kong were private Chinese schools and those run by Christian missionary organizations, such as the Morrison Education Society School (named after Robert Morrison, the first Protestant missionary to China), which moved to Hong Kong from Macau in 1842, and the London Missionary Society's Anglo-Chinese College, which came from Malacca in 1843. In 1847, in accordance with similar programs in Britain, the British government allowed the colonial government to provide a limited grant to several Chinese village schools. Although funding Chinese education in Hong Kong represented a break from British colonial policy (in India, the Orientalists, who believed that Western knowledge and values could be spread through Indian languages, lost out to the Anglicists, who were convinced that the government should support only English), from 1850 to 1859 the number of Chinese village schools in Hong Kong increased, while the number of Anglo-Chinese missionary schools decreased.

Although Christian churches continued to play an important role in Hong Kong's education system, the government, with the guidance of James Legge, began to take a more active role in education and to stress the teaching of English. (Although he was a missionary, Legge opposed church control of education and compulsory religious education. He also admired Confucianism and saw no need to replace it with Christianity.) This shift was partly shaped by changing attitudes toward education in Britain, where church control of education had fallen out of favor, and by colonial officials' conviction that teaching English would help improve Sino-British relations. But the shift also reflected the attitudes and demand of a rising Chinese middle class, which increasingly called for English education. The government Central School for boys, founded in 1862, quickly became far more popular with the local Chinese middle class than the village schools. (Wealthier Chinese generally sent their sons to China or hired private tutors; a government school for girls opened in the late 1880s.) Many Chinese boys considered the Central School an avenue to a good job with European firms or the Imperial Chinese Maritime Customs. By the 1870s, graduates were acquiring jobs with local trading houses, in the Chinese treaty ports, in Japan, and in the United States.

Central School graduates soon became some of the most successful businessmen in the colony, many making their fortunes as compradors to foreign firms or by starting their own businesses. The best known of these graduates were the Eurasian Ho brothers. Robert Ho Tung, who entered the school in 1873, became an internationally known tycoon. At age seventeen he joined the Imperial Chinese Maritime Customs but resigned in 1880 to become comprador of Jardine and Matheson. He was considered to be the wealthiest man in Hong Kong and was associated with practically every large business in the colony. Ho Tung was a renowned philanthropist, both in Hong Kong and in China. His brother Ho Kam Tong was Jardine and Matheson's assistant

Schoolboys, circa 1900. Courtesy of the Prints and Photographs Division,
Library of Congress, Washington, D.C.

comprador, a successful businessman on his own, and a Tung Wah Hospital
Committee member. Even more so than his brother, Ho Kam Tong was
known in Hong Kong and China for his public service and philanthropy. Another brother, Ho Fook, graduated from the Central School in 1881, later succeeding Robert as head comprador of Jardine and Matheson.

Policing Prostitution and Contagious Diseases

The regulation and licensing of prostitution in Hong Kong has often been
seen as another form of control—as a way for the government to intervene

in the lives of its colonial subjects, especially Chinese women, and as an example of how the colonial government could choose which local laws and customs to keep or abolish. As with education, here too the situation was considerably more complicated. The colonial government did not always have such a free hand. It had to answer to the Colonial Office and the British Parliament, and it was often bound to comply with legislation in other parts of the empire. Nor could it afford to offend the Chinese community. The colonial government also often had help from Chinese elites who, for example, especially supported the licensing and regulation of prostitution to keep brothels from infiltrating into respectable parts of town.

Brothels and venereal disease were part of the colony's history from the start. Because the overwhelming majority of Chinese and Europeans who came after the British occupation were men, Hong Kong's gender balance was always heavily skewed. The large military presence made the situation even worse. Although the influx of Chinese during the Taiping Rebellion brought more women, according to the first proper census in 1872 the ratio of Chinese men to women was seven to one; the ratio for Europeans was five to one. By the 1850s, Hong Kong was known as a center for prostitution and venereal disease, especially syphilis. According to the 1876 census, five-sixths of the almost twenty-five thousand Chinese women in Hong Kong were prostitutes. In 1877 the police magistrate estimated that only one out of every six Chinese women in Hong Kong were either married or concubines, the rest being prostitutes.

This assumption that Chinese women who were either not married or concubines must necessarily have been prostitutes says more about European attitudes toward the Chinese community than about the actual number of prostitutes. Because Europeans in Hong Kong often considered Chinese women to be sexual and moral hazards, from 1857 to 1890 prostitution was licensed and regulated, with brothels strictly confined to separate areas depending on whether they catered to Western or Chinese clients. Similar to ordinances passed that year in Malta and the Ionian Islands (both British possessions), Hong Kong's first contagious disease ordinance, passed in 1857, called for the licensing of brothels by the registrar general, compulsory weekly medical inspections of prostitutes, punishment of prostitutes (and the brothel keepers) who transmitted venereal diseases to clients, and the detainment of infected prostitutes in a lock hospital. After the British Parliament passed the Contagious Diseases Acts of 1866 in England and Wales, the 1857 ordinance was replaced in Hong Kong by the Contagious Diseases Ordinance of 1867. The colonial government now had even more power to regulate prostitution, for the new ordinance gave the registrar general and the police superintendent the right to enter suspected brothels without a warrant. This, explains historian Philippa Levine, justified "a greater invasiveness into colonial lives, especially those of Chinese women."[18]

Colonial officials claimed that these ordinances saved girls and women from brothel slavery and from being exploited by brothel owners and kept prostitution from spreading into the respectable parts of town. However, the ordinances were designed mainly to protect soldiers, sailors, and policemen from venereal diseases by maintaining a supply of disease-free Chinese women. Only prostitutes who serviced Westerners had to be inspected, while in practice only the prostitutes servicing European police and soldiers were regulated. In December 1880, Governor Hennessy explained to the secretary for the colonies that the "real purpose of the brothel legislation" in Hong Kong had not been the protection of prostitutes but rather "the provision of clean Chinese women for the use of the British soldiers and the sailors of the Royal Navy in this Colony." Here the legislation had been successful. However, "far from checking this odious species of slavery," the ordinances had "undoubtedly intensified it."[19] In June 1881, Hennessy explained how "women are bought and sold in nearly every brothel in the place."[20] Although the Colonial Office did not support Hennessy's plans to overhaul the ordinances, it approved minor amendments to them.

When the Colonial Office ordered colonial governments to end their contagious diseases laws after the British Parliament repealed the Contagious Diseases Acts in 1886, Governor William Des Voeux tried desperately to maintain the status quo. Des Voeux argued that the colony's security depended on the health of its soldiers and police and that the system was the only way to keep girls from being sold into prostitution, check the spread of venereal diseases, and keep brothels from spreading into the more respectable parts of town. Finally, in 1889, the Legislative Council passed the Women and Girl's Protection Ordinance, which repealed the Contagious Diseases Ordinance of 1867 but then reinstated almost all of the provisions for licensing and registering brothels. Although this ordinance was repealed in 1890 because it violated the orders of the secretary for the colonies, its repeal seems to have had little effect because the same prostitutes who had heeded or ignored the earlier laws continued to do the same.

While it did little to prevent brothel slavery or the exploitation of prostitutes, the licensing and regulation of prostitution met its main goal of helping to prevent the transmission of venereal diseases among soldiers and sailors and keeping brothels from spreading into more respectable areas of town (which appears to have been the main concern of the Chinese elite). In 1893, however, fiery speeches in Parliament and pressure from groups in Britain forced the colonial government to stop all registration and inspection schemes. Unlike in 1890, this time the change was dramatic. Prostitutes stopped going for their medical inspections, new brothels opened in areas where they had not been before, and by 1897 about half of the soldiers in Hong Kong were being treated for venereal diseases (compared to about 15 percent a decade earlier).

What do we know about the prostitutes themselves? Many of the Chinese prostitutes were either kidnapped and sold into prostitution or sold by their impoverished parents. Contemporary reports mention how young girls in Hong Kong often disguised themselves as boys in public to avoid being kidnapped. Other prostitutes came from the already well-developed sex trades in Canton and Macau. Most of the European prostitutes had been prostitutes before they came to Hong Kong, but some resorted to prostitution after falling on hard times. Toward the end of the nineteenth century, among the European prostitutes were a large number of Jews who had fled the pogroms in Russia. Shunned by other European women, these prostitutes lived mainly on the margins of the European parts of town or in the predominantly Chinese sections such as Wanchai. The life of European prostitutes was not always one of humiliation and despair, however, for some rose high enough in society to retire comfortably in Europe or America.

In a group of their own were so-called protected women—Chinese women who served as mistresses to European men, especially before European women came in larger numbers later in the nineteenth century. Many of these women were Tankas, some having been purchased by their European masters from brothels in Canton and Hong Kong. Known to the Chinese as saltwater maids, these women lived in a marginal area of Hong Kong that was nestled between the European business and residential sections of town and was inhabited by a mixed group of European prostitutes, Indian merchants and shopkeepers, Portuguese, and Chinese prostitutes who serviced European and middle- and upper-class Chinese clients. Although some of these protected women did well for themselves, the status of their protection could be very fragile. Most European men eventually returned home, leaving their Chinese mistresses in Hong Kong, where they were often despised by the mainstream of the Chinese community. The children of these women formed the beginnings of the Eurasian community.

Mui-Tsai

Many of the girls and women in Hong Kong were *mui-tsai* ("little sisters") who had been sold to wealthier families through an intermediary known as a pocket mother. Found throughout China under a variety of names, this arrangement helped poor families find better homes for their daughters, while providing domestic help for wealthier families. Although Hong Kong's first ordinance, passed in 1844, banned slavery, neither the colonial government nor the majority of the Chinese population considered this to include the *mui-tsai*. Despite some sporadic criticism, mainly from missionaries in Hong Kong and officials in Britain, the legal status of the system did not come into question until the late 1870s.

Young upper-class women with servant, circa 1900. Courtesy of the Prints and Photographs Division, Library of Congress, Washington, D.C.

The reason that the *mui-tsai* issue became so controversial had much to do with timing. By the late 1870s, an extensive network of kidnapping had developed to feed the need for prostitutes and servants in Hong Kong. Girls were kidnapped from their native villages in China and then sold in Hong Kong. With the opening of the Suez Canal in 1869, the colony was becoming a popular destination for European and American tourists, many of whom were shocked that such a practice could be tolerated in a British colony. The Victorian traveler Isabella Bird described the *mui-tsai* system as a "peculiar hateful form of slavery which is recognised by Chinese custom, and which has attained gigantic proportions in Victoria."[21] The issue had also attracted the attention of reformist groups in Britain, such as the Anti-Slavery Society and the Society for the Protection of Aborigines. In California, American politicians used evidence of the *mui-tsai* to support restricting Chinese immigration to the United States. Furthermore, local Chinese elites had become strong enough to protect a time-honored Chinese custom from which they benefited. In November 1878, four prominent Chinese merchants—including Fung Ming Shan, a founder of the Nam Pak Hong Kung So—petitioned Governor Hennessy for permission to form an agency to stop the kidnapping of children from Dongguan, the four merchants' native district in Guangdong.

In October 1879, Chief Justice John Smale condemned the *mui-tsai* practice for violating British and Hong Kong laws prohibiting slavery. Smale estimated that between ten thousand and twenty thousand girls were enslaved in Hong Kong. "The more I penetrate below the polished surface of our civilization," he declared, "the more convinced am I that the broad under-current of life here is more like that in the Southern States of the America when slavery was dominant, than it resembles the all-pervading civilization of England."[22] Smale's attack caused a stir among the Chinese community, and less than two weeks later a group of Chinese merchants petitioned Governor Hennessy for permission to form an association to protect kidnapped women and children. After reminding Hennessy of Charles Elliot's proclamation of February 1841 guaranteeing Chinese in Hong Kong the right to practice their traditional customs, the petitioners went to great lengths to explain the difference between kidnapping and the *mui-tsai* system. They also warned that banning the system would lead even more poor families in Guangdong to practice another traditional Chinese custom: drowning unwanted female babies at birth.

Many people in Hong Kong felt that Smale had unnecessarily condemned a perfectly acceptable, time-honored Chinese custom. Complicating matters was the ambiguous status of the *mui-tsai* within the adoptive household—half servant, half family member—with some *mui-tsai* even eventually becoming concubines and inheriting their husbands' wealth. And one of the cardinal rules of British colonial administration was that tampering too much with native customs could be risky. But critics considered the system a form of slavery that often encouraged sexual abuse. Defenders, however, insisted that the girls were treated as family members and that the system saved girls from prostitution.

By asking for permission to form a society to stop kidnapping, the Chinese elites were trying to distinguish between kidnapping and the *mui-tsai* system, thus attempting to preserve a custom in which they were so heavily invested. Their petition was also a declaration that the Chinese elites had the wherewithal to handle the situation. After a series of studies on whether the system constituted slavery, the matter went to the British House of Lords, which agreed that the colonial government should not interfere with customs that were so deeply ingrained in Chinese society. In 1880 Hennessy approved the Chinese merchants' plan, and the Po Leung Kuk (Society for the Protection of Women and Children) was officially opened in August 1882. The Colonial Office eventually decided that the only thing necessary was to ensure that the *mui-tsai* were not being sold into prostitution, passing an ordinance to this effect in 1887.

Especially compared to the movement to end the *mui-tsai* system after World War I, the debate in the late 1870s and the early 1880s was short-lived and confined mainly within Hong Kong. Nor did the debate and the subsequent establishment of the Po Leung Kuk lead to any significant changes to the *mui-tsai* system. Although Hennessy hoped that the Po Leung Kuk would end the practice, some critics considered the society a clever scheme for ensuring that wealthy Chinese families always had a steady supply of young servants and that wealthy Chinese men had a pool of potential concubines. As Elizabeth Sinn argues, the Chinese merchants' "triumph had long-term consequences." Despite its many commendable charitable and philanthropic activities, the Po Leung Kuk upheld a "peculiarly Chinese form of patriarchy at a critical point of its development in Hong Kong." Once the controversy had subsided, "official inertia set in again," and the *mui-tsai* system was left "unquestioned" until 1917.[23] Sociologist Henry Lethbridge concluded that instead of ending the system, the Po Leung Kuk "helped, indirectly, to maintain in servitude numbers of Chinese girls until long after the First World War."[24]

NOTES

1. Christopher Munn, "The Hong Kong Opium Revenue, 1845–1885," in Timothy Brook and Bob Tadashi Wakabayashi, eds., *Opium Regimes: China, Britain, and Japan, 1839–1952* (Berkeley: University of California Press, 2000), 107.

2. Quoted in G. B. Endacott, *A History of Hong Kong*, rev. ed. (Hong Kong: Oxford University Press, 1973), 122.

3. Christopher Munn, *Anglo-China: Chinese People and British Rule in Hong Kong, 1841–1880* (Richmond, Surrey, UK: Curzon, 2001), 64.

4. Elizabeth Sinn, *Power and Charity: The Early History of the Tung Wah Hospital, Hong Kong* (Hong Kong: Oxford University Press, 1989), 1.

5. Quoted in James Pope-Hennessy, *Half-Crown Colony: A Hong Kong Notebook* (London: Jonathan Cape, 1969), 53.

6. G. B. Endacott, *A Biographical Sketch-Book of Early Hong Kong* (Singapore: Eastern Universities Press, 1962; reprint with new introduction by John M. Carroll, Hong Kong: Hong Kong University Press, 2005), viii.

7. "Betty," *Intercepted Letters* (Hong Kong: Kelly and Walsh, 1905), reprinted in Barbara-Sue White, ed., *Hong Kong: Somewhere between Heaven and Earth* (Hong Kong: Oxford University Press, 1996), 147.

8. May Holdsworth, *Foreign Devils: Expatriates in Hong Kong*, with additional text by Caroline Courtauld (Hong Kong: Oxford University Press, 2002), 186.

9. Vicky Lee, *Being Eurasian: Memories across Racial Divides* (Hong Kong: Hong Kong University Press, 2004), 24.

10. Quoted in Munn, *Anglo-China*, 323.

11. Reprinted in Steve Tsang, ed., *A Documentary History of Hong Kong: Government and Politics* (Hong Kong: Hong Kong University Press, 1995), 65.

12. Munn, *Anglo-China*, 2–4.

13. Ibid., 159.

14. Quoted in Peter Wesley-Smith, "Anti-Chinese Legislation in Hong Kong," in Ming K. Chan, ed., *Precarious Balance: Hong Kong between China and Britain* (Armonk, NY: Sharpe, 1994), 97; also quoted in Munn, *Anglo-China*, 285.

15. Quoted in Wesley-Smith, "Anti-Chinese Legislation in Hong Kong," 91.

16. Quoted in G. B. Endacott, *Government and People in Hong Kong, 1841–1962: A Constitutional History* (Hong Kong: Hong Kong University Press, 1964), 101.

17. Alice Lun Ngai Ha Ng, *Interactions of East and West: Development of Public Education in Early Hong Kong* (Hong Kong: Chinese University Press, 1984), viii.

18. Philippa Levine, "Modernity, Medicine, and Colonialism: The Contagious Diseases Ordinances in Hong Kong and the Straits Settlements," *positions* 6(3) (Winter 1998): 685.

19. Hennessy to Kimberly, November 13, 1880, in *Correspondence Relating to the Working of the Contagious Diseases Ordinances of the Colony of Hong Kong* (London: Her Majesty's Stationery Office, 1881), 46–47, reprinted in Irish University Press Area Studies Series, *British Parliamentary Papers, China, 26: Correspondence, Annual Reports, Conventions, and Other Papers Relating to the Affairs of Hong Kong, 1882–99* (Shannon, Ireland: Irish University Press, 1971), 624–25.

20. Hennessy to Kimberly, June 15, 1881, in *Correspondence Relating to the Working of the Contagious Diseases Ordinances of the Colony of Hong Kong*, in *British Parliamentary Papers, China, 26*, 625.

21. Isabella L. Bird, *The Golden Cheronese and the Way Thither* (London: John Murray, 1883), 41.

22. Smale's declaration, October 6, 1879, enclosed in Hennessy to Hicks Beach, January 23, 1880, in *Correspondence Regarding the Alleged Existence of Chinese Slavery in Hong Kong, Presented to Both Houses of Parliament by Command of Her Majesty, March 1882* (London: Her Majesty's Stationery Office, 1882), 13, reprinted in *British Parliamentary Papers, China, 26*, 177.

23. Elizabeth Sinn, "Chinese Patriarchy and the Protection of Women in 19th-century Hong Kong," in Maria Jaschok and Suzanne Miers, eds., *Women and Chinese Patriarchy: Submission, Servitude, and Escape* (Hong Kong: Hong Kong University Press, 1994), 143.

24. Henry J. Lethbridge, "Evolution of a Chinese Voluntary Association in Hong Kong: The Po Leung Kuk," in his *Hong Kong: Stability and Change: A Collection of Essays* (Hong Kong: Oxford University Press, 1978), 82.

3

Colonialism and Nationalism

In 1891, Hong Kong observed its fiftieth anniversary under British rule with a celebration truly befitting of a proper British jubilee: ships decorated with lights, church services at the Anglican and Catholic cathedrals, a royal salute fired from ships in the harbor, a review of military forces at the horse racing course in Happy Valley, sporting contests, and a public ball at City Hall. Although the jubilee reiterated the familiar, self-congratulating themes of British colonialism, it was truly a collaborative affair, for local European, Chinese, Eurasian, and Indian leaders all helped organize the festivities. This collaboration was reflected in the jubilee rhetoric, which emphasized Hong Kong as a meeting point of East and West: "a curious commentary on the relative characteristics of Western and Oriental enterprise."

Jubilees and other commemorations create idealized representations of societies and their histories. What the 1891 jubilee rhetoric did not explain was that the segregated Chinese and European communities often remained highly suspicious of each other, as would become evident during the bubonic plague of 1894. Many disgruntled Europeans wanted more political representation and a larger role in managing the colony they had helped to build. Alarmed by the rise of Chinese nationalism and the potential threats from other powers in the late 1800s, these Europeans also became increasingly worried about the colony's defense, a fear partly assuaged by Britain's acquisition of the New Territories in 1898. And even as they became more concerned about the fate of their ancestral homeland, many Hong Kong Chinese—especially among the rising bourgeoisie—began to see themselves as a special group of Chinese.

THE PLAGUE OF 1894

In May 1894, Hong Kong was stricken with bubonic plague believed to have originated in Canton, where some one hundred thousand people died. The known death toll in the colony over the next five months was more than twenty-five hundred, mainly among the Chinese lower classes. Governor William Robinson reported on May 17 that the plague was "entirely confined to the poorer classes of Chinese."[1] The colonial government responded by conducting house-to-house searches for infected people and quarantining victims on board the *Hygeia,* a hospital ship supervised by European doctors. These plague measures met with great resistance from much of the Chinese community. Many Chinese distrusted Western medicine, with its emphasis on disinfection and surgery. Resenting house-to-house searches by male inspectors, which they considered a violation of women's privacy, some residents hid their sick relatives from the inspectors. Approximately eighty thousand people left Hong Kong during the epidemic. All sorts of rumors spread: doctors were cutting open pregnant women and gouging out their babies' eyes to make medicine; the government was planning to select children from local schools and surgically remove their livers to obtain bile, the only known cure, and to send any child with the slightest pimple or boil to the *Hygeia.* Placards in Canton warned people against going to Hong Kong, where Western doctors were allegedly cutting up Chinese women and children. The colonial government issued its own proclamations, warning inhabitants not to believe such "wild and baseless rumours."[2] The Tung Wah Hospital Committee was divided. Some committee members resisted the government's plague measures; others openly supported the government and criticized the Chinese for not complying.

Europeans generally dismissed this resistance to the government's plague measures as xenophobia, superstition, and hostility toward Western medicine, but the situation was considerably more complex. Like most colonial governments, the Hong Kong government had never taken such an interventionist role in colonial medicine and public health. Until the mid-1800s, colonial medicine had been concerned mainly with protecting Europeans from the harmful effects of their tropical environments. Only after the bacteriological revolution of the late 1800s was disease associated with contagious persons rather than with unhealthy tropical environments. In response to an 1882 report by Osbert Chadwick, an engineer sent by the British government to examine health and sanitary conditions in Hong Kong, in 1883 the colonial government established the Sanitary Board, which was given the power to inspect and disinfect private homes and to quarantine contagious persons in hospitals. However, the board was unable to carry out most of these measures. It was opposed mainly by landlords and merchants, who worried that measures to reduce overcrowding and im-

Plague inspectors, 1894. Courtesy of the Prints and Photographs Division, Library of Congress, Washington, D.C.

prove sanitation would be too expensive and who often justified their arguments by pointing to the colonial government's historical promise to let the Chinese keep their own customs.

Furthermore, there was no reason for the Chinese population to necessarily accept the validity of the government's plague measures. To Europeans, the plague seemed to prove the latest theories about disease, for it appeared to be confined to the poorer and more crowded Chinese parts of town. Although some colonial officials derided the Chinese for believing that the plague emanated from the ground after long periods of hot, dry weather, Western medical theory had not yet established that plague was transmitted by rats; most medical officials believed that it was caused primarily by poor hygiene and overcrowding. Thus, the government's antiplague policies focused mainly on controlling and isolating the contagions of the disease: the Chinese population (the death rate for infected Europeans was substantially lower than for Chinese). The Sanitary Board, now given more power, ordered troops to search homes, remove and burn corpses, and isolate plague victims in the *Hygeia*. Many houses were burned down, leading to massive dislocation. As the Chinese were responding to what they saw as the government's intrusive policies, their resistance was both rational and remarkably similar to responses in other colonial and noncolonial societies.

The plague of 1894 had several important effects on Hong Kong society. Although some Chinese leaders had helped distribute medicine, many colonial officials and European residents criticized both Chinese medicine and the Tung Wah Hospital. In 1896, medical officials demanded that the hospital be abolished. This prompted an inquiry commission, which recommended that the hospital be supervised by the Medical Department, that Western medicine be offered on a voluntary basis, and that a Chinese resident surgeon trained in Western medicine be appointed. In 1897, the government appointed a Chinese steward to oversee the sanitation of the hospital. As the resistance to the government's plague measures seemed to prove how little the Chinese population understood Western ideas of health and sanitation, Europeans and some Chinese elites demanded more English in schools. The plague also reaffirmed many Europeans' conviction that they needed to stay as far away as possible from the Chinese.

Still, the suppression of the plague was not a victory for either the colonial government or Western medicine. Although local colonial medical officials criticized the Tung Wah Hospital for continuing to offer Chinese medicine, which was dismissed as empiricism and quackery, the Colonial Office opposed any attempts to close the hospital. And even though by the end of the nineteenth century half of the patients at the Tung Wah Hospital were choosing Western medicine, the fatality rate for these patients was initially higher than for those who chose Chinese medicine. The Hong Kong plague was also probably responsible for the one that afflicted India in 1896–1900. As in Hong Kong, part of the Western-educated Indian middle class was critical of the way that hospitalization and segregation were carried out. As in Hong Kong, all kinds of rumors spread, although in India they were compounded by rumors of general catastrophe and the collapse of British rule: inoculation brought instant death, hospitals were poisoning victims and cutting up bodies to extract their *momiai* (vital oil), and even healthy people were being hospitalized and would never leave alive. Only after widespread resistance from the Indian population did the colonial government agree to end or modify some of the more coercive plague measures.

THE REFORM MOVEMENT OF 1894

By the end of the nineteenth century, Hong Kong was the only British colony with such a limited form of self-government. Although the Chinese community rarely questioned this system, many Europeans believed that they deserved a larger role in running the colony they had helped build. In 1894, the Constitutional Reform Association petitioned for the right to elect British nationals as unofficial members in the Legislative Council and for more control over the colony's finances. The British government, however, rejected this as a poorly disguised attempt to gain power for Europeans. Secretary for the Colonies Lord Ripon, formerly the viceroy of India, argued that because Hong Kong had "become a Chinese rather than a British community" and Chinese settlement formed the "one main element in its prosperity," he could not sanction any representation that would exclude the Chinese.[3] The Colonial Office also feared that giving in to any European demands would encourage the Chinese to make similar requests. Although he raised the possibility of appointing a Chinese to the Executive Council, Lord Ripon warned that granting representation to Europeans would mean giving more representation to the Chinese.

Ironically, the 1894 petition for constitutional reform ended up benefiting the Chinese community more than the European community. The Legislative Council was increased by one official and one unofficial member, but the latter was Wei Yuk, a comprador and entrepreneur appointed in 1896. In May 1896, Lord Ripon's successor, Joseph Chamberlain, ordered that two unofficial members be added to the Executive Council. They were to be selected "at the discretion of the Governor" from the unofficial members of the Legislative Council and "by consideration of personal merit" and with "no reference to the particular class or race."[4] A Chinese was not appointed to the Executive Council until 1926, but given how the 1894 movement for reform inadvertently benefited the Chinese community, the European community did not seriously mention constitutional reform again until after World War I.

THE ACQUISITION OF THE NEW TERRITORIES

In June 1898, according to the Convention of Peking and "for the proper defence and protection of the Colony," Britain leased the predominantly rural area between Kowloon and the Shenzhen River from China for ninety-nine years. Around 365 square miles—approximately ten times the size of Hong Kong and Kowloon combined—these New Territories also included some 230 outlying islands, one of them (Lantau) considerably larger than Hong Kong Island. More than eighty thousand people lived in the region.

Colonial officials and British merchants in Hong Kong had advanced various arguments for taking the New Territories throughout the second half of the nineteenth century. The area would be a buffer zone with China and would provide land for real estate and for housing and training troops. The British government had resisted such calls. Even though proponents of expansion continued to harbor designs of making China into another India, the government had decided by the 1860s against more territorial expansion in China. Most British leaders were convinced that the "China hands" had exaggerated China's economic potential (by the late 1800s, less than 2 percent of Britain's exports were to China) or that this potential did not warrant territorial control because goods such as silk and tea could be obtained easily enough without territorial control (more than half of China's foreign trade was already with Britain). Making China into another India could overstretch British imperial power, and further expansion might lead to China's being carved up like Africa, which would only hurt free trade. Territorial expansion in China risked provoking other European powers into doing the same—perhaps even into war—and drawing resistance from the United States, which was actively involved in trade and missionary work in China.

The change in British policy toward the New Territories in the late 1890s reflected growing concerns about the defense of Hong Kong, not so much from China but from the other powers that were now challenging Britain's supremacy in China. Russia, having expanded rapidly westward in the second part of the nineteenth century, had a stretch of coastal territory in northeastern China. Despite earlier reservations about the value of empire, Germany had also become a colonial power and longed for a port along the Chinese coast. France, which enjoyed considerable influence in southern China after its victory in the Sino-French War (1884–1885), had signed an alliance with Russia in 1893. Although relations with the United States were generally good, the U.S. Navy used Mirs Bay—less than twenty miles northeast of Hong Kong—to conduct its operations in the Philippines during the Spanish-American War. (Mirs Bay was included in the lease of the New Territories, as was Deep Bay, northwest of Hong Kong.)

Even more important for the change in British policy was the rise of a new Asian power. This was Japan, which emerged victorious from the Sino-Japanese War of 1894–1895. The Treaty of Shimonoseki showed how much Japan had learned from the Western imperialists. Apart from awarding Japan an indemnity, opening four Chinese ports, and granting Japanese citizens the right to trade and manufacture in China, the treaty gave Japan control of the Liaodong Peninsula in northeastern China (although Germany, France, and Russia forced Japan to return it in exchange for higher reparations), the Pescadores (Penghu) Islands, and the island of Taiwan.

Apart from showing Japan's new power, the Sino-Japanese War led to the Scramble for Concessions from 1897 to 1899. Although Britain and the United States urged the other powers to maintain an open door and not take more territory in China, in late 1897 Germany occupied Jiaozhou, on the southern part of the Shandong Peninsula in northeastern China, after two German missionaries were killed there. The following year, the Germans leased Jiaozhou for ninety-nine years. In December 1897, Russia occupied Port Arthur and Dalian on the Liaodong Peninsula; the following spring Russia leased the two ports for twenty-five years. Eager not to be left out of the scramble, Britain leased the port of Weihaiwei on the northern part of the Shandong Peninsula. When the French leased Guangzhouwan, near Hainan Island and only two hundred miles from Hong Kong, for ninety-nine years, the British made their move on the New Territories.

Compared with the earlier treaties between Britain and China, the negotiations for the Convention of Peking were remarkably smooth. Although the British hoped for a permanent cession, their chief negotiator and minister in Beijing, Claude MacDonald, assumed that a ninety-nine-year lease would in fact be permanent. The Qing government had been reluctant to lease the region but, like the British government, hoped that conceding a relatively small area so quickly and without fanfare would prevent the other powers from using the British acquisition of the region as a pretext for demanding more concessions. Led by the seasoned statesman and reformer Li Hongzhang, the Qing negotiators had at one point demanded that the British pay rent for leasing the area, but they soon decided against this because it might prove the increasingly loud charges by Chinese nationalists that the Manchus and their Chinese helpers were literally selling out the country. Britain thus got what it had demanded, free of charge and without harming relations with China or the other powers.

Unlike when the British took control of Hong Kong Island and Kowloon, the occupation of the rural New Territories provoked widespread resistance from both sides of the new border, perhaps encouraged by Guangdong authorities. Villagers promptly burned down temporary structures erected by the new colonial administration. In October 1898, the residents of Kam Tin, a village in the northwest, raised a fund to resist the British if they tried to interfere with traditional practices of land ownership. After British troops fired on the village walls, village elders presented the wall gates as a sign of their submission. (Governor Henry Blake quickly had the gates sent back to his home in Ireland, where they remained until 1925.) In the spring of 1899, placards called on villagers to resist the invaders. Although the British had not expected such fervent and well-organized resistance, they had no trouble defeating the several thousand villagers who rose up throughout the region. British forces proceeded to arrest resistance leaders, confiscate weapons, and destroy the gates to village walls.

Some of this resistance was organized by local leaders who worried that the British regime would threaten the power that their families had enjoyed for several centuries. Other concerns were similar to those that inspired resistance against colonial expansion elsewhere. Villagers feared that the British invaders would impose new taxes, confiscate land, interfere with traditional customs, and disrupt feng shui. Rumors spread that women would be raped. Although the Convention of Peking stipulated that there would be "no expropriation or expulsion of the inhabitants of the district included within the extension" and that any land required for official purposes would be purchased at "a fair price," the villagers had good reason to believe otherwise. To persuade villagers to sell their land cheaply, the two Chinese members of the Legislative Council, Ho Kai and Wei Yuk—along with other Chinese businessmen—had spread rumors that the British were going to seize all land. Robert Ho Tung, the Eurasian tycoon, had helped the colonial authorities gather information on the region for the takeover. A local investment company had dispatched representatives to purchase land deeds in hopes that the value of the land would increase under British occupation.

Most of the resistance subsided once the British showed that they had little intention of interfering radically in local life, and the British occupation of the New Territories formally began on April 16, 1899. Here the British applied a form of indirect rule similar to that in other parts of the British Empire, such as West Africa. Governor Blake, who had been governor of the Bahamas, Newfoundland, and Jamaica before arriving in Hong Kong in late 1898, believed that the New Territories could not be governed in the same way as the more urbanized areas of Hong Kong Island and Kowloon. Instead, he intended to run the region as Chinese officials had: by interfering as little as possible except for collecting taxes and relying instead on village elders whenever possible. Blake divided the region into districts and sub-districts, each managed by a committee of village elders charged with maintaining order. The entire area was administered by a British district officer who was in actuality the chief police officer, magistrate, and chief administrative officer. After 1909, the area was divided into two districts, each with its own district officer. Over time, the district officer system expanded, with officers in charge of various parts of the region. This system lasted until after World War II.

Still, the colonial government retained considerable power over the New Territories. For example, the Summoning of Chinese Ordinance of 1899 allowed the registrar general to "enquire into and report as to any matter which is connected with the New Territories . . . if such matter exclusively concerns persons of Chinese race." The registrar general could also summon any Chinese person to appear before him for questioning. Despite some reservations, the two Chinese members of the Legislative Council did not oppose the ordinance. Ho Kai explained how he was "quite prepared to sacrifice a certain amount of our liberty with the object of helping the Government to carry out their policy for the good of the Chinese inhabitants of the New Territory."[5] Although a European Legislative Council member argued strongly that the bill gave too much power to the registrar general, Ho demanded only that the ordinance be administered tactfully and discretely and that it be used only temporarily.

In theory and in practice, most of the New Territories ended up being administered differently from the rest of Hong Kong—not from the benevolence of the colonial government but mainly because the region had been so tightly integrated with the rest of Guangdong province for so long. The region produced numerous administrative hassles for the colonial government, which, confounded by confusing and inconsistent patterns of land ownership, set about resurveying the land. Much of the land was not very fertile (as now, most food in Hong Kong came from China). In the first year or so, the colonial government spent over thirty times more money administering the region than it received in revenue. From the beginning of the British occupation, the region was exempt from many ordinances that applied to Hong Kong, including some dealing with abattoirs and markets, public health, opium, licensing, and registration. Over time, the New Territories came to play an increasingly vital role in Hong Kong's economy. Nevertheless, many traditional Chinese customs that had begun to fade away in urban Hong Kong and in mainland China—especially after the Communist revolution of 1949—persisted in the rural New Territories well into the 1970s. For example, the practice preventing women from inheriting land remained legal until the 1990s, long after it was abolished on the mainland and on Taiwan. Alexander Grantham, governor from 1947 to 1957, described the New Territories as "almost more Chinese than China itself."[6]

A peculiar feature of the Convention of Peking was the exclusion of a Chinese walled garrison that the Qing had expanded substantially after the British occupation of Hong Kong Island and after the cession of Kowloon. According to the convention, the area would remain under Chinese administration "except so far as may be inconsistent with the military requirements for the defence of Hong Kong." When Qing imperial troops helped villagers resist British rule in the New Territories in 1899, however, the British unilaterally declared the area no longer under Chinese jurisdiction. The area would later become a source of contention between the British and Chinese governments. When the British tried in the 1930s, 1940s, and 1960s to clear the area for sanitary reasons and to resettle the residents, local residents appealed to the respective Chinese governments, which reminded the British that the area was still technically under Chinese jurisdiction. Indeed, the Walled City became such a powerful symbol of Chinese sovereignty in British Hong Kong that patriotic protesters torched the British consulate in Canton in 1948 after the colonial government tried to destroy the city and build a park in its place. Thus, explains writer Jan Morris, the old garrison eventually evolved into "a sort of no man's land, known simply as the Walled City. The Chinese objected whenever the British proposed to pull the place down; the British never applied to it all their usual municipal regulations, and as late as the 1970s it was said that its only real administration was provided by the Triads."[7]

In the long run, the Convention of Peking that leased the New Territories to the British was, in the word of historian Steve Tsang, "a major blunder for British diplomacy."[8] The convention left unresolved issues that would eventually hurt the same colony it was designed to protect. Although the convention leased the region to Britain, the permission to extend British jurisdiction came from the Royal Order in Council of October 20, 1898, according to which the New Territories formally became part of the colony of Hong Kong. Because the order stipulated that British jurisdiction last only as long as the ninety-nine-year lease, British jurisdiction would expire on June 30, 1997. The region became more closely linked with the rest of Hong Kong, especially after the Communist revolution of 1949, by which time Britain was no longer in a position to seek any revisions to the convention. By signing the convention, the British had not ensured the future of Hong Kong; rather, they had made "an appointment with China." Eighty years later, they would have to keep this appointment by beginning negotiations with a new, much more powerful Chinese government. This time, they would not be successful.

THE RISE OF THE HONG KONG CHINESE BOURGEOISIE

In the late 1800s and early 1900s, a new class of Chinese businessmen and professionals began to emerge in Hong Kong, which had become the center of a Chinese capitalist expansion that ranged from China to Southeast Asia. Apart from controlling trade with China and Southeast Asia, Chinese began to dominate the industrial sector of Hong Kong's economy. In the late 1880s and 1890s the colony received a new group of immigrants in the form of overseas Chinese from Australia, Canada, and the United States—the result of restrictive immigration laws introduced by the British Dominions and by the American Exclusion Acts of 1887. Political instability in China supplied a steady influx of wealthy Chinese immigrants, who brought with them new capital, entrepreneurial skills, and valuable business connections. By the early 1900s, Chinese also owned the most real estate in Hong Kong. The completion of the Kowloon-Canton Railway in 1910 linked Hong Kong with Chinese and international markets, helping local industrialists import and export raw materials and manufactured goods.

The rising economic status of the Chinese bourgeoisie was also evident in the growth of consumer culture and conspicuous consumption. Department stores such as the Sincere Company, founded in 1900 by Ma Ying Piu, a Chinese who had made his fortune in Australia, and the Wing On Department Store, founded in 1907 by the Kwok brothers, who had also made their money in Australia, signaled the growth of a bourgeois Chinese com-

Queen's Road on Chinese New Year, 1902. Courtesy of the Prints and Photographs Division, Library of Congress, Washington, D.C.

mercial culture. Here, Chinese shoppers could purchase almost anything they desired—Cuban cigars, Italian felt hats, American razors, French champagne, Swiss chocolate, American gramophones, Japanese robes made from Chinese silk, and English suits, shoes, and cigarettes. With the improved economic status came an increase in cohesiveness and organization, enhanced by the emergence of a new group of retailers, bankers, and industrialists in the early years of the twentieth century. New organizations represented the interests of the Chinese business community, such as the Chinese Chamber of Commerce, founded in 1896 by prominent merchants and compradors.

Despite their status and wealth, the members of the Chinese bourgeoisie, like all Chinese in Hong Kong, continued to face racial discrimination at every turn. Racial segregation was enforced both legally and informally. In 1901 a group of Europeans petitioned the colonial government for a separate school for Europeans, arguing that integrated education harmed the morality and character of European children. Although one Chinese resident complained in the local press that "to exclude Chinese from certain schools means to go against the law of nature and to aggravate the hatred between Chinese and foreigners"[9] and Secretary for the Colonies Chamberlain condemned the proposal, it enjoyed great support among European parents and the colonial government. Ironically, the new school, the Kowloon British School, had originally been built and presented to the colonial government by the Eurasian Robert Ho Tung as a school for all races. Ho Tung now reluctantly agreed, regretting a decision "so opposed to the spirit which prompted my offer of the school to the Colony."[10] Chinese were barred from the Hong Kong Club and the Hong Kong Jockey Club, and in some hotels Chinese guests could stay only in certain rooms or could not stay overnight.

A particularly visible example of this government-enforced racial divide was Victoria Peak, the exclusive hill district on Hong Kong Island where no Chinese, except for the servants, cooks, houseboys, and drivers working for Europeans, were to live. In 1902 this residential segregation became law when the Colonial Office allowed the Peak to be used solely by residents approved by the governor. Subsequent ordinances passed in 1904 and 1918 explicitly barred Chinese and Eurasians from living on the Peak. As in India and other British colonies, Europeans in Hong Kong worried that close contact with Chinese posed serious physiological and moral risks. Most Europeans in Hong Kong believed that the fate of the colony depended on the health of its European population. Amid the fears of increased contact with Chinese and rising economic competition from the Chinese bourgeoisie, these restriction movements were attempts to preserve the status and social structure of the elite European community of Hong Kong.

How did Chinese and Eurasians in Hong Kong respond to the racial discrimination that was so prevalent in Hong Kong? Irene Cheng, Robert Ho Tung's daughter, insisted that the Peak District Bill of 1918, which prohibited non-Europeans from living on the Peak, was "bitterly resented by the Chinese and other Asian residents of Hong Kong."[11] But the Chinese members of the Legislative Council did not oppose the Peak ordinance, and only during the general strike of 1925–1926 was there a demand that Chinese be allowed to live on the Peak. And even this demand came from the strike organizers, who could hardly have afforded to live on the Peak even had they been allowed to do so. In 1919, a similar ordinance reserved part of the island of Cheung Chau as a vacation reserve for British and American mis-

Hong Kong, Kowloon, and Victoria Harbour as viewed from the Peak, early 1900s. Courtesy of the Prints and Photographs Division, Library of Congress, Washington, D.C.

sionaries. This time, however, the Chinese members of the Legislative Council objected. Lau Chu Pak expressed his surprise and disappointment that even missionaries could behave in such a manner, while Ho Fook, Robert Ho Tung's brother, condemned the bill as little more than "racial legislation." A few Chinese were permitted by the Executive Council to live on that section of the island in the 1930s, but the Peak and Cheung Chau ordinances were not repealed until 1946.

For the most part, wealthy Chinese and Eurasians responded to racial discrimination by creating their own exclusive social world. These leaders often considered themselves members of a special class, distinct from the rest of the local Chinese population and from their counterparts in China. In March 1901, for example, a group of Chinese elites asked Governor Blake to establish a special school exclusively for their own children. The signatures on the petition belonged to some of Hong Kong's most prominent Chinese residents. Ho Kai was a barrister, physician, financier, and unofficial member of the Legislative Council. Wei Yuk, a close friend of Ho Kai and one of the first Chinese to study in Britain, was an unofficial Legislative Council member, comprador to the Mercantile Bank of India, and former chairman of the Tung Wah Hospital. Tso Seen Wan was a prominent solicitor educated in England. The petitioners argued that "the indiscriminate and intimate mingling of children from families of the most various social and moral standing" rendered the existing government schools "absolutely undesirable as well as unsuitable for the sons and daughters of respectable Chinese families." Although some members of the Chinese community objected, the new school was built the next year.

The leaders of the Hong Kong Chinese bourgeoisie also established several exclusive clubs and associations to enhance and perpetuate their elite status. Barred from the Hong Kong Club, several prominent Chinese and Eurasians formed their own club in 1899: the Chinese Club. Among the founders were the Eurasian brothers Robert Ho Tung and Ho Kam Tong. Another founder, Kwan Sun Yin, was one of the first Chinese practitioners of Western medicine in Hong Kong. Membership and directorship were restricted to some of the most prominent Chinese and Eurasian businessmen and professionals in Hong Kong. Another elite club was the Chinese Recreation Club, founded in 1912 by Ho Kai, Wei Yuk, and several other prominent Chinese. Apart from enjoying such British sports and games as cricket, tennis, and billiards, members could practice Chinese martial arts or play mah-jongg. Even more important than the sports were the institutions and functions surrounding them. As in the British clubs, the Chinese Recreation Club's screening process was rigorous, and membership fees were high. Club rules were strict, and proper cricket and tennis whites were required. The club's directors and members were some of the best-known Chinese and Eurasian men of the colony.

HONG KONG AND CHINESE NATIONALISM

Historians have often stressed Hong Kong's contributions to China's nation-building in the late 1800s and early 1900s. Graduates of local schools such as the Central School served widely in the Chinese Civil Service and the Imperial Chinese Maritime Customs. Other Hong Kong–educated Chinese ended up working in China as teachers, doctors, scientists, and engineers. Local entrepreneurs invested heavily in commercial and industrial activities in southern China and donated to charitable, educational, public works, and medical projects in their native districts. Hong Kong was also the main remittance center for southern China, handling more than 50 percent of the money remitted to China by overseas Chinese.

Many Chinese in Hong Kong also participated in nationalist boycotts such as the Anti-American Boycott of 1905–1906. Throughout the 1880s and early 1890s, the American government issued a series of exclusion acts prohibiting Chinese workers from entering the United States, but other Chinese in America were also the targets of discrimination and violence. In July 1905, a Chinese who had been arrested without a warrant by immigration officers in Boston committed suicide in front of the American consulate in Shanghai. This led to a massive boycott of American goods in China. Although many local Chinese business leaders opposed the boycott on the grounds that it would hurt Hong Kong's economy, teachers, students, journalists, and merchants kept it going. Some stores refused to carry American goods. Chinese newspapers publicized the progress of the boycott, refused to take advertisements for American goods, and listed the names of merchants who sold American goods. Sedan-chair carriers and rickshaw pullers refused to carry visiting American Secretary of War William Taft (who, weighing more than three hundred pounds, would have been a very heavy load indeed) and his entourage. A group of wealthy Chinese merchants, including Li Yuk Tong, who had started his career in California, formed the Society to Oppose the American Exclusion Treaties Against Chinese Laborers.

A similar display of Chinese nationalism was the Anti-Japanese Boycott, which lasted from March to December 1908. After the Japanese government forced the Chinese government to apologize for seizing the *Tatsu Maru II*, a Japanese freighter that had been smuggling arms and munitions into Guangdong, Chinese in Canton protested this national humiliation by boycotting Japanese goods. Organized mainly by local merchants, the Hong Kong boycott was even more extensive than the one in Canton. Merchants who violated the boycott faced fines, while the Dare to Die Society threatened to kill and slice off the ears of Chinese merchants who broke the boycott. In early November, rioters attacked shops that sold Japanese goods. Although the boycotters did not attack any Japanese companies, the colonial government had to protect Japanese firms. After the colonial police shot two Chinese rioters, arrested at least one hundred more, and banished the boycott leaders without trial, Chinese firms protested by stopping business for two weeks; others withdrew large sums from the Hong Kong and Shanghai Bank. Worried that the crackdown would hurt trade by panicking the Chinese population, the European business community persuaded the government to ease up on the arrests. When Japanese exports to Hong Kong dropped by more than one-quarter, the Japanese vice-consul tried to patch up relations with the Chinese business leaders. The boycott ended by January 1909, although it was revived later that year in protest against the expansion of Japanese influence in northeastern China.

Hong Kong's colonial situation also enabled it to play an important role in the 1911 revolution, which toppled the Qing dynasty and established the Republic of China. Sun Yat-sen, who is celebrated throughout the Chinese world as the "father of the nation," was educated partly in Hong Kong, first at the Central School and later at the College of Medicine. Although the government was eager to prevent Hong Kong from becoming a center for subversion, the colony served as a base for recruiting and training Chinese revolutionaries. Here Sun established a local branch of the Revive China Society, which he had founded earlier as a student in Honolulu. The United League, a revolutionary group founded by Sun in Tokyo in 1905, was also active in Hong Kong. In a free port with easy access to arms and munitions from Japan and the West, Sun and his revolutionaries were able to organize a range of clandestine activities. The first revolutionary uprising in Canton in 1895 was orchestrated from Hong Kong, as was the second uprising, which occurred in 1900 in Huizhou—only ten miles from the New Territories. An aborted uprising scheduled for January 1903 outside Canton was also partly planned in Hong Kong. The colony was home to a host of local organizations that supported the revolutionaries, while local Chinese businessmen offered financial support for the movement.

Given Hong Kong's relatively wide freedom of the press, revolutionary newspapers such as the *China Daily*—published in Hong Kong and distributed to overseas Chinese communities—could not only debate more conservative newspapers advocating less radical reforms for China but could even openly call for revolution. Hong Kong also served as a sanctuary for Chinese reformers and revolutionaries. Sun Yat-sen took refuge there after the failed 1895 uprising. When the moderate reformer Kang Youwei fled to Hong Kong with help from British authorities after the aborted Hundred Days of Reform in the summer of 1898, he was initially protected by the colonial government. Yang Quyun, a leader of the Revive China Association, was allowed to take refuge in Hong Kong after the 1900 uprising. Embarrassed and outraged when Qing agents assassinated Yang in 1901, colonial authorities provided police protection to Chen Shaobai, another revolutionary, and gave him a permit to carry a gun for self-defense.

Like colonial governments elsewhere, the Hong Kong government inadvertently helped to encourage the growth of Chinese nationalism. Eager not to encourage anti-Manchu or revolutionary feelings, the government did not include recent Chinese history in local schools. By including topics such as parliamentary government, however, the colonial educational curriculum encouraged students to think about politics in ways that helped shape their political consciousness. Furthermore, students in schools such as the Central School were exposed to teachers and students of different nationalities and backgrounds, and the school library had works from all over the world. In a speech at the University of Hong Kong in 1923, Sun Yat-sen declared that he had developed his revolutionary ideas "entirely in Hong Kong." The extreme contrast between the peace and order in Hong Kong and the disorder and corruption in China, Sun explained, had made him a revolutionary. "I began to wonder how it was that foreigners, that Englishmen, could do such things as they had done, for example, with the barren rock of Hong Kong, within 70 or 80 years, while China, in 4,000 years, had no places like Hong Kong." (Sun did not mention this part, but, having observed the anti-French strikes of 1884, he knew that Hong Kong would provide a favorable environment for his revolutionary activities.)

Although the official government policy toward the Chinese revolutionaries was one of neutrality, the colonial government had to walk a very narrow tightrope. Like most Chinese in Hong Kong, it supported political change in China. The colonial government was under orders from the British government not to let Hong Kong become a base for subversion, but it could not afford to alienate its Chinese subjects by clamping down on revolutionary activities (although in 1907 it passed the Chinese Publications Ordinance, aimed at preventing Hong Kong from becoming a bastion of anti-Qing sentiment). Thus, in March 1896 Governor Robinson rejected a request by Canton authorities to extradite one of Sun's followers. Nor did the government try to close down revolutionary groups such as the Revive China Association. In March 1896, however, Robinson ordered that Sun, en route from a fundraising trip in Hawaii, be banished from Hong Kong for five years. Robinson insisted that the Hong Kong government would not allow the colony "to be used as an Asylum for persons engaged in plots and dangerous conspiracies against a friendly neighbouring Empire."[12]

Sun's banishment became an embarrassment to both the Hong Kong and British governments in 1897, when Qing agents kidnapped him in London and temporarily imprisoned him in the Chinese legation. He was saved only after a friend from Hong Kong, James Cantlie, who had been dean of medicine at the College of Medicine, intervened with the Foreign Office on his behalf. After a British soldier leaked the banishment case to the local press, the press and British politicians demanded to know why Sun was a political refugee in Britain yet did not enjoy the same rights in a British colony. In the end, Chamberlain ruled that because Sun had left before the banishment order was issued, the order could remain in effect. When moderate Kang Youwei returned to Hong Kong in October 1899, the Qing government demanded that he be expelled for plotting against the Qing government. As Governor Blake explained that Kang had not been causing any trouble, the British Foreign Office rejected the Qing government's request. By December of the same year, however, the Foreign Office had decided that allowing Kang to remain in Hong Kong might lead other powers to accuse Britain of encouraging rebellion in China. The Foreign Office diplomatically suggested that Kang go to Singapore, on the grounds that he would be safer there.

There are, however, good reasons not to overemphasize the role of Hong Kong in the growth of Chinese nationalism. As historian Chan Lau Kit-ching argues, concern with events in China was "lukewarm" at best.[13] Revolutionary publications were all very short-lived, and the activities of the Hong Kong branch of the United League were neither as extensive nor as effective as they are often described in revolutionary accounts that portray Hong Kong as a breeding ground for revolution. Nor was Hong Kong involved in organizing the 1911 revolution itself. The influence of newspapers such as the *China Daily* was also quite small. And the Revive China Association lost much of its vigor after the failed uprisings of 1895 and 1900. Rather, what appears to have evolved in Hong Kong was a kind of conservative Chinese nationalism that was shaped by Hong Kong's status as a British colony.

Consider the experience of Ho Kai, who was part of a small group of reformers that arose in Hong Kong and the treaty ports and is credited with influencing the political ideas of Sun Yat-sen. On the one hand, men like Ho Kai—born and educated in Hong Kong—saw themselves as members of a privileged group, in not only Hong Kong but also the greater Chinese world and the British Empire. Yet, like many Chinese inside and outside of China, they became increasingly concerned about the fate of their ancestral homeland. The son of a Protestant minister, land speculator, and merchant, Ho embodied a nationalism that was inseparable from the colonial situation in which he lived. He was educated entirely in British schools, both in Hong Kong and in Britain. He received his early education at the Central School, and then went to Britain for training in both medicine and law.

Ho returned in 1882 to Hong Kong, where after running a short-lived medical practice, he began his career as barrister at law and, like his father, invested in real estate and local businesses. He also developed a distinguished career in public service. In 1890 he was appointed as the Chinese unofficial member of the Legislative Council. He was the main founder of the Alice Memorial Hospital (named after his deceased wife, Alice Walkden, whom he had married while in England) and of the College of Medicine, where he taught physiology and medical jurisprudence. He was also a member of the advisory committees of the Po Leung Kuk and the Tung Wah Hospital, meaning that he was a government appointee and not elected by the Chinese themselves. For his services to the colony and the British Crown, he was made a Companion of the Order of St. Michael and St. George in 1892 and was knighted in 1912.

Inspired by liberal thinkers such as John Locke, Adam Smith, Jeremy Bentham, and John Stuart Mill, Ho saw British rule as liberating rather than oppressive. He believed that Hong Kong could be a commercial and political model for China and that, like Britain, China should be a constitutional monarchy with people's rights. He was proud of Hong Kong, which he considered more prosperous and politically stable than any Chinese city, its government less corrupt and repressive and its education and civil service systems better than anything China had to offer. Hong Kong represented the best of two worlds: Chinese entrepreneurship encouraged and protected by British free trade and liberal government. Just as commerce had made Hong Kong more prosperous and stable than China, the cure for China would also be commerce, supported by British liberalism and parliamentary government. With his friend Hu Liyuan, Ho expressed this belief in a series of political treatises that were later published in 1900 in a six-volume work called the *True Meaning of New Government*.

Ho was involved with the revolutionary movement at the turn of the century and played an important role in the history of the Revive China Society. Along with several other local Chinese merchants, he helped finance the society's newspaper, the *China Daily*. He also helped organize the aborted 1895 uprising in Canton. During the planning of the Huizhou uprising in 1900, he tried to use his connections with the Hong Kong English press on behalf of Sun Yat-sen's rebels to obtain British aid or at least ensure a friendly Hong Kong government (under pressure from the Foreign Office, the colonial government allowed Qing troops to pass through Hong Kong territory to suppress the uprising). Although Ho's involvement with the revolutionary movement declined greatly after the 1900 uprising, as did his attempts to act as a middleman between the Chinese revolutionaries and the Hong Kong government, his concern for Chinese affairs was not diminished. Rather, Ho, who believed that China should be a constitutional monarchy like England instead of a republic, had come to believe that the republican ideas of Sun and his revolutionaries were too radical. Still, Ho would remain committed to the welfare of China for the rest of his life. He is still regarded as an influential reformer. One historian has called his writings "a symbolic turning point" in the Chinese reform movement.[14]

THE 1911 REVOLUTION AND ITS EFFECTS ON HONG KONG

On October 10, 1911, units of the Qing government's New Army based in the city of Wuchang seized the local munitions depot. After similar mutinies in two other neighboring cities, Wuchang declared itself independent of the Qing dynasty. This sparked a rash of defections, with ten provinces declaring their independence in two weeks and others seceding one after another from the Qing. The rebels established the Chinese Republic on January 1, 1912, with the capital at Nanjing and Sun Yat-sen as provisional president.

The 1911 revolution aroused Chinese of all classes in Hong Kong. Governor Frederick Lugard wrote that the news of the revolution was received with "the most amazing outburst which has ever been seen and heard in the history of the Colony. . . . The entire Chinese populace appeared to have been temporarily demented with joy."[15] On October 18, 1911, four hundred people marched on the local offices of the Bank of China and a promonarchy newspaper, forcing both to remove the Qing imperial flag. Businessmen such as Ma Ying Piu and Li Yuk Tong formed the East Canton Red Cross Society to provide medicine and personnel for those wounded in the revolution. The Tung Wah Hospital collected food for war refugees. Students and merchants raised money to support the rebels. Barbers cut queues (the Manchu hairstyle imposed on all men within the empire) for free, while patriotic prostitutes announced that they would donate half of their profits to the revolutionary cause. Hong Kong also became a haven for former Qing officials after the revolution. Here these officials and their families became a sort of displaced aristocracy, building Chinese-style villas, listening to music, composing poetry, and playing mah-jongg.

Although the revolutionaries, eager to keep the foreign powers neutral, discouraged antiforeign sentiments, many Chinese in Hong Kong felt that since the Manchus had been driven out of China, the British should be next. Colonial authorities discovered factories for making bombs, and civil unrest erupted throughout the colony. Crowds looted shops, threw stones at the police and at the governor when he appeared in public, and tried to rescue prisoners in jail. Europeans rushed to purchase firearms after some were attacked on the streets. The police made so many arrests that the prison authorities had to release some prisoners before they had finished their terms. In July 1912, a young Chinese man tried to assassinate the new governor, Francis May. While the assassination attempt does not appear to have been connected with any political plot, it nevertheless revealed the tensions that the revolution had provoked in Hong Kong.

Partly because it was confined mainly to the lower classes of Hong Kong and partly because the new Canton government publicly disapproved of it, this civil unrest was short-lived. Although they supported the revolution, the Chinese elites of Hong Kong were determined not to let it harm Hong Kong's economic and political stability. Shortly after the revolution, Ho Kai and Wei Yuk, the two Chinese unofficial members of the Legislative Council, voted for an amendment to the Peace Preservation Ordinance authorizing the flogging of rabble-rousers in the local jail. In 1912 the registrar general reported that although the "excitement bred of the Revolution" in China and an "unintelligent passion for politics" had posed an "element of danger" and "opportunity for the unscrupulous," the "unostentatious work of the gentlemen" on the District Watch Committee "helped in no small degree the observance of the Colony's regulations and the keeping of the peace."[16] Still, the wake of the revolution left the colonial government anxious about revolutionary activities in China and Hong Kong. In 1913, Governor May pushed through his Education Bill, which required all private schools to register with the government. Although May claimed that his intention was to improve the standard of education in these schools, his correspondence with the Colonial Office shows that he was trying to keep schools from becoming centers for anti-British propaganda. The Seditious Publications Ordinance of 1914 was aimed at any publications that might undermine the stability of Hong Kong or China.

The 1911 revolution is known throughout the Chinese world as a glorious page in the annals of Chinese history. Like most revolutions, however, it caused as many problems as it solved. Yuan Shikai, the army commander who replaced Sun as president in March 1912, was unable to hold the young republic together. Although Yuan was committed to preserving order and unity and to modernizing China, he was equally committed to maintaining his own power. In 1913 he assassinated the leader of the Nationalist Party and suppressed a second republican revolution led by Sun in five breakaway provinces. The following year Yuan abolished the provincial assemblies. In 1915 he declared himself emperor of the Chinese Empire after being convinced by an American political scientist that China was not ready for democracy. Even before Yuan died in 1916, power in China had begun to flow outward into the hands of warlords or military leaders, who emerged as the new power brokers. China remained politically fragmented until the late 1920s.

The failure of the 1911 revolution to make China a stable republic had two important effects for Hong Kong. By 1913, many Chinese in Hong Kong had lost their enthusiasm for Sun Yat-sen, who was largely ignored when he visited in June that year. Indeed, both the Hong Kong government and the local Chinese elites welcomed Yuan Shikai's suppression of Sun's second revolution. The 1911 revolution had simply caused too much trouble: refugees poured in from China by the day, and by 1914 the population had reached half a million. The revolution also radically changed Hong Kong's political relations with China. Because the government in Beijing ruled China only in name, the Hong Kong government had to deal directly with a succession of regimes in Canton, several of which tried to undermine Hong Kong's political and economic stability. Yet because the British Foreign Office continued to recognize whoever was in charge of Beijing as the rightful government of China, this often led to friction between the Foreign Office and the Hong Kong government.

THE TRAM BOYCOTT OF 1912–1913

The Tram Boycott of 1912–1913 showed how dramatically the political changes in revolutionary China could affect Hong Kong. In April 1912, the

Hong Kong government banned the circulation of Chinese coins. The economies of Canton and Hong Kong had been intertwined since the early days of the colony, and Chinese coins had been used in Hong Kong since then. As conditions in Guangdong deteriorated after the 1911 revolution, however, the colonial government became worried about the effects of an influx of depreciated Chinese coins from Guangdong. Many Chinese in Hong Kong took the ban as an insult to the new Chinese republic. In November of the same year, Governor May encouraged the Star Ferry Company and the colony's two tramways to stop accepting Chinese coins. This caused even more resentment among the Chinese population because the shortage of Hong Kong coinage in comparison to Chinese left local residents with less money for their tram fare. When a colony-wide boycott broke out, its organizers used various means to intimidate those who violated the boycott.

In December 1912, May encouraged prominent Chinese to help end the boycott. He insisted that the tram companies' decision not to accept Chinese currency was purely an economic move and was not intended to insult China and that the boycott would only hurt both Hong Kong and China since so much Chinese capital was invested in the tram companies. On December 20, during a meeting at the Chinese Commercial Union, Ho Kai and Wei Yuk, both unofficial Legislative Council members, defended the tram companies and condemned the boycott for harming the economies of both Hong Kong and Guangdong. A weakened Hong Kong economy, they argued, would mean that Hong Kong residents would have less money to help their kin in Guangdong. With help from local Chinese merchants, the boycott ended by early February 1913. Although several of the Chinese who collaborated with the government to end the boycott received threatening letters, May was disappointed by the lack of influence that the more prominent Chinese now seemed to have over the Chinese population. He was particularly annoyed that Ho Kai and Wei Yuk had waited so long to help end the boycott. Indeed, Ho's failure to help the government earlier was part of the reason he was not reappointed to a fifth term on the Legislative Council. Nevertheless, the defeat of the boycott boosted the government's authority.

THE UNIVERSITY OF HONG KONG

It was shortly after the 1911 revolution that the first university was established in Hong Kong. The driving force behind the university was Lugard, governor from 1907 to 1912. Best known in British imperial history for his system of indirect rule in Africa, whereby indigenous rulers retained power under the supervision of a British resident, Lugard came up with the idea of a university only five months after arriving in Hong Kong. The only tertiary school at the time was the Hong Kong College of Medicine, established in 1887.

Getting the money for the new university was no small feat and reveals concerns about radicalism and higher education in Hong Kong, both locally and in Britain. Hormusjee Mody, a Parsee merchant who was later knighted for his generosity and his service to the British Crown, offered almost eighteen thousand pounds to start the building and a generous endowment. Already reluctant to contribute to an institution in which they would have no supervisory role, however, many Chinese elites were concerned that students who attended universities abroad often returned to Hong Kong imbued with radical ideas. The local British business community was even more hesitant, dismissing Lugard's plan to establish "the Oxford and Cambridge of the Far East" as simply another example of "the university fad" that was so strong in Britain and the colonies. As Lugard wrote to his wife Lady Lugard (a prominent journalist named Flora Shaw), "the money-grabbing traders fear that if we educate the Chinaman he may become a serious rival."[17] The Colonial Office called the idea of a university "Sir Frederick's pet lamb," and some officials in London feared that providing purely secular education would promote antiforeignism and radicalism.

Eventually the necessary funds were raised. Ng Li Hing, a local Chinese merchant, donated money for the anatomy building. A Chinese merchant from the Straits Settlements contributed to the arts faculty. The Eurasian Robert Ho Tung later endowed a chair in surgery. Only after Lady Lugard began to canvass their London headquarters, however, did the local British merchant community agree to contribute. Butterfield and Swire made a large donation of forty thousand pounds, mainly to prevent a boycott of their company after one of their ticket collectors had been accused of kicking an elderly Chinese to death. Whereas the Beijing and Canton governments each sent twenty-five thousand pounds, the British government was especially stingy, sending a paltry three hundred pounds to be used for the King Edward VII Scholarships.

The University of Hong Kong officially opened on March 11, 1912, with approximately seventy students from Hong Kong, Canton, and the other treaty ports and as far as the Straits Settlements (women were not admitted until 1921, and only after a struggle). In 1917 the editor of a local English-language newspaper wrote that "commercially, industrially, and educationally the colony of Hongkong, a mere spot on the map, is keeping the lamp of British traditions and high standards burning in far-off East Asia, and is also passing on the light." However, Lugard's dream of the University of Hong Kong becoming the Oxford and Cambridge of East Asia never quite materialized. Despite hopes that the university would attract students from the mainland, Japanese universities and those run by American missionaries in China remained far more popular. Only after World War II would the university truly fulfill its potential.

HONG KONG AND WORLD WAR I

Hong Kong was not directly involved in the hostilities of World War I, and there was no real military threat at any point, although between sixty thousand and one hundred thousand Chinese residents sought temporary refuge in Guangdong out of fear that the colony might be attacked. Nor, with the exception of inflation and restrictions on certain goods, did the war pose a serious economic threat. The deflection of European trade from Asia helped local Chinese firms. Chinese entrepreneurs benefited from the departure of approximately one-quarter of the colony's European men for the war front, moving into businesses dominated by Europeans such as banking and shipping. Older and smaller Chinese industries, such as camphor wood, preserved ginger, rattan, soap, soy sauce, tobacco, and vermilion, continued to develop, but they no longer remained the primary focus for Chinese industrialists. The most serious problems during the war were not even related to the war: a disastrous fire at the Happy Valley race track in February 1918 left more than six hundred dead and four hundred wounded, and an outbreak of cerebrospinal meningitis in the crowded Chinese tenements later that year killed more than one thousand people. The war did, however, affect the European community significantly, for all German women and children were repatriated, the men interned until the end of the war.

Like the rest of the empire, Hong Kong played a role in the British war effort. Almost 25 percent of British males volunteered for war service, and a large number of Chinese workers served in the Chinese Labour Corps in France. Both the Chinese and European communities raised money by subscribing to war charities. Chinese property owners agreed to an additional rate assessment of 7 percent, which raised more than two million Hong Kong dollars in the last two years of the war. Robert Ho Tung, the Eurasian tycoon, donated the cost of two airplanes and several ambulances to the British government. Chau Siu Ki, a Chinese insurance and shipping magnate and real estate developer, served on the War Charities Committee.

The formal end of World War I in July 1919 brought the entire Hong Kong community together in celebration, marked with fireworks, motorcades and parades, lanterns, and Allied flags. A mile-long parade organized by the Chinese business community went from Happy Valley to Central District, with lanterns shaped like various forms of animals and culminating with a great dragon at the end. So many people came from Guangdong to watch the festivities that the trams had to be suspended. One week after the victory celebrations, however, rice riots broke out—the first such activities that the colony had seen for many years. Although the riots ended soon, they nevertheless foreshadowed some of the events that would affect Hong Kong in the 1920s.

NOTES

1. Robinson to Ripon, May 17, 1894, in *Correspondence Relative to the Outbreak of Bubonic Plague at Hong Kong* (London: Her Majesty's Stationery Office, 1894), 4, reprinted in Irish University Press Area Studies Series, *British Parliamentary Papers, China, 26: Correspondence, Annual Reports, Conventions, and Other Papers Relating to the Affairs of Hong Kong, 1882–99* (Shannon, Ireland: Irish University Press, 1971), 390.

2. Enclosed in Robinson to Ripon, May 23, 1894, in *Correspondence Relative to the Outbreak of Bubonic Plague*, 4, reprinted in *British Parliamentary Papers, China, 26*, 395.

3. Quoted in G. B. Endacott, *Government and People in Hong Kong, 1841–1962: A Constitutional History* (Hong Kong: Hong Kong University Press, 1964), 121.

4. Great Britain, Colonial Office, Original Correspondence: Hong Kong, 1841–1951, Series 129 (CO129), Public Record Office, London, CO 129/274/119, May 29, 1896, Chamberlain to Robinson, reprinted in Steve Tsang, ed., *A Documentary History of Hong Kong: Government and Politics* (Hong Kong: Hong Kong University Press, 1995), 110.

5. Quoted in Peter Wesley-Smith, "Anti-Chinese Legislation in Hong Kong," in Ming K. Chan, ed., *Precarious Balance: Hong Kong between China and Britain* (Armonk, NY: Sharpe, 1994), 97.

6. Alexander Grantham, *Via Ports: From Hong Kong to Hong Kong* (Hong Kong: Hong Kong University Press, 1965), 11.

7. Jan Morris, *Hong Kong: Epilogue to an Empire* (New York: Vintage, 1997), 264.

8. Steve Tsang, *Hong Kong: An Appointment with China* (London: Tauris, 1997), 12.

9. Letter to the editor, *Hongkong Daily Press*, February 7, 1901, reprinted in Anthony Sweeting, *Education in Hong Kong, Pre-1841 to 1941, Fact and Opinion: Materials for a History of Education in Hong Kong* (Hong Kong: Hong Kong University Press, 1990), 273–74.

10. Quoted in G. B. Endacott, *A History of Hong Kong*, rev. ed. (Hong Kong: Oxford University Press, 1973), 281.

11. Irene Cheng, *Clara Ho Tung: A Hong Kong Lady, Her Family and Her Times* (Hong Kong: Chinese University Press, 1976), xiv.

12. CO 129/283, October 4, 1897, Lockhart to Sun, reprinted in Tsang, *Government and Politics*, 278; also quoted in Chan Lau Kit-ching, *China, Britain and Hong Kong, 1895–1945* (Hong Kong: Chinese University Press, 1990), 35.

13. Chan Lau, *China, Britain and Hong Kong*, 4.

14. Lloyd E. Eastman, "Political Reformism in China before the Sino-Japanese War," *Journal of Asian Studies* 27(4) (August 1968): 698, 709.

15. Quoted in Frank Welsh, *A Borrowed Place: The History of Hong Kong* (New York: Kodansha, 1993), 353.

16. "Report of the Registrar General for the Year 1912," *Administrative Report for 1912*, reprinted in Tsang, *Documentary History of Hong Kong*, 209–10.

17. Quoted in James Pope-Hennessy, *Half-Crown Colony: A Hong Kong Notebook* (London: Jonathan Cape, 1969), 129.

4

The Interwar Years

Interwar Hong Kong is sometimes characterized as a sleepy colonial back-water, particularly when compared with Shanghai, the "Paris of the Orient." This image overlooks how during the 1920s and 1930s Hong Kong was drawn more tightly than ever into the orbits of Chinese, British imperial, and world history. The revolutionary nationalism in China ushered in an era of strikes and boycotts, both in China and in Hong Kong. Struggles for political unity in China were accompanied by increasing vocal calls for abolishing the unequal treaties, extraterritoriality, and foreign concessions. Such sentiments never led to any serious anticolonial movements in Hong Kong, but they helped make the 1920s considerably more politically charged than any other time in Hong Kong's history. With the rise of Socialism and the ascendancy of the Labour Party, colonialism and imperialism came increasingly under fire in Britain. Although the British Empire reached the peak of its territorial expansion after World War I by inheriting some of the former Ottoman and German colonies and dependencies, the British share of industrial production and world trade declined, while the Washington Treaty of 1922 restricted Britain's military power to protect its commercial interests in Asia.

Because of the various interparty and provincial rivalries in China, Hong Kong was more affected than ever by events on the mainland—especially by the turbulent developments in neighboring Guangdong. Not only was the city of Canton ruled by several successive regimes, but it also became a center for Chinese Communism. The strife in Guangdong boosted Hong Kong's population significantly: in 1921 the population was around 600,000; by 1931 it had risen to almost 850,000. Furthermore, the crime encouraged by the political chaos in Guangdong often spilled over into

Hong Kong. In the 1920s, for example, piracy occurred weekly in Hong Kong waters. In an especially notorious case in 1924, pirates seized a ferry from the island of Cheung Chau en route to Hong Kong. After taking the passengers to a mainland lair, the pirates sent three of the victims' ears to their relatives in demand for a ransom.

In the absence of a strong central government, some Hong Kong merchants tried to influence Chinese politics in order to protect their business interests on the mainland. As historian Stephanie Chung writes, these men thus "developed a national orientation in politics outside the colony."[1] On the other hand, contrasting the stability of Hong Kong with the turbulence in China led many local Chinese, especially wealthier residents whose fortunes depended on Hong Kong's colonial status, to identify increasingly with Hong Kong—witnessed by the way in which they collaborated with the colonial government to end the strikes of the 1920s. A Western political scientist who visited Hong Kong on the eve of World War II observed that "one factor which has played a part in creating a class of Chinese who regard Hong Kong as their home is the insecurity which prevailed for many years in China."[2] This sense of belonging deepened as the colonial government became more willing to incorporate Chinese opinion, especially after the general strike of 1925–1926.

Advances in communications and transportation helped connect Hong Kong to the rest of the world and make the colony a popular tourist destination. A 1920 guide for British tourists described Hong Kong as "the most interesting Port of Call for Visitors to the Far East, as it is also the most important commercial and shipping centre in this part of the world."[3] The prominent Chinese scholar and reformer Hu Shi recalled a trip to Hong Kong in the late 1920s, insisting that the city's night skyline was among the world's best. An airfield opened in 1928 at Kai Tak, in Kowloon, and by 1936 Imperial Airways offered a flight from Hong Kong to Penang (in Malaya), from which passengers could eventually reach Britain. Pan American Airways operated a flight to Manila, linking Hong Kong to San Francisco, while China National Airways Corporation connected the colony with the mainland.

Hong Kong was also attracting British writers fascinated by the colony "as an outpost of empire, a minute enclave enveloped by the vastness of China, an exotic entrepôt pulsating with life and adventure, yet paradoxically a speck of normality on the brink of a forbidding continent."[4] In *The Painted Veil* (1924), renowned novelist Somerset Maugham presented Hong Kong's European community as a den of passion and scandal. So scathing that colonial officials protested and the leading characters won a libel suit against Maugham, the novel later became a Hollywood film starring Greta Garbo. In 1930, Putnam Weale, a less well-known but prolific author on China and Asia, wrote *The Port of Fragrance*, a fictional work that focused on

Tourist poster, 1930s. Courtesy of the Prints and Photographs Division, Library of Congress, Washington, D.C.

the general strike of 1925–1926 but also dealt with the unhappy lives of bored European women in Hong Kong. Stella Benson, who was married to a British official, wrote several books based on her experience in Hong Kong: *The Poor Man* (1923), *The Little World* (1925), and *Mundos* (1935). Benson spent the last years of her life fighting child prostitution in Hong Kong by writing reports for the League of Nations.

CHINESE INDUSTRY AND BANKS

Thanks to World War I and developments on the mainland, Chinese businessmen played an increasingly large role in Hong Kong's modern economy during this period. The war had diverted European business from Asia, allowing smaller Chinese firms to move in, while the chaos after the 1911 revolution in China brought an influx of wealthy Chinese entrepreneurs—especially during the general instability of the early 1920s, when Sun Yat-sen's Kuomintang (Nationalist Party) in Canton was receiving help from Soviet advisors. Chinese came from Guangdong in large numbers yearly until the Japan invasion in 1941. The rising social and economic status of Hong Kong's Chinese population was reflected in the number of Chinese moving to residential areas previously dominated by Europeans and in the growth of Chinese department stores, restaurants, and teahouses.

Most scholars have assumed that Hong Hong's industrialization did not take off until the late 1940s, when entrepreneurs came from China to escape civil war and Communist rule. In the late 1970s, however, scholar Frank Leeming argued that Hong Kong's industry "did not arise transformed within a year or two in the late forties, but was already geared to transformation before the Second World War, on the basis of an industrial inheritance of expertise in labour and capital going back for a century."[5] Whereas colonial reports as late as the 1940s consistently underestimated the number of Chinese-owned factories in Hong Kong, reports by Chinese business groups showed that Hong Kong's Chinese industry was much larger and more modernized. The idea of Hong Kong having little industry persisted in colonial government publications until the 1960s, by which time Hong Kong had become well known for its industry.

There is much evidence to support Leeming's claim. In 1881, Governor John Hennessy reported a wide range of industries run by local Chinese, including boat building, glass-making, and rope-making. In the early 1900s, Chinese entrepreneurs tried vigorously to compete with foreign industries. The Nanyang Brothers Tobacco Company had a factory in Hong Kong that produced cigarettes to compete with the British American Tobacco Company. In 1912, a group of Chinese businessmen opened the Kwong Sang Hong, which produced cosmetics, perfumes, and soaps. After World War I,

Chinese capitalists began to turn parts of Kowloon into factories for producing flashlights, batteries, and underwear. Hong Kong's industries were so developed that by the 1930s local exports were holding their own in the international market. Goods of all kinds—from automobile parts to salt, hemp, and burlap—were exported to China and across Southeast Asia. Pharmaceutical factories founded in the late 1910s and early 1920s exported their products to China and worldwide. Other important industries included dyeing, knitting, and fireworks. In 1939, Labour Officer H. R. Butters noted that while most of the heavy industry such as docks and cement works were owned and managed by Europeans, most of the recently founded companies and factories were "purely Chinese."[6]

The reason that the colonial government consistently played down Hong Kong's industry says much about Hong Kong's historical purpose in the British Empire. As political scientist Tak-Wing Ngo argues, the official colonial account of Hong Kong's industry as not beginning until after 1949 ignores any "activities not sanctioned by the ruling authorities," such as industrial development by Chinese entrepreneurs, while focusing on the China trade under British merchants.[7] Fearing that colonial imports would compete with British goods, until the 1930s the British government discouraged colonial governments from promoting industry. Large British firms, which had little interest in industry, enjoyed considerable influence in Hong Kong's legislative and executive councils as well as in the British Parliament. Thus, even though Hong Kong's industries were highly developed before 1949 and Chinese industry was the largest employer in the colony, the colonial government maintained that Hong Kong's economic success was due to the China trade. An economic commission formed in 1934 by Governor William Peel (and including representatives from all the major British firms) to study the local effects of the Great Depression concluded that Hong Kong's economy still depended primarily on the China trade rather than on industry. Yet by this time Hong Kong–made goods such as cosmetics and leatherware had replaced imports, while locally made flashlights took over the Southeast Asian market that had previously been dominated by British and Japanese firms. British officials complained about cheap imports from Hong Kong, prompting the British and Canadian governments to impose tariffs.

The steady growth of Chinese industry both helped and benefited from the growth of Chinese banks in Hong Kong. Before 1919, the colony had two main types of banks: large Western banks and smaller Chinese banks. For most Chinese in Hong Kong, writes Elizabeth Sinn, "foreign banks were irrelevant." The main source of credit was the small banks in the Western District, the center of Chinese business. While these banks were much more in touch with the needs of local business, they were risky ventures based mainly on the reputation of the proprietor or a few partners. Interest rates

*Central District, 1930s. Courtesy of the Prints and Photographs Division,
Library of Congress, Washington, D.C.*

were high, loan periods short. The banks could not meet many of the demands for modern business, such as checking accounts, bills of exchange,
or letters of credit. By the early twentieth century, there was a "gaping chasm
between modern foreign banks and native Chinese banks." Astute Chinese
entrepreneurs saw that the "market was ripe for banks which could offer all
the modern facilities and, at the same time, be attuned to Chinese business
culture."[8] The Bank of East Asia, established in 1919, was the first public
Chinese-capitalized bank traded on the Hong Kong Stock Exchange. The
bank's directors were among the most influential Chinese men in Hong
Kong, with huge commercial interests in China, Japan, Indonesia, Indochina, and elsewhere in East Asia.

CONSTITUTIONAL DEVELOPMENTS

The rise of Chinese commercial power and influence helps explain some of the constitutional developments of the interwar period. In the 1910s and early 1920s, demands arose for political representation and more control over the colony's finances. None of these movements, orchestrated mainly by Europeans, succeeded. The Colonial Office rejected a petition for constitutional reform in 1916, and little resulted from the short-lived Constitutional Reform Association, founded in May 1917 and dismissed by Governor Reginald Stubbs in 1920 as a "farcical body."[9] In 1919 a group of residents, mainly British and some of them unofficial members of the Legislative Council, pushed for more representation. Neither Governor Francis May nor the home government approved of the demands. Another political organization, the Kowloon Residents' Association formed by a group of Europeans in 1921, pressed for more roads and public works in Kowloon as well as for a European reserve similar to that on Victoria Peak. In 1922, Governor Stubbs rejected another petition for representation as coming from "a numerically insignificant transitory European population."[10]

As earlier, the Colonial Office resisted demands for constitutional reform because it distrusted the local European business community. The Colonial Office also feared that giving in to such demands would encourage wealthy Chinese to make similar demands. In 1923, Stubbs explained that giving voting rights to Europeans or Eurasians would lead to demands for the same from the Chinese in Hong Kong. The British government opposed constitutional reform in Hong Kong for another reason. The colony, explains historian John Darwin, was "merely one square on the larger chessboard of Anglo-Chinese relations."[11] In the 1920s, the British government became even more insistent on this policy. For example, in 1922 the Foreign Office criticized Stubbs for trying to forge better relations with the left-wing government in Canton, arguing that Stubbs had violated the official British policy of encouraging Chinese unity. Similarly, in the late 1920s the Foreign Office rejected Governor Cecil Clementi's proposal to formally convert the leased New Territories, maintaining that it violated British policy of conciliating Chinese nationalism.

Several significant constitutional reforms did, however, take place during the interwar period. In May 1926, Clementi shocked the Colonial Office by proposing to nominate a Chinese, Chow Shouson, to the Executive Council. Chow, a prominent merchant and community leader who had attended Columbia University in the 1870s as one of the first Chinese to study in the West and subsequently distinguished himself in the Qing government, remained on the council until 1936, when he was replaced by Robert Kotewall, a Eurasian businessman. In 1928, the Colonial Office accepted Clementi's proposal to expand the Legislative Council by two official and two nonofficial members. However, Clementi dashed the British business-men's hopes for increased representation by selecting a Chinese physician, Tso Seen Wan, and a Portuguese merchant, Jose Pedro Braga, the first Portuguese appointed to the council.

STRIKES AND BOYCOTTS

More than anything else, interwar Hong Kong was characterized by strikes and boycotts. Although World War I had not greatly affected Hong Kong, the aftermath of the war did. Having sent more than two hundred thousand laborers to Europe during the war, China hoped to regain control of the German concessions in Shandong. Instead, the victorious Allied powers gave the German concessions to Japan as part of a secret deal made during the war. The Treaty of Versailles had been inspired by American president Woodrow Wilson's calls for open diplomacy and self-determination, but the settlement convinced many Chinese that such talk was a sham. When news of the settlement reached Beijing, university students held a mass demonstration in Tiananmen Square on May 4, 1919. Part of what became known as the May Fourth Movement, the demonstrations in Beijing spread like wildfire to other cities and led to a massive boycott of Japanese goods. In Hong Kong, students and journalists organized anti-Japanese demonstrations, while merchants led a boycott of Japanese goods and urged local Chinese to buy only Chinese goods. World War I showed the barbarism of the West and led colonized people around the world to question the legitimacy of colonialism, while the Treaty of Versailles ending the war and prompting the May Fourth demonstrations stimulated the growth of revolutionary nationalism. Influenced by the rise of Chinese nationalism and by workers' movements in China and around the globe, labor consciousness in Hong Kong soared.

The Mechanics' Strike of 1920

The mechanics' strike of spring 1920 was the first strike in Hong Kong organized by a labor union, the Chinese Mechanics Institute. The union demanded a 40 percent increase in wages. Although the Hong Kong dollar had depreciated by 50 percent since the outbreak of World War I and prices had risen significantly, Chinese workers' wages were no higher than before the war. (European workers, who already enjoyed higher wages than Chinese workers, had received increases of around 15 percent.) Rice had been sent to Europe in 1919 to relieve food shortages there, leading to such severe shortages and price increases in Hong Kong that the government had to impose price limits. To support their demands, the Chinese Mechanics

Institute enlisted the services of Lo Man Kam, a prominent Eurasian lawyer. After employers—mainly the dockyards, electric companies, and the government itself—turned down four requests, the workers went on strike on March 31. Within a week, almost ten thousand workers were on strike, bringing Hong Kong's economy to a standstill. Many of the strikers went to Canton, where they were supported by Sun Yat-sen's government and local labor unions. Although most people in Hong Kong, including many Europeans, considered the workers' demands justified, the employers refused to yield. The strike lasted for more than three weeks, and only after pressure from Secretary for Chinese Affairs E. R. Hallifax did the employers eventually concede to a 32.5 percent pay increase for the workers.

The 1920 strike was mainly economic, but it had important ramifications beyond the economic realm. A victory for organized labor, the strike showed how workers had learned the importance of organizing—more than one hundred unions were formed in 1920 alone—and how to use strikes for collective bargaining. The strike also revealed how organizations such as the Tung Wah Hospital were no longer able to mediate between the Chinese working classes and the colonial government. By this time, organized workers had the power to deal directly with their employers. The government, which had been completely unprepared for a labor union to gain so much power, subsequently took a more proactive role in managing Chinese guilds, unions, and other associations. The Societies Ordinance of 1920 prohibited any society having "unlawful purposes or purposes incompatible with the peace and good order of the Colony." While the ordinance banned triad groups, it also banned a dozen considerably less controversial groups—including the Hotel Boys and Cook Guild, the Knitters' Union, the Christian Youth Groups, and the Barbers' Union. Finally, the strike affected workers in neighboring Canton, who subsequently went on their own strike and obtained better wages. In 1921 alone, workers there organized successful strikes in every major industry.

The Seamen's Strike of 1922

Organized by the Chinese Seamen's Union, the seamen's strike of January–March 1922 began as a strike by about fifteen hundred workers. Under the leadership of three seamen—Su Zhaozheng, Lin Weimin, and Chen Bingsheng—the strikers demanded wage increases of 30–40 percent to match the rises in the cost of living and that seamen be hired through the union rather than through compradors. By the end of January, more than ten thousand seamen had left for Canton, where the cost of living was lower and where they were welcomed by the mayor, Sun Fo, son of Sun Yat-sen. Although Chinese merchants asked the Tung Wah Hospital and the Chinese Chamber of Commerce to mediate, the negotiations soon broke down.

Lasting more than fifty days, the seamen's strike was the "first real demonstration in Hong Kong of the strength of the Chinese worker."[12] When servants, clerks, waiters, and tram conductors all left their jobs, the privileged European and Chinese communities found themselves helpless. Although any initial sympathy for the strikers eventually evaporated, for many Europeans the strike was a sobering experience. "It will have done some good," an English-language newspaper argued, "if it teaches us that we are living in a wholly different world from that which existed before the war."[13] The colonial government enlisted the support of Chinese and Eurasian community leaders such as Chow Shouson, Lau Chu Pak, Robert Ho Tung, and Robert Kotewall, but these elites seemed more concerned about preventing labor unions from taking over their leadership of the Chinese community than with mediating. Lau Chu Pak and Chow Shouson, the two Chinese unofficial members of the Legislative Council, insisted that the strike was political rather than economic and was inspired by "Bolshevism." The two denounced the strikers as selfish and ignorant, insisting that the colonial government ban all unions and not "retreat one inch."[14]

Colonial authorities, Chinese elites, and the European community blamed the strike on left-wing agitators in China, who have historically taken credit for this "first angry wave" of labor struggles. But the seamen always insisted that the strike was economic and not political (although this was a common justification for strikes, in Hong Kong and elsewhere, and Su Zhaozheng and Lin Weimin later joined the Chinese Communist Party). Governor Stubbs mismanaged the strike by overreacting and insisting that it was political and led by agitators in Canton. When the seamen's union posted armed pickets along the coast and seized food from trains on the Canton-Kowloon Railway, on February 1 Stubbs banned the union as "an unlawful society" that was being "used for purposes incompatible with the peace and good order of the Colony." After colonial police arrested some of the union leaders, closed down the union headquarters, and pulled down its signboard, written in the calligraphy of Sun Yat-sen, the union responded by beckoning all workers in Hong Kong to strike and leave for Canton. More than one hundred thousand additional workers heeded the call, including the entire staff at Government House. The Legislative Council retaliated by passing the Emergency Regulations Ordinance, which prohibited posters and public gatherings and authorized wide police powers for censoring mail and conducting random body searches. After Stubbs stopped train service to Canton, on March 4 colonial police shot dead five workers and wounded eight more trying to leave on foot through Sha Tin, in the New Territories.

As historian Ming Chan argues, the colonial government's measures helped to transform the strike "from an economic strike into an all-out political confrontation between British colonial might and Chinese patriotic pride and national interests."[15] Following extensive negotiations among the seamen, the shipping companies, and the Canton and Hong Kong governments, the workers won a settlement close to what they had demanded. The colonial government agreed to lift the ban on the Seamen's Union, release the arrested leaders, and pay compensation to the victims of the shootings in the New Territories. The end of the strike on March 7 resulted "in a total victory for the Chinese seamen but complete capitulation of the British establishment, with its dignity and prestige in shambles."[16] As part of the strike settlement, Stubbs had to rescind his ban on the Seamen's Union, while the same policeman who had pulled down the union's signboard had to put it back up. The strike also showed that the Chinese workers had become a class of their own, no longer relying on the Chinese merchant elite for support. More strikes occurred in 1922, although few were as successful as the seamen's strike.

The Strike-Boycott of 1925–1926

The most significant event of the interwar period was the strike-boycott of 1925–1926, which showed how the revolutionary nationalist movements in China could affect Hong Kong. On May 30, 1925, Sikh police under British command opened fire on a crowd of Chinese demonstrators in the International Settlement of Shanghai. At least 9 demonstrators were killed, and many others were wounded. News of this so-called May Thirtieth Incident spread like wildfire, prompting protests all across China but especially in the two cities where British interests were most heavily concentrated, Shanghai and Canton. On June 23, during a particularly heated demonstration in Shamian (known to Europeans as Shameen), the British and French concession in Canton, troops under foreign command killed more than 50 Chinese protesters and wounded almost 120 more. As news of the massacre spread, labor and union leaders in Canton called for a general strike in southern China—especially in Hong Kong, the most visible example of British imperialism. Kuomintang leaders and their Soviet advisors even considered attacking the International Settlement in Shamian. Anti-British pamphlets and placards in Hong Kong implored Chinese to rise up and drive out the British colonialists and their Chinese "hunting dogs." Strike leaders in Canton called on all Chinese to leave Hong Kong, spreading rumors that the colonial government planned to poison the colony's water supplies and offering free passage to Canton by train or steamer.

In the first two weeks after the massacre in Shamian, more than 50,000 Chinese left Hong Kong in protest. Food prices soared, prompting a run on banks. Hong Kong's economy nearly came to a halt, and by early July the colony was "like a ghost town."[17] Pickets in Canton prevented strikers from returning to Hong Kong. On July 10, Stubbs wrote that "all regular trades are practically at a standstill." The police had been deporting vagabonds and other "undesirables."[18] By the end of July, some 250,000 Chinese had left for Canton. On September 18, Stubbs described the colony's financial situation as "most serious."[19] One prominent Chinese bank had already gone into liquidation, other firms were on the verge of bankruptcy, and Stubbs feared that more would follow suit. The Chinese Chamber of Commerce had asked for a trade loan from the British government. Although the worst was over by early 1926, the strike lasted for more than a year, and the British government had to provide a trade loan of three million pounds to prevent the colony's economy from collapsing. And even after the strike itself ended, the accompanying boycott against British goods, which helped make the strike so devastating, lasted for several more months.

Governor Stubbs and his successor, Clementi, were adamant that the strike was directed by Bolshevik agitators in Canton and their Soviet advisors and had nothing to do with economic or political conditions in the colony. Stubbs in particular has often been criticized for not understanding the political situation in China and for failing to differentiate between Chinese nationalism and Communism, but he was not necessarily exaggerating the extent of these influences from Canton. Even before the strike, left-wing intellectuals and union organizers had tried to encourage nationalist sympathies in Hong Kong by distributing handbills urging workers to strike. Nor were Stubbs and Clementi exaggerating the importance of funding from outside the colony. The bulk of the financial support came from the revolutionary Kuomintang government in Canton, with other funds coming from overseas Chinese, Russian workers, and an anonymous British trade union. And the colonial government had another reason to convince the British government that the strike had nothing to do with conditions in Hong Kong or with the Chinese business community: many people in Britain believed that the strike represented a just revolt of workers against conditions that had long been abolished in England and were unsympathetic toward the European expatriates in Hong Kong.

Why did the strike become so powerful? Although it was sparked by events in China, the strike derived part of its local force from genuine economic concerns and from the popular feeling against the privileged status of foreigners. This was apparent from the demands of the strike commission, which apart from standard issues—such as an eight-hour workday, the abolition of contract and child labor, freedom of speech and press, the right to organize, and reductions in rent—also had a strong local component: that labor unions be allowed to vote for a Chinese member on the Legislative Council and that Chinese be treated as the equal of Europeans and be able to live on the Peak. Second, although many Chinese left Hong Kong for Canton to show their nationalism and patriotism, others left because they were pressured to do so, while those who tried to return to Hong Kong could not. In early February 1926, Clementi reported that the strike pickets had intensified their aggression against Hong Kong. They were shooting at Indian troops on the Hong Kong side of the border and at police launches in the Shenzhen River between Hong Kong and China, blocking trains to and from China, and preventing villagers from crossing back into Hong Kong. And in Guangdong, the general strike was limited mainly to the city of Canton and its environs. Although many of the rural counties along the Guangdong–Hong Kong border supported the strike-boycott, peasants often resisted the boycott and its restrictions against selling crops and fish to Hong Kong.

Having anticipated such a strike ever since the seamen's strike of 1922, the colonial government had taken precautions by increasing the garrison, improving intelligence gathering, and building supply depots for coal. Although Stubbs inflamed local tensions by overreacting rather than trying to understand the cause of the strike, the emergency measures that he passed may have prevented the strike from expanding. Under the Peace Preservation Ordinance and the Emergency Ordinance that had been enacted during the 1922 strike, Stubbs declared a state of emergency, mobilizing volunteers and prohibiting the export of foodstuffs and money. Stubbs also granted Chinese bankers their request for a moratorium on Chinese banks. He limited the amount of currency that could be taken out of the colony, dispatched policemen to guard water supplies, sent troops to operate the Star Ferry and patrol the streets, closed schools early for summer vacation, and imposed a curfew. He also ordered the main Chinese and European department stores to remain open for at least four hours per day. In July, he authorized all Chinese mail and telegrams to be censored. He also ordered the secretary for Chinese affairs to examine and censor all Chinese newspapers. Three workers in shifts from dawn to dusk worked to remove any seditious or prostrike material, and no group related to the strike was allowed to place advertisements in the newspapers. Stubbs also tried to use public and private funds to assist Chinese antirevolutionary forces in Canton and to persuade the Foreign Office to bribe the Beijing government into wiping out the revolutionary government in Canton.

The Chinese and foreign communities assisted the government during the strike. Volunteers worked at hospitals and drove the trams. Tung Wah Hospital Committee members operated food stalls and sold food at low prices, while many Chinese and Eurasians joined the Volunteers, the Special Police Reserve, and the St. John's Ambulance Service. Tso Seen Wan coordinated the Chinese Labour Office, recruiting volunteers to fill the empty jobs. Only three days after the strike broke out, Tso had assembled more than 500 Chinese volunteers; three weeks later, he had 3,000 volunteers, much to the European community's surprise. Other loyal Chinese helped the government censor cables, mail, and newspapers. Many Chinese joined the volunteer fire brigade and formed street committees and street guards to patrol their neighborhoods. The District Watch Force helped maintain order, mediate, and prevent intimidation. A group of Chinese business leaders founded the Commerce Protection Bureau, using their connections to import food from Macau, Shanghai, Saigon, Singapore, and Penang. Many government employees resisted the call to strike. By September 1925, only 1 of the 105 Chinese clerks, telephone operators, and interpreters working for the colonial government had left his post, while only 7 of the 335 policemen had deserted. Similar performances were reported among the Water Police and the Chinese detectives stationed along the border in the New Territories.

The colonial government especially benefited from the help of two of the unofficial members of the Legislative Council, Chow Shouson and Robert Kotewall, the latter of whom, although Eurasian, held one of the two positions on the council reserved for Chinese and was generally considered a representative of the Chinese community. Although they received anonymous letters threatening violence and murder and although rewards for their heads were posted in Canton, Chow and Kotewall orchestrated an intensive propaganda campaign to fight the strike. They formed the Counter-Propaganda Bureau, which plastered posters and distributed leaflets encouraging the population to resist the strikers. The two also established the *Commercial Press,* a counterpropaganda newspaper circulated widely in Hong Kong and among overseas Chinese in the United States and Australia who had been supporting the strikers. Chow and Kotewall also recommended that the governor order routine military marches and demonstrations as a show of strength. They persuaded the government to establish the Labour Protection Bureau, a secret bureau to protect laborers from intimidators and to launch a counterattack against such intimidators. Led by a retired Chinese pirate and general, the Labour Protection Bureau hired thugs and former pirates to protect workers who stayed at their jobs and to intimidate anyone who encouraged the strikers. Officials in London expressed some concern about the bureau's staff members and their previous experience, but Kotewall and Chow were unconcerned.

For supporting the colonial government during the strike, Chow and Kotewall were branded in Canton as "running dogs" of the British imperialists. Like other Chinese and Eurasian businessmen in Hong Kong, one reason the two helped the government end the strike was of course to protect their own interests. However, this was more than an issue of protecting class interests: the two saw the strike as an ideological and economic war launched by Canton against Hong Kong. Fighting the strike meant protecting the colony that they had helped fashion from the fabled barren rock and preserving a new way of life that they had helped shape. Nor did these men see collaborating with the British as betraying China. Because they viewed the Canton government as radical leftists, they considered working with the colonial government to stop the strike as a sign both of their loyalty to Hong Kong and of their patriotism to China.

After various attempts at negotiations by Governor Clementi—as well as threats of military force—and after a series of negotiations and political swings in Canton, in October 1926 the Canton government finally ended the strike. Although Hong Kong's economy eventually recovered, relations with Canton remained tense. In the confusion leading up to Chiang Kai-shek's attempt to unify China during the Northern Expedition of 1926–1927, Hong Kong was again the target of anti-British attacks. In March 1927, Clementi reported that gunmen from Canton had been sent to assassinate him, Hallifax, Chow, Kotewall, and other loyal Chinese. Better relations with Canton eventually developed, however, especially after Chiang Kai-shek's Kuomintang brutally purged the Communists in 1927. Realizing that the strike had shown the power of Chinese nationalism and had also shown that Hong Kong and Canton society, politics, and economics could not be separated, Clementi and subsequent governors made sure to stay on good terms with the Canton government.

The general strike did not have a long-term impact on Hong Kong's political or economic stability, but it had several important effects, not just on Hong Kong but also on Britain's position in China. The colonial government made it harder to express antigovernment views by requiring newspapers to pay a security fee. In 1927 the Printers and Publishers Ordinance was revamped to prevent attacks against the colonial administration. The Illegal Strike and Lockout Ordinance of 1927 made strikes illegal if they tried to coerce the government or had any objective beyond a dispute within a certain industry. The government also banned all unions that had been involved in the strike and all politically motivated strikes. Union funds could not be used for political purposes outside of Hong Kong, and no branch of any union in China could be formed in Hong Kong.

Well after the strike had ended, groups involved in anti-imperialist movements were forbidden to place advertisements in local newspapers, while news stories from abroad that dealt with imperialism, Communism, or Socialism were edited. The government was so successful in harassing the Hong Kong branch of the Chinese Communist Party that this discouraged local residents from joining the party (although Hong Kong was where Ho Chi Minh founded the Vietnamese Communist Party in 1930). Whereas in the 1920s Hong Kong had been an important base for Communist activities in Guangdong, after Chiang Kai-shek's White Terror in 1927 the Hong Kong government worked hard to suppress Communist activities in the colony. Often acting on tips from Guangdong authorities, the government arrested Communists and deported them to Guangdong, where they were executed. The combination of Chiang's suppression of Communism and the Hong Kong government's "determination to crush any such movement" inhibited the growth of labor unionism in Hong Kong for twenty years.[20]

The colonial government also tried to use education to curb the growth of radical nationalism in Hong Kong. During the general strike, Kotewall recommended that more emphasis in schools be placed on Confucianism as an antidote to the revolutionary nationalism engulfing China. In 1927, Clementi encouraged some of the most distinguished Chinese scholars in Hong Kong—most of whom had left China after the 1911 revolution and during the May Fourth Movement—to promote traditional Chinese culture and morality in Hong Kong, promising to provide government support for a Chinese Department at the University of Hong Kong to train teachers for local schools. By patronizing these scholars, Clementi tried to provide a cultural, moral, and political alternative to the revolutionary nationalism that had inspired the strikers.

The strike failed to change the political status of Chinese in Hong Kong, but it showed the government that its Chinese subjects were to be taken seriously. The government realized that it could no longer take workers for granted and that it needed to work more closely with leaders of the Chinese community. Thus, in May 1926 Clementi appointed Chow Shouson as the first Chinese member of the Executive Council. A strategic move designed to show strikers in Hong Kong and Canton that the government was willing to compromise, the appointment also represented a major shift in local colonial policy. The important role that Canton had played as a sanctuary for strikers who returned "home" demonstrated to the colonial government that Chinese nationalism could not be taken lightly. Clementi paid a visit to Canton in 1927, "symbolically inaugurating an era of rapprochement between China and the British colony."[21]

Finally, the strike showed how Chinese nationalism could provoke enough of a crisis in Hong Kong to affect British policy toward China. The strike hurt Hong Kong's economy enough to convince the Foreign Office of the need to make concessions to China, which it did by surrendering the concessions at Hankou and Jiujiang in 1927–28 and Weihaiwei in 1930. The Foreign Office became more convinced that working with the Kuomintang was the best way to protect British interests in China. However, this strained relations among the British consul general at Canton, the British legation in Beijing, and the Hong Kong government, which feared that the others might sacrifice Hong Kong to improve Britain's political and commercial position in China. On several occasions during the interwar period, British officials suggested surrendering Hong Kong as a gesture of British goodwill in the face of rising Chinese nationalism, arguing that Britain no longer needed a colony to maintain its trading interests in China. Exacerbating these tensions was the fact that although the Hong Kong government logically had to deal directly with Canton, the British diplomatic corps was in Beijing and insisted on being the only diplomatic channel for dealing with China. The Foreign Office often criticized Hong Kong governors for trying to interfere with

Canton politics, dismissing them as being out of touch with broader British goals in China and with China's political situation.

SEPARATE WORLDS, SEPARATE LIVES

The strike-boycott of 1925–1926 showed that outside influences were never fully able to transform Chinese nationalism in Hong Kong into anticolonialism. Many Chinese remained loyal to the colonial government, and Canton politics were too divided and volatile to create and sustain any serious anticolonial feelings. On the contrary, the strike strengthened many Hong Kong people's appreciation for the colony's political and economic stability—especially in contrast to the political turbulence in neighboring Guangdong—and reaffirmed their sense of belonging and commitment to Hong Kong. As sociologist Henry Lethbridge explains, "Hong Kong had come of age in 1925: it was no longer simply a congeries of various groups, composed of acquisitive, rootless, transient individuals, but was beginning to coalesce into a community and, if all racial divisions are included, into a plural society, its members bound together, as it were, in a network of contractual arrangements. It had begun to acquire an identity."[22]

Even though they could come together to combat strikes, the Chinese and British communities lived largely separate lives. Often blaming the failure to mix with Chinese on the latter's preference for not mixing with foreigners, the British created an extensive social world that revolved around clubs, music, parties, formal dinners, and the annual St. George's and St. Andrew's balls. British men who worked for firms such as the Hong Kong and Shanghai Bank were expected to participate in bank-sponsored sports such as cricket that were seen as vital for both physical and mental health and for meeting European colleagues in other firms. Chinese were generally excluded from most of these activities, as were most Eurasians (as late as the 1940s, for example, Chinese and Eurasians could not join the Cricket Club). In both the colonial government and the European firms, there was a level that Chinese simply could not rise above. European firms hired Chinese staffs, but almost never at the upper levels. The Hong Kong and Shanghai Bank had a policy of not having any Chinese on its board. This often provoked resentment among the Chinese who had been educated at English schools and universities.

Foreign firms generally had strict, though often unwritten, rules about their employees becoming involved with Chinese women. European officers of the Hong Kong and Shanghai Bank were discouraged from marrying non-British women; until World War II no bank officer had married a Chinese. Although marriage between European civil servants and non-European women was not legally forbidden, it was discouraged. Some

Horse racing at Happy Valley, 1902. Courtesy of the Prints and Photographs Division, Library of Congress, Washington, D.C.

members of the Public Works Department had to sign an agreement that if they married Chinese women or took Chinese concubines they could be dismissed; those who married Chinese or Eurasians were not allowed to live in government quarters. A few higher-ranking officers did marry Chinese, but this was frowned upon and ruined their chances for being promoted to another position in a different colony. European policemen who married Chinese or Eurasians were not allowed to reenlist after their contracts expired.

The general feeling among Europeans was that Hong Kong was not a healthy place for European children to grow up. These children were sent to schools in England or in China, where the weather was better and it was easier to get to Hong Kong for the holidays. Those who stayed in Hong Kong generally attended one of the special schools for Europeans. Eurasians usually went to Diocesan Boys' School or Diocesan Girls' School, while Chinese attended one of the government schools, such as Queen's College or King's College. Many expatriates lived in constant fear that the Chinese would rise against them. In June 1934, five young European children were allegedly thrown into a ditch by a Chinese man. One child was killed, his body later found in the sea.

Some Chinese and Eurasian leaders tried to curb the racial discrimination that permeated Hong Kong society. In 1921 leaders of the various communities—including Jose Pedro Braga, later the first Portuguese appointed to the Legislative Council, and Lo Man Kam, the prominent Eurasian solicitor—formed the League of Fellowship, whose goal was to eliminate "racial disabilities" and to "promote good fellowship within the Colony, irrespective of race, class and creed." For the most part, however, the various communities continued to keep their distance from each other—almost comfortably. The political scientist who visited Hong Kong on the eve of World War II explained that "the racial bitterness which has caused so much trouble in India is not found in Hong Kong, although British and Chinese have separate clubs and, on the whole, social intercourse between the races is limited. Many individuals however are on friendly terms; and perhaps also one may hazard the guess that the Chinese is too content with the society of those of his own race to trouble himself with his exclusion from European circles. He has a robust sense of his own superiority, and has none of the hypersensitiveness and inferiority complex which make so many Indians, for example, bitterly resent their exclusion from Western society."[23]

PUBLIC WORKS AND SOCIAL WELFARE

The interwar period saw a greater interest in public works and in social legislation and welfare, both because of similar developments in Britain—where laissez-faire economics was losing popularity to the welfare state ideal—and because of the colonial government's determination to limit the growth of Chinese nationalism and labor consciousness. Completed in 1937 and named in honor of King George V, the Jubilee Reservoir in the New Territories boasted the tallest dam in the British Empire. New roads were built, and land reclamation projects occurred on both sides of the harbor. Medical and sanitary services also expanded. The Malaria Bureau was established in 1930, and the Urban Council replaced the Sanitary Board in 1936. The government Kowloon Hospital opened in 1926; begun in the late 1920s, the Queen Mary Hospital opened in Pokfulam on Hong Kong Island in 1937. The Building Ordinance of 1935 set standards for lighting and ventilation, although overcrowding continued because of the influx of refugees from China. More schools were built, both for Chinese and Europeans, as were several teachers' training colleges.

As in Britain and the rest of the empire, there was more interest in social welfare. Social protection in Hong Kong before the British arrived had traditionally come from family, clan, and lineage organizations. Although European missionaries ran orphanages and other charitable institutions, until the 1920s social welfare was largely confined to Chinese organizations such as the Tung Wah Hospital and the Po Leung Kuk and to rich residents such as Clara Ho Tung, wife of Robert Ho Tung and a devout Buddhist who established temples and free schools for poor children in Hong Kong and Macau. In the 1920s, however, the government began to take a more active role in providing social welfare. This was a gradual process shaped by developments in Britain, China, and Hong Kong. The idea of trusteeship rather than colonialism was becoming the norm, while new social legislation in Britain due mainly to the rise of the Labour Party, trade unions, and Socialists made the welfare state a popular alternative to the nineteenth-century ideal of laissez-faire individualism. The flow of refugees from China soon exceeded the capacity of voluntary organizations to provide social welfare. And although workers in Hong Kong were less politically conscious than those in Canton, partly because they (especially those working for European employers, who usually paid more than Chinese employers) were generally paid better than in Canton, the government hoped to limit the growth of labor consciousness by marginally improving working and living conditions.

Social welfare and legislation in Hong Kong were relatively progressive, at least in theory and when compared to other colonies such as Singapore or other Chinese cities such as Shanghai. The Industrial Employment of Children Ordinance of 1922, the first in East Asia, prohibited the employment of children under age ten in factories or under age twelve in "dangerous trades" such as carrying coal, building materials, or debris; by the 1930s, child labor in factories had been largely eliminated. The Factory Ordinance of 1927 appointed factory inspectors. The same year, a labor division was established within the Secretary for Chinese Affairs. The Industrial Employment of Women, Young Persons and Children Amendment Ordinance of 1929 regulated the employment of women in certain industries. The Factories and Workshops Ordinance of 1932 kept children under age sixteen and women out of dangerous trades such as fireworks, glass-making, lead processing, and vermilion-making. In 1938 the government appointed a labor officer to deal with unions, labor conditions, and trade disputes.

Still, the colonial government always tried not to spend too much on social welfare, worrying that more immigrants would pour in from China if conditions in Hong Kong were too good. "Even at its mightiest," writes historian David Faure, "Britain had no social policy on Hong Kong as such."[24] In 1935 the government conceded that the "struggle for existence" in Hong Kong was "very severe" and that it would soon have to provide some sort of subsidized housing.[25] Corpses were frequently abandoned in the streets, the families too poor to arrange for proper burials; the government reported more than thirteen hundred such corpses in 1937 alone. Although colonial governors were encouraged to apply innovations from other colonies, they were rarely under great pressure from the Colonial Office to make any dramatic changes in their respective colonies. Twice during the interwar period, for example, the Hong Kong government declined to pass legislation for compulsory workers' compensation, even though it had been urged to do so. Although in 1938 Governor Geoffrey Northcote argued that the government must increase taxation to keep from reducing social services, neither government nor management paid much attention to the welfare of workers. A handful of companies—usually European—provided their workers with decent housing and working conditions, but most workplaces were dangerous and overcrowded. In 1939, Labour Officer Butters reported that a tailoring establishment was "so overcrowded that one male worker engaged in ironing was found suspended from the roof on a beam with his ironing board suspended in front of him."[26]

PROSTITUTION AND *MUI-TSAI*

The increased interest in social welfare and British reformers' stronger interest in Hong Kong led to the revival of debates about prostitution and *mui-tsai* in the 1920s and 1930s. Although the colonial government had been ordered by the Colonial Office to abolish licensed prostitution in Hong Kong at the turn of the century, by the 1920s it had devised a complex and extralegal system of regulating prostitution, using the various discretionary powers of the governor to close down any brothel that failed to comply with these regulations. The secretary for Chinese affairs classified brothels into those dealing with Europeans, Indians, and Chinese. As in the 1800s, the controls on prostitutes dealing with Europeans were much stricter. The result was that venereal disease was kept under control among the European population but much less so in the Chinese population. In the early 1920s, 30–40 percent of Chinese men were estimated to suffer from venereal diseases.

The pressure to end licensed prostitution came from three main sources: reformers in Britain, the League of Nations, and a group of local European women. The latter group included Penelope Clementi, wife of Governor Clementi; Mrs. Wolfe, wife of the inspector general of police; Mrs. Tratman, wife of Secretary for Chinese Affairs D. W. Tratman; and Bella Woolf

Southorn, wife of the colonial secretary, Wilfred Southorn. Licensed brothels were gradually closed down in Hong Kong from 1931 to 1935, with pre-
dictable results: more soliciting on the streets, higher incidence of venereal
disease among European soldiers and sailors, and an increased number of
so-called sly brothels disguised as massage parlors, saunas, and bathhouses.
The Japanese instituted a system of regulated and inspected brothels when
they took over in 1941, but these were closed down after the British returned in 1945.

The *mui-tsai* issue had drawn quite a bit of local publicity in 1917 during
a legal case involving two *mui-tsai* who had allegedly been kidnapped. A
British member of Parliament who happened to be passing through town
took the case to the Colonial Office, asking how slavery could not only be
tolerated but could even be protected by law in the British Empire. The
Colonial Office was terribly embarrassed and seemed unaware that the system had been discussed back in the 1880s. In August 1918, Governor May
explained that although slavery was illegal in Hong Kong, the *mui-tsai* system was not slavery and was so prevalent that almost every family that
could afford a *mui-tsai* had at least one. Because the Colonial Office agreed
that it could not interfere too much with local customs, it recommended
that the issue be allowed to drop. In 1921 the secretary of Chinese affairs reported that half of all Chinese families in Hong Kong had *mui-tsai*.

One of the most intense and protracted British colonial policy disputes
in the interwar period, the anti-*mui-tsai* campaign had three main differences from that in the 1880s. It focused more on the system itself rather
than on the prostitution aspect. This time, the campaign had help from all
sorts of places: British women in Hong Kong, a small group of local Chinese, members of Parliament in Britain, religious leaders (including the
archbishops of York and Canterbury), and international women's groups.
And since the system had been banned in China after the 1911 revolution
(although the ban had never been effectively enforced), no one in Hong
Kong could claim that it should be allowed simply because it was a Chinese
tradition.

A key mover in the anti-*mui-tsai* campaign was Clara Haslewood, wife of
a commander in the Royal Navy stationed in Hong Kong. After a barrage of
critical letters to the press offended leaders of the Chinese community, Governor Stubbs asked the Admiralty to transfer Haslewood's husband. But the
two spent their retirement in Britain rallying against the *mui-tsai* system by
writing the press and members of Parliament. Soon the Colonial Office was
receiving complaints from groups such as the Anti-Slavery and Aborigines
Protection Society, the Fabian Society, the International Woman Suffrage
Alliance, and the League of Nations Union. As the campaign gained steam
in Britain, the Hong Kong Anti-Mui Tsai Society was founded in 1921, its
organizing committee almost all Chinese. The two Chinese members of the

Legislative Council responded by establishing the Society for the Protection of Mui Tsai to help regulate the system instead of ending it. The Anti-Mui Tsai Society, which also received backing from local groups such as the Young Women's Christian Association, established in 1920, was able to win over many of the labor unions and to gain support from the foreign community, especially since its English secretary, C. G. Anderson, wrote regularly to the newspapers in Hong Kong and Britain. But the Society for the Protection of Mui Tsai had the Tung Wah Hospital Committee, the District Watch Committee, and the Po Leung Kuk on its side.

In February 1922, Secretary for the Colonies Winston Churchill, who had previously defended the system, argued to the House of Commons that the system should be abolished. Although Governor Stubbs argued that the timing was bad—the colony was still recovering from the seamen's strike—and the Chinese bourgeoisie opposed abolishing the system, Churchill promised the House of Commons that the system would be ended within a year. The leaders of the Chinese community insisted that the system benefited the girls and their parents and prevented infanticide, and Stubbs warned the Colonial Office that interfering too much in local customs might even turn the Chinese against their British rulers. Still, the Female Domestic Service Ordinance was passed in 1923, although Stubbs distanced himself from the ordinance by insisting that the well-meaning reformers in Britain simply did not understand the system or Chinese customs. (As in the late 1800s, there was no single Chinese view toward the practice, but the colonial government dismissed to the British government as not representative the Chinese who opposed the *mui-tsai* system.) And the bill ended up doing very little, except mainly to prohibit any new *mui-tsai* transactions and domestic service for girls under ten years of age. But after Stubbs reported in 1924 that no new *mui-tsai* had been engaged and that the number of *mui-tsai* had dropped considerably, the Colonial Office let the issue go. Although reports in the mid-1930s suggested that the number of *mui-tsai* had probably increased after 1923, the bill temporarily ended all agitation in Britain.

The *mui-tsai* issue reemerged, however, after the Canton government abolished all forms of slavery in March 1927 and canceled the deeds for the transfer of *mui-tsai*. In October 1928, the newly revived Anti-Mui Tsai Society declared that conditions had become even worse since 1923 and sent details to groups in Britain. When the secretary of the Anti-Slavery and Aborigines Protection Society learned about the situation, he wrote a letter to the liberal *Manchester Guardian* that was soon published in a widely circulated pamphlet. The Colonial Office was in a spot: it had failed to fulfill Churchill's promise to Parliament, and now the new governor, Clementi, was defending the system. Clementi argued that there was no evidence that the number of *mui-tsai* had increased and that the system could not be abolished any faster without alienating the Chinese population, especially as long as the system continued to exist in China, where the laws against it were not being enforced. Convinced that reforming or abolishing the system would be more harmful than useful, Clementi may have been right: the number of abandoned dead babies and children was 1,851 in 1929, some 300 more than in 1928 and about 700 more than in 1927.

Many of the Britons who had been involved in the campaign in the early 1920s now resurfaced, distributing articles with such inflammatory titles as "Little Yellow Slaves under the Union Jack." As historian Susan Pedersen argues, the issue was "not only about the definition of 'slavery,' but also about the wider character and the obligations of British rule."[27] Part of a maternalist trend in Britain and throughout the British Empire, the campaign showed how British women were beginning to play an activist role in the expansion of social services in their empire. But there was also more than a hint of racism, for many of the British reformers were convinced that only British women, not any Chinese groups, could care for the freed *mui-tsai*.

In response to so much pressure, in 1929 the Legislative Council passed an amendment stipulating that *mui-tsai* were to be registered and paid wages. Although registration eventually increased and the Colonial Office was generally satisfied, the 1929 amendments did not please everyone. Legislative Council member Tso Seen Wan argued that far from being a slave, a *mui-tsai* was treated as a foster daughter. As such, she might be asked to "do such service as a natural daughter might be called upon to at any time."[28] Many Chinese resented the amendment for stigmatizing having a *mui-tsai*. The Anti-Mui Tsai Society claimed that fewer than half of the *mui-tsai* were actually registered. After more pressure from societies in Britain, in July 1931 the government added a police inspector and two Chinese female inspectors to help register *mui-tsai*. Finally, in response to increased pressure in Britain and a colonial inquiry (the Woods Commission) prompted by the League of Nations' Permanent Advisory Committee of Experts on Slavery, in April 1938 the Legislative Council passed legislation making it compulsory to register all adopted girls with the secretary for Chinese affairs. However, this affected only girls who were actually registered (of which there were still more than one thousand) and did little to end the large number of girls being sold into prostitution. The *mui-tsai* system lasted beyond the end of World War II, with cases being reported even into the 1970s.

RETRENCHMENT

Partly because it benefited from the Imperial Preferences system instituted after the Imperial Economic Conference of 1932 in Ottawa, Hong Kong was not seriously hurt by the Great Depression. Still, officials in Britain and in Hong Kong grew concerned about the colony's expenditures and began to demand retrenchment in the civil service by appointing more non-Europeans. Although governors frequently drew attention to the large number of Europeans in the public sector compared to other British colonies, until 1930 there was no local demand to replace Europeans with local Chinese civil servants. On the contrary, in 1914 the European unoffi-cial members of the Legislative Council requested that the government hire more European nurses at the government civil hospital, even though the hospital already had more Europeans than in similar hospitals in the British Empire. In 1921, there were more than 180 Europeans in the police force, compared with 40 in Singapore and 23 in Ceylon (whose population was more than six times that of Hong Kong). Not only was this an issue of racial discrimination, it was also very costly. In 1914 a European police con-stable received more than seven times the pay of a local Chinese or Indian constable, while in 1939, the lowest-ranking European policeman received almost eight times the pay of a Chinese of the same rank.

Colonial officials and European residents often justified the large num-bers of Europeans in government service by arguing that they were less cor-rupt and more trustworthy and efficient than Chinese as well as more loyal to Britain. Fearing that Cantonese policemen would be neither able nor willing to control their fellow Cantonese, the government recruited police-men from Britain, India, or Weihaiwei. Only on the eve of World War II were Chinese police admitted at the rank of subinspector, and even then they were under the control of more junior British officers. Many clerical positions held by Europeans were subsequently filled by their sons. (Some of these Europeans were in fact more connected to Hong Kong than most Chinese residents were. According to the 1931 census, Europeans in Hong Kong were slightly less migratory than urban Chinese, for 8.5 percent of them had been in Hong Kong for more than thirty years, compared to 6.4 percent for the urban Chinese.) Neither the European nor the Chinese un-official members of the Legislative Council urged the government to hire more local residents. Although the Colonial Office preferred more local ap-pointments as a way to lower salaries, it rarely tried to pressure the Hong Kong government into doing so.

After 1930, when a report on government salaries led to a public uproar, governors and the Chinese, Eurasian, and Portuguese members of the Leg-islative Council increasingly called for more local hires. Lo Man Kam, the Eurasian lawyer and one of the "Chinese" unofficial members of the Leg-islative Council, vigorously supported this policy, which was accepted by Governor Andrew Caldecott in 1935. In 1936 the government agreed, in principle, that before vacancies were advertised in Britain, qualified local candidates would be considered. Progress was slow, however, not just be-cause of the entrenched vested interests of the European community but also because the low salaries compared to those for Europeans discouraged qualified Chinese candidates from applying. Although differences in pay actually increased during the 1930s because of the depreciation of the Hong Kong dollar, the Chinese and Eurasian unofficial members of the Legislative Council never insisted that Chinese should draw the same salaries as Europeans. Chinese did not serve in large numbers until after World War II, and even though in 1946 Britain's Labour government ordered that civil service positions throughout the empire should be opened to local recruits, up to 1966 only a handful of Chinese had been appointed to senior government positions. "Until localization was the order of the day, in the 1980s," concludes David Faure, "no Hong Kong Chinese, however well educated and however well established in his or her own profession, could reasonably have seen that he or she could have gone very far in government service."[29]

NOTES

1. Stephanie Po-yin Chung, *Chinese Business Groups in Hong Kong and Political Change in South China, 1900–25* (Basingstoke, UK: Macmillan, 1998), 19.

2. Lennox A. Mills, *British Rule in Eastern Asia: A Study of Contemporary Government and Economic Development in British Malaya and Hong Kong* (London: Oxford University Press, 1942), 390.

3. R. C. Hurley, *Handbook to the British Crown Colony of Hong Kong and Dependencies* (1920), reprinted in John and Kirsten Miller, eds., *Chronicles Abroad: Hong Kong* (San Francisco: Chronicle Books, 1994), 171.

4. C. Mary Turnbull, "Hong Kong: Fragrant Harbour, City of Sin and Death," in Robin W. Winks and James R. Rush, eds., *Asia in Western Fiction* (Honolulu: University of Hawaii Press, 1990), 117–18.

5. Frank Leeming, "The Earlier Industrialization of Hong Kong," *Modern Asian Studies* 9(3) (1975): 342.

6. *Report by the Labour Officer Mr. H. R. Butters on Labour and Labour Conditions in Hong Kong* (Hong Kong: Noronha, 1939), 109.

7. Tak-Wing Ngo, "Industrial History and the Artifice of *Laissez-faire* Colonialism," in Tak-Wing Ngo, ed., *Hong Kong's History: State and Society under Colonial Rule* (London: Routledge, 1999), 119.

8. Elizabeth Sinn, *Growing with Hong Kong: The Bank of East Asia, 1919–1994* (Hong Kong: Bank of East Asia, 1994), 4–5.

9. Stubbs to Milner, July 29, 1920, quoted in John Darwin, "Hong Kong in British Decolonisation," in Judith M. Brown and Rosemary Foot, eds., *Hong Kong's Transitions, 1842–1997* (London: Macmillan, 1997), 19.

10. Stubbs to Duke of Devonshire, March 14, 1923, quoted in Darwin, "Hong Kong in British Decolonisation," 19.

11. Darwin, "Hong Kong in British Decolonisation," 20.

12. Paul Gillingham, *At the Peak: Hong Kong between the Wars* (Hong Kong: Macmillan, 1983), 32.

13. Quoted in Gillingham, *At the Peak*, 32.

14. Quoted in Chan Wai Kwan, *The Making of Hong Kong Society: Three Studies of Class Formation in Early Hong Kong* (Oxford, UK: Clarendon, 1991), 190.

15. Ming K. Chan, "Labour vs. Crown: Aspects of Society-State Interactions in the Hong Kong Labour Movement before World War II," in Elizabeth Sinn, ed., *Between East and West: Aspects of Social and Political Development in Hong Kong* (Hong Kong: Centre of Asian Studies, University of Hong Kong, 1990), 139. This article is also reprinted in David Faure, ed., *Hong Kong: A Reader in Social History* (Hong Kong: Oxford University Press, 2003), 575–95.

16. Chan, "Labour vs. Crown," 139.

17. Gillingham, *At the Peak*, 37.

18. CO 129/488, July 10, 1925, Stubbs to Amery, 580–81, quoted in John M. Carroll, *Edge of Empires: Chinese Elites and British Colonials in Hong Kong* (Cambridge: Harvard University Press, 2005), 133–34.

19. CO 129/489, September 18, 1925, Stubbs to Amery, 212, quoted in Carroll, *Edge of Empires*, 134.

20. Chan, "Labour vs. Crown," 137.

21. Ibid., 141.

22. Henry J. Lethbridge, *Hong Kong, Stability and Change: A Collection of Essays* (Hong Kong: Oxford University Press, 1978), 25.

23. Mills, *British Rule in Eastern Asia*, 410.

24. David Faure, ed., *A Documentary History of Hong Kong: Society* (Hong Kong: Hong Kong University Press, 1997), 1.

25. Report of the Housing Commission, 1935, reprinted in Faure, *Documentary History of Hong Kong*, 205.

26. *Report by Labour Officer Mr. H. R. Butters*, 135.

27. Susan Pedersen, "The Maternalist Moment in British Colonial Policy: The Controversy over 'Child Slavery' in Hong Kong 1917–1941," *Past and Present* 171 (2001): 164.

28. *Hong Kong Legislative Council Sessional Papers, 1930*, 255–60, reprinted in Faure, *Documentary History of Hong Kong*, 175.

29. David Faure, *Colonialism and the Hong Kong Mentality* (Hong Kong: Centre of Asian Studies, University of Hong Kong, 2003), 50.

5

War and Revolution

In July 1937, Japan launched a full-scale invasion of China. Despite resistance from Nationalist Chinese troops under Generalissimo Chiang Kai-shek, Japanese troops soon occupied most of China's major cities. In October 1938, Chiang retreated to Chongqing, in Sichuan province, which became the capital of Free China. Some thirty thousand Japanese troops landed that same month at Daya (Bias) Bay, only thirty miles northeast of Hong Kong, taking the city of Canton within two weeks. Almost overnight, Hong Kong assumed a new importance for China. The colony became a haven for refugees fleeing the Japanese invasion—some five hundred thousand came in 1938 alone—and a crucial source of arms for the Chinese war effort. Until the Japanese took Canton in October 1938, more than fifty tons of munitions and supplies purchased overseas entered China per month via the Kowloon-Canton Railway. Even after the fall of Canton, strategic materials were smuggled into China over land and by boat. Many Chinese newspapers moved to Hong Kong, while local organizations such as the Chinese Merchants' Relief Association, the Chinese Women's Relief Association, and the Hong Kong Chinese Women's Club helped raise money for the war effort.

The Sino-Japanese War had a dramatic effect on Hong Kong's economy. After the Japanese blockaded Shanghai and other Chinese ports, by early 1938 half of China's foreign trade was diverted through Hong Kong. Banks such as the Bank of China and the Communications Bank moved their headquarters to Hong Kong, making it the exchange banking center for all of China. The massive influx of refugees from China exacerbated the colony's already crowded housing conditions and strained its resources, but it also created a boom in land sales that boosted government revenues. Chinese entrepreneurs not only brought capital but also transplanted entire factories, some of which produced military equipment for the Chinese war effort. This helped build an industrial base that would greatly assist Hong Kong's economic recovery after the war.

The Hong Kong government's policy toward the war in China was both shaped and constrained by the concerns of British defense policy. Although the British military leadership had expected another world war and a conflict with Japan, it was eager to prevent any action against Japan that might drive Germany and Italy toward war in Europe. The colonial government could not afford to provoke the Japanese government, especially when Hong Kong was declared a neutral zone in September 1938. (The colonial government had been embarrassed in 1931 after the Japanese invasion of Manchuria provoked a rash of riots in which angry crowds looted Japanese shops, attacked Japanese residents, and murdered a Japanese family. The hostilities continued for five days, and the army had to be called in to help the police keep order.) Thus, the Hong Kong government rejected the Chinese government's pleas to arm local Chinese for helping the war effort on the mainland. Similarly, the colonial government turned down requests by the Chinese unofficial members of the Legislative Council to send relief money to China. The Hong Kong Red Cross Society was forbidden to send workers into the war zone.

Yet the colonial government sympathized with China and was reluctant to alienate its Chinese subjects by clamping down on activities supporting the Chinese resistance. It thus turned a blind eye to efforts by both the Chinese Nationalists and the Communists to funnel resources and draw international support for China's war effort. For the Chinese Communist Party (CCP), Hong Kong was a link to the outside world. In January 1938, the colonial government allowed the CCP to establish a local office (disguised as a tea company in order not to violate British neutrality laws) of the Eighth Route Army, which raised donations of medicine and money from overseas Chinese. The CCP also opened the Hong Kong News College and the China News Agency to train reporters and promote the Chinese war effort. The Hong Kong branch of the Chinese National Anti-Japanese Literary Association and the Defend China League, headed by Song Qingling, widow of Sun Yat-sen, drummed up support for the Chinese cause. Chiang Kai-shek's Nationalist party, the Kuomintang, also had a strong presence in Hong Kong, where it published newspapers and continued its propaganda war. Wang Jingwei and his faction, who later collaborated with the Japanese from Nanjing, broadcast their own propaganda through the *South China Daily.*

DEFENDING THE INDEFENSIBLE

While some British military officials had doubted that the Japanese were capable of challenging the mighty British Empire, more farsighted leaders realized as soon as full-scale war broke out with Germany in 1940 that Hong Kong could not be defended. But they also stressed the need to hold on to the colony to maintain face and to prevent the harbor from falling into enemy hands. Prime Minister Winston Churchill decided against reducing the local garrison, which would weaken both the prestige of the empire and the morale in China. Yet the Hong Kong government was in a weak position to prepare for an invasion. The huge number of refugees from China drained resources (by early 1941, the colony's population was well over 1.5 million), while the colony's status as a free port, coupled with its open border with China, made controlling immigration—not to mention the movement of Japanese agents and sympathizers—impossible.

The colonial government was thus in the unenviable position of preparing to defend a colony that could not be defended, even while maintaining its neutrality. In September 1938 the government reinstated the Emergency Powers Ordinance of 1922, which allowed the police to deport anyone not employed; prohibit public meetings and organizations; censor Chinese newspapers, pamphlets, and placards; and call up a special force of constables. They also allowed the government to control food prices, intern Chinese and Japanese soldiers taking refuge in Hong Kong, and prohibit repairing and provisioning Japanese or Chinese vessels involved in the hostilities.

Even as the government was professing Hong Kong's neutrality, it was preparing to defend the colony against a Japanese invasion. In July 1939, all British male subjects of European origin between the ages of eighteen and fifty-five were made liable for compulsory service in the Defence Reserve. After criticism from the local press and Chinese unofficial members of the Legislative Council, in summer 1940 the government began a program of air-raid tunnels. In 1940, the colonial government evacuated a number of British women and children to Australia. Among the evacuees were Eurasians holding British passports, who because of the Australian government's White Australia policy were dropped off in Manila. This provoked an outcry from Eurasian and Chinese leaders in Hong Kong. In July 1941, Japanese assets in Hong Kong were frozen (as they were in Britain and the United States), although barter trading continued for a while.

Like all British colonies, Hong Kong became part of the British war effort once Britain declared war on Germany for invading Poland in September 1939. Hong Kong had already been part of the Chinese war effort, its formally neutral status notwithstanding, but the fact that both China and Britain were now at war joined the Chinese and the British communities in common cause. In April 1940 the colony contributed to the British war effort through new taxes and several gifts of cash. The *South China Morning Post* organized a Bomber Fund, while both Chinese and expatriates contributed to campaigns such as the British Prisoners of War Fund, the British

War Organization Fund, the Chinese Relief Association, and the Hong Kong and South China Branch of the British Fund for the Relief of Distress in China. Under the Chinese Defence League's "Bowl of Rice" campaign, donors ordered meals at participating restaurants but ate only a bowl of steamed rice, donating the price of the meal to the Chinese war effort. Robert Ho Tung, the Eurasian tycoon, donated a vessel to the Hong Kong Naval Volunteer Force.

Despite the Chinese community's generous contributions to both war efforts, the colonial government doubted that it could rely on the Chinese to help defend the colony. The official view was that because most Chinese considered Hong Kong a temporary home, they were incapable of making any sacrifice for Hong Kong. Yet the government had done little over the previous century to evince the type of loyalty that it now sought from its Chinese subjects. Nor had the government shown that it trusted the Chinese enough to enlist them to defend the colony. Only in May 1938 was a Chinese company added to the Volunteer Defence Corps, founded in 1855 before the Second Opium War. And only after the Chinese members of the Legislative Council had assured the governor of Chinese support were British subjects of Chinese extraction allowed to register for the Defence Reserve. Although the British War Office finally agreed to accept Chinese infantry forces in October 1941, the minimum height and weight restrictions kept many of them out: of the six hundred who applied, only thirty-five were accepted.

THE FALL OF HONG KONG

On December 8, 1941, Hong Kong time, Japanese bombers attacked Hong Kong, Malaya, Pearl Harbor, and the Philippines. Within as many minutes, five Royal Air Force aircraft at Kai Tak airfield in Kowloon had been destroyed. As Japanese troops moved swiftly across the New Territories and into Kowloon, propaganda leaflets declaring "Asia for the Asians" called on Chinese and Indians in the colony to rise up and drive out their British exploiters. Within seventeen days, the Japanese took Hong Kong Island, occupying the entire colony until August 30, 1945. On Christmas Day, one week after the Japanese launched a three-pronged attack on Hong Kong Island, Governor Mark Young, who had arrived in the colony in September from Barbados, surrendered unconditionally to Lieutenant General Sakai Takashi. By February 1942, after the fall of Malaya and Singapore, the sun had set over Britain's empire in East Asia.

Why did the British resistance fall apart so quickly? A better question might be, given the overwhelming strength of the Japanese forces, why did Hong Kong not fall even earlier? Although critics later complained that the

British should have put up a stiffer resistance, both regular troops and volunteers followed Churchill's orders to fight to the end. When Governor Young finally surrendered, he did so after rejecting three earlier offers of surrender and partly to prevent the Japanese invaders from committing the kind of atrocities they had inflicted on the city of Nanjing in 1938. On the eve of the invasion, the Hong Kong side, led by Major General Christopher Maltby, had approximately ten thousand forces—including two British battalions, the Hong Kong Volunteers, two Indian infantry battalions, and two battalions of infantry offered by the Canadian government—and a small number of airplanes and ships, with no chances of any naval reinforcements. A false announcement by the British military on December 20 that some sixty thousand Chinese troops were on their way may have raised morale, but it could not alter the fact that the Japanese side enjoyed clear superiority at sea, on land, and in the air. The Japanese had more than twenty thousand troops as well as more and better planes and ships and could always count on reinforcements from within China. By the time three of Chiang Kai-shek's divisions arrived in Canton to attack the Japanese forces there, Hong Kong had already fallen. As the title of Tony Banham's recent study of the invasion suggests, the colony had "not the slightest chance."[1]

Whereas the British commanders were almost all new to Hong Kong (Maltby had arrived only in August) and the two battalions of Canadian infantry were still being trained, the Japanese had several years of experience fighting in China, and many of their troops had been training together for the assault on Hong Kong. British defense plans changed late in 1941 from defending only Hong Kong Island to holding down the Japanese at the Gin Drinkers' Line—a series of pillboxes running eleven miles from Gin Drinkers' Bay in western Hong Kong to Port Shelter in the eastern region—and then retreating to defend Hong Kong Island. This did not leave enough time for effective planning and training. The British also failed to use the local Chinese effectively; the some 450 who volunteered were used primarily in service positions. The British, who moved mainly by road, were hamstrung when their military transport system fell apart. Helped by spies along the way, the fit, organized, and well-equipped Japanese moved quickly by foot, often at night.

The British had weak, outdated, and insufficient artillery and ammunition. Their persistently weak intelligence underestimated the size and quality of the Japanese forces. The Japanese had much better intelligence, obtained over several years by placing agents throughout Hong Kong in various civilian positions. (Several Japanese residents suddenly appeared in Japanese military uniforms shortly after the surrender.) Large numbers of Japanese merchants had been in Hong Kong since the 1930s, and almost one hundred Japanese remained in Hong Kong in late 1941. A Japanese intelligence map, now housed in the Harvard University Map Collection, shows just how well the Japanese knew their target. Based on British maps, this meticulously detailed map includes administrative boundaries, railway tracks, roads and paths, telephone and telegraph lines, wireless transmitters and underwater cables, police stations and post offices, telegraph and telephone offices, schools, hospitals, churches, temples, pagodas, cemeteries, wells, orchards, marshes and wetlands, uncultivated and barren areas, and both deciduous and coniferous forests.

The human costs of the invasion are unclear. British sources estimated 2,311 troops killed or missing and around the same number wounded, but a recent study places the number closer to 1,560 dead or missing. Japanese figures are less reliable, ranging from initial reports of only 675 killed or missing and 2,079 wounded to the equally dubious report by Tokyo later of 7,000 killed and 20,000 wounded; a more realistic estimate is around 2,000 killed and between 5,000 and 6,000 wounded. As in most wars, it is impossible to tell how many civilians were killed in the invasion. One estimate places the dead at 4,000 and the wounded at 3,000, but the actual numbers were probably much higher.[2]

THE JAPANESE OCCUPATION

Thus began the three years and eight months of "The Captured Territory of Hong Kong," which although touted as part of Japan's "Great East Asian Co-Prosperity Sphere" was little more than Japanese colonialism. Despite their anticolonial rhetoric, the Japanese quickly transformed Hong Kong from a British colony into a Japanese one. Statues of British royalty were removed, while street and place names were replaced with Japanese names (Queen's Road, for example, became Meiji Road). Even the racehorses at Happy Valley were bestowed with Japanese names. The new rulers also Japanized the landscape with various monuments and a cemetery in Causeway Bay for the Japanese horses killed during the invasion, to which Chinese residents were forced to bow. Replacing the Gregorian calendar with the Japanese calendar (based on the contemporary emperor's reign), the Japanese introduced their own holidays, such as the emperor's birthday, the Yasukuni Festival for Japanese war dead, and Empire Day or National Foundation Day. In May 1943, the new authorities established the East Asia Academy to introduce potential government servants, teachers, and businessmen to Japanese morals and customs. As an official Japanese publication explained, since Hong Kong was now a "Hong Kong for the East Asians," it was time for the "poisonous remains of British cultural leftovers" to be "thoroughly eradicated."[3]

Although they portrayed their invasion as liberation from colonialism, as elsewhere in their new empire the Japanese in Hong Kong soon showed

Japanese victory parade, December 28, 1941. Photo courtesy of Tim Ko.

that they could be far more brutal than the British had ever been. On January 4, 1942, all of Hong Kong's British, American, and Dutch residents were arrested. The Japanese displayed their victory over the British for Hong Kong's non-European population to see, parading prisoners of war through the streets and forcing Allied captives to bow to Chinese, pull rickshaws, and clean the streets. Most of the British civilians were imprisoned in Stanley, on the south side of Hong Kong Island, while the military prisoners were held at a former British camp at Sham Shui Po in Kowloon. Although most of the Americans were repatriated, the head of the Stanley internment camp, Frank Gimson, who had arrived as colonial secretary the day before the Japanese invasion, insisted that the British civilians remain in Hong Kong as a show of force. Many civilian and military prisoners were executed; others died of disease and malnourishment. But even though Prime Minister Tojo Hideki ordered that the European prisoners have only the barest of rations, the British in Hong Kong had it better than their counterparts in some of the Japanese camps in Southeast Asia. In Hong Kong, writes historian Philip Snow, "the keynote of their treatment was humiliation rather than brutality for the sake of it." Still, the "combined shock of the defeat and internment" undermined the "entire pre-war edifice of British supremacy in Hong Kong."[4]

Those who suffered the most, both in the invasion and during the occupation, were the same people the Japanese repeatedly insisted were not their enemies: the Chinese. The Japanese authorities tried to reduce Hong Kong's population by repatriating the refugees who had come from China in the years leading up to the invasion. In early January 1942, they announced that anyone without residence or employment would have to leave. Although the Japanese had a hard time enforcing this policy, within a year Hong Kong's population had dropped from more than 1.5 million to 1 million. By the end of the occupation in August 1945, it was under six hundred thousand. In three and a half years, at least ten thousand Hong Kong civilians were executed, while many others were tortured, raped, or mutilated. Army officers were even more vicious than their men, but the most systematically brutal were the Kempeitai, the notorious Japanese military police who routinely performed executions by beheading at King's Park in Kowloon and used Chinese for shooting or bayonet practice. Dorothy Lee, a social worker, recalled how everyone lived "in fear of the 'midnight knock.' The Japanese might come to your door at any time to take over your house or flat and, in the early days, they came into rape." Lee saw one Japanese corporal known as "the killer" personally behead twelve civilians within several minutes.[5]

Although the Japanese created countless atrocities throughout their empire, Hong Kong's unique situation may have encouraged the scope and intensity of this brutality. As they did in Malaya, Indochina, and Indonesia, many Japanese administrators and soldiers resented the Chinese of Hong Kong for supposedly having served their European overlords so willingly. Unlike the colonies of Southeast Asia, however, Hong Kong lacked the natural resources to make conquest worthwhile. Although the new regime introduced a program for reopening factories to produce goods such as shoes made with rubber from Indochina and Malaya, the Japanese economic record was disastrous. Shortages and price increases were exacerbated by orders from Tokyo to confiscate anything of value and send it to Japan. By late 1942, when the war was going badly for Japan, the governor tried even more vigorously to restrict Hong Kong's scarce resources for the Japanese troops. In January 1943, the Kempeitai set two German shepherds on a group of Chinese women who had been gathering grass for fuel. Only after the dogs had chewed pieces of flesh out of them were the women released. As the colony's overseas trade suffered, by mid-1943 the food shortage became even more unbearable. Several hundred corpses—some with parts of their thighs and buttocks removed for food—littered the streets every day, and many residents survived only by eating rats. The weakening of central government control and the expansion of corruption that accompanied Japan's failing war effort made conditions even worse and "opened the way to an orgy of private greed." Uncontrolled and free to do as it pleased, the

Kempeitai in Hong Kong created an "empire unmatched by the Kempeitai branches in any other Japanese-occupied zone" and "waxed fat on the narcotics trade."[6]

Despite some provisions under the Japanese for educating Hong Kong's poor, the education system practically fell apart. Whereas more than one hundred thousand children were enrolled in school before the war, by the end of the war this number had plummeted to around three thousand. Yet any account of the Japanese occupation must also include some of the more positive changes. Snow argues that the Japanese brought more Chinese into the "central administration of the colony than the British had ever done."[7] The Japanese practice of delegating tasks gave Chinese a larger role than under the British, while the Japanese also created a network of district bureaus, which the British never had. Unlike the British, the Japanese went to great lengths to publicize and explain their policies to the Chinese. The Japanese also made some positive changes in public health and agriculture. With "something close to a mania" for preserving public health—mainly to protect the health of Japanese soldiers—they kept outbreaks of smallpox and cholera minor compared with the prewar years.[8]

Collaboration took different forms and assumed various levels of intensity. As soon as the Japanese flag was raised in Central District on December 27, Japanese flags appeared all over the area, and Hong Kong's new rulers had no trouble finding recruits for their administration. Some Chinese may have believed in Japan's rhetoric of "Asia for the Asians," but most people in Hong Kong, relieved that the invasion was over, collaborated simply to get by. For the Eurasians who were recruited for the same kinds of clerical and secretarial posts that they had held under the British and had nowhere else to go, collaboration must have seemed a rather logical choice. The writers for the *Hong Kong News*, which had been published before the war by Japanese businessmen and was revived by the occupation authorities, were mainly Eurasians and Indians. Many Eurasians and Portuguese became brokers between the Japanese administration and the Chinese population, running various black or gray markets. The Japanese also tried hard to win over the Indian population, promising to help them drive the British out of India. Some Britons also worked with the Japanese; for example, high-level bankers chose to collaborate to ensure some level of financial stability. Similarly, P. S. Selwyn-Clarke, the former director of medical services, worked with the Japanese for the sake of the Chinese community and the interned Europeans and prisoners of war.

To consolidate their rule, the Japanese tried to recruit the same community leaders who had worked with the British. On January 10, 1942, two weeks after the British surrender, Lieutenant General Sakai invited some 130 of the leading Chinese and Eurasians to a formal luncheon at the Peninsula Hotel in Kowloon. Sakai insisted that the war in Hong Kong was against Britain, not China, and that the Chinese and Japanese should work together for the prosperity of all the races of Greater East Asia. Lieutenant General Isogai Rensuke, who became governor later that month, established two councils consisting of Chinese and Eurasian leaders for managing the Chinese population. On the Chinese Representative Council were Robert Kotewall, the chair; Lau Tit-shing, manager of the Communications Bank and chairman of the Chinese Bankers' Association; Li Tse-fong, manager of the Bank of East Asia (which had maintained extensive contacts with Japanese firms before the war) and former unofficial member of the Legislative Council; and Chan Lim-pak, who had once been comprador to the Hong Kong Shanghai Bank in Canton. The Chinese Cooperative Council, whose 22 members were selected by the Chinese Representative Council from the leading professionals, was chaired by Chow Shouson.

Some Chinese leaders were enthusiastic about working with the Japanese. Lau Tit-shing, for example, was president of the Chinese-Japanese Returned-Students Association and, according to sociologist Henry Lethbridge, was "very pro-Japanese," having been "thoroughly brainwashed by his early education in Japan."[9] When Lau died in April 1945, he was honored by the Japanese governor. Chan Lim-pak had been arrested by the British during the Japanese invasion on charges of "defeatist talk" and aiding the enemy. He was killed in 1944 by an American bomber while en route to Japan. But most Chinese and Eurasian leaders probably collaborated with the Japanese in the same way the majority of Hong Kong's population did: "with reluctance and misgiving, and as a matter of physical survival."[10] Fear and pragmatism were no doubt strong reasons for collaborating, as was preserving their own class interests. And many collaborated with the Japanese to help the local community. Indeed, three colonial officers testified after the war that they had met secretly with Chow Shouson and Robert Kotewall shortly before the fall of Hong Kong and requested that they cooperate with the Japanese to protect the interests of the Chinese community. That there was so little Chinese resentment toward the two Chinese councils during the occupation suggests that most Chinese understood that the Chinese and Eurasian leaders had to cooperate.

Just as collaboration during the Japanese occupation took many forms, so did resistance. As they had under the British, many Chinese simply ignored the regulations and proclamations issued by the Japanese authorities. Chinese staff in the governor's office often failed to show up for their mandatory Japanese classes; clerks at Chinese-run department stores refused to sell goods to Japanese, pretending that they were out of stock; and entire schools moved to unoccupied parts of the mainland rather than comply with the new curriculum. By summer 1943, people in Hong Kong realized that the war no longer favored the Japanese. By 1944, Chinese and Eurasian leaders started to avoid their duties on the two Chinese councils.

Given Hong Kong's urban nature, most organized resistance occurred in the rural New Territories, especially along the Chinese border. Led by Lindsay Ride, a professor at the University of Hong Kong and a member of the Volunteer Defence Corps who had escaped from the Sham Shui Po prison camp, and with help from local Chinese such as Paul Tsui, a recent graduate of the University of Hong Kong, the British Army Aid Group (BAAG) helped European and Chinese residents escape from Hong Kong, gathered intelligence, and rescued Allied airmen shot down by the Japanese. Based in Guilin in southern China, the BAAG was technically a noncombat unit of the Indian Army. By late 1942, the Chinese Nationalists had revived an underground movement, while the Communist guerrillas of the East River Column were active in the New Territories and in the urban areas of Hong Kong. Despite the mutual suspicions among the British, Nationalists, Communists, and their respective agendas, this joint resistance helped to break down racial divisions between Britons and Chinese and to create a "camaraderie unimaginable in the pre-war years."[11]

WARTIME PLANNING AND THE RACE TO RECOVER HONG KONG

British planning for postwar Hong Kong began almost immediately after the fall to Japan, which, compounded by the loss of Singapore and Malaya, was a terrible blow to British morale. As the Colonial Office began to reassess the British failure to defend Hong Kong, one of the conclusions was that the British should have relied more on local Chinese and accepted help from Chiang Kai-shek's Nationalist forces. Some wartime planners argued that the invasion might even be a chance for the British to start afresh in Hong Kong after the war by building a better sense of community between the British and the Chinese, including by opening higher-level government positions to local Chinese. They were especially eager to prevent the type of anticolonial nationalism that had erupted in India and would eventually lead to independence in 1947.

The British plans for recovering Hong Kong, however, faced opposition from both China and the United States. With help from American president Franklin Delano Roosevelt (whose grandfather had been a partner in the American firm of Russell and whose mother had once lived in Hong Kong), in January 1942 Chiang Kai-shek became the supreme allied commander of the China-Burma-India Theater. Chiang hoped to use the war to recover Hong Kong and to end the embarrassing unequal treaties. Supported by the United States, in mid-1942 Chiang's Nationalists approached Britain to give up Hong Kong, or at least the New Territories. In late 1942, Sino-British negotiations began for abolishing extraterritoriality in China and revising the status of the New Territories after the war. At the Cairo Conference of November 1943, Roosevelt promised to help Chiang recover Hong Kong if he agreed to help the Chinese Communists fight the Japanese.

Even while wartime planners in Britain were committed to restoring Hong Kong to British rule after the war, they also realized that the Chinese Nationalists' demands would have to be taken seriously and that conditions in postwar Hong Kong would have to be different. Although the Nationalists suddenly aborted their campaign to recover the New Territories—content for the time being with the agreement that China would reserve the right to raise the issue at a later time—some British officials believed that Hong Kong might have to be surrendered for Britain to focus on its other possessions, especially India and Egypt. Realizing that many American officials supported China, some British officials even suggested giving up Hong Kong before the United States applied pressure on Britain to do so. In mid-1942, the Colonial Office conceded that Hong Kong might have to be surrendered after the war. Even in late 1945, George Kitson, head of the China Department at the Foreign Office, suggested that Britain return Hong Kong for both symbolic and practical purposes: as a token of gratitude for China's help in defeating Japan, as a gesture of friendship in a new postwar world, as proof that British colonialism was entering a new phase, and as a preemptive move to prevent possible confrontation with China over the region.

As the war turned against Japan's favor, however, by early 1943 the Colonial Office resolved to retain Hong Kong after the war. The Colonial Office became particularly optimistic in February 1944 when Li Shu-fan, a prominent Chinese surgeon who had made his way to London, assured the Colonial Office and the Foreign Office that most members of the Chinese upper classes would prefer British rule to Chinese rule after the war. That summer, the Hong Kong Planning Unit was established under Frank Smith, the former colonial secretary. After 1944 the unit was led by David MacDougall, a Hong Kong cadet who had escaped during the Japanese occupation. By mid-1945, Winston Churchill realized that Chiang Kai-shek could not try to recover Hong Kong without support from the United States, which now considered the continuation of the British Empire vital to its own interests in the postwar world. As victory became imminent, in the summer of 1945 the Hong Kong Planning Unit and the China Association, a powerful lobby representing British business interests in China, began to consider various proposals for constitutional reform, among them giving a greater role to local Chinese. Churchill now declared that Hong Kong would be removed from the British Empire "over my dead body."

As the British planned for recovering Hong Kong, the problem of what to do with the old business and professional elite arose. The British needed a local support base, but some of the Europeans interned during the war had criticized leaders such as Robert Kotewall and Chow Shouson for being too compliant with the Japanese. Yet the returning colonial government would have great difficulty finding anyone to replace these old leaders. Furthermore, there was the problem of convincing the local Chinese population that Britain, rather than Nationalist China, deserved to rule Hong Kong after the war. This explains both why the British, who could not afford to lose the people they had depended on for so long, decided to keep the old leaders and why these leaders worked so hard to restore British rule. The Colonial Office eventually decided that Chow and Kotewall had been acting in the colony's best interest.

Just as victory against Japan became certain, a more immediate challenge arose. Japan surrendered on August 14, earlier than most British military planners had predicted. American and Nationalist Chinese troops were making progress in China, getting closer by the day to Canton. Knowing that Roosevelt wanted Chiang Kai-shek to accept the Japanese surrender as supreme commander in almost all of the China Theater, the British feared that Chiang's troops would try to accept the surrender in Hong Kong. Although Chiang assured them that he would not try to retake Hong Kong after accepting the surrender, the British dispatched Rear Admiral Cecil Harcourt from Sydney with a fleet to reach Hong Kong first. When Britain and China asked the United States to help them resolve the matter, Chiang proposed delegating surrender authority to a British official in Hong Kong, but only if Britain agreed not to accept the Japanese surrender until after Chiang had formally accepted the surrender for the China Theater. Britain agreed, and on September 16 Harcourt accepted the Japanese surrender on behalf of Britain and China in the presence of a Chinese and an American official.

This arrangement briefly soured Sino-British relations, but it was as pragmatic as it was symbolic. It also helps explain why Hong Kong remained a British colony after the war. Although there were loud calls in China for recovering Hong Kong and although he had almost sixty thousand troops within three hundred miles of Hong Kong when the Japanese surrendered, Chiang realized that Britain would not give up Hong Kong easily and that a failure to recover Hong Kong would discredit him in China. Furthermore, he needed the support of both the United States and Britain to be a major player in the new world order. Preoccupied with recovering northern China and keeping Chinese Communist troops from recapturing Japanese-held territory, he did not want to provoke the Communists into entering the race for Hong Kong, especially since their East River Column was closer to Hong Kong than were his own troops. Concerned about the postwar order, the United States had now softened its stance toward colonialism. Harry Truman, who became president after Roosevelt died in April 1945, was less committed than his predecessor to restoring Hong Kong to Chinese sovereignty, while General Douglas MacArthur, commander of the Allied forces in the Southwest Pacific, supported outright the continuation of the British Empire in East Asia. The British realized that they could not prevent Chiang's troops from recapturing Hong Kong and that the United States, regardless of its new attitudes toward colonialism, would not help the British resist such an attempt. They also realized that such an arrangement would play out better among the Chinese population of Hong Kong, some of whom, proud of China's new status, thought that this might be a chance to get rid of the British.

REBUILDING HONG KONG

Postwar Hong Kong was plagued by the problems that face all societies reeling from the ravages of war: inflation, unemployment, looting, poor health and sanitary conditions, and shortages in currency, housing, personnel, and food (some 80 percent of the population suffered from malnutrition). Compounding these problems was the task of imprisoning and repatriating thousands of Japanese soldiers and civilians. Recovery was not easy, but David MacDougall's interim military administration, which managed the colony for eight months, did a remarkable job of restoring order by setting price controls, providing emergency food supplies, and restoring the fishing industry. Anne Sorby, who came to work in the interim military administration from the mainland, where she had been stationed with the British Special Operations Executive unit, recalled that "there was a real team spirit between the military, naval and civil. . . . It was all very inspiring. We were determined to make it work, and it did."[12]

Hong Kong's recovery could not have been accomplished, however, without an enterprising and resourceful population that, having endured the Japanese occupation for more than three years, was ready to help rebuild Hong Kong. By November 1945, the economy had recovered so well that government controls were lifted and free markets restored. By early 1946 the population had returned to around one million, although this had as much to do with the chaotic conditions in China, which provided a steady influx of immigrants, as with the efforts of the interim government. Trade had returned to almost 60 percent of its prewar level. During the same year, Hong Kong got its own airline, Cathay Pacific, a predominantly British corporation. The economy recovered so quickly that the government enjoyed a budget surplus for the 1947–1948 financial year. Hong Kong's economy also benefited greatly from the Chinese civil war between the Nationalists and the Communists. Although Hong Kong's industry had already been reasonably well developed before the war, it was rejuvenated by Chinese entrepreneurs escaping the war. The colonial government later estimated that the infusion of Shanghai capital and business experience gave the colony a ten- to fifteen-year head start over the rest of East Asia.

When Rear Admiral Harcourt landed at Hong Kong on August 30, observers noted that for every British flag that welcomed him, there were about four Nationalist Chinese flags. Yet even though pro-Chinese sentiment was strong, there was very little overt anti-British sentiment, let alone the type of anticolonial nationalism that developed after the war in other European colonies. The speed of Hong Kong's postwar recovery helped restore confidence in British rule, especially compared with the suffering during the Japanese occupation and with the political and financial instability in postwar China. Still, many Chinese—and even some Europeans—agreed that some of the old racial barriers had to be removed. Criticism of the many failures of prewar British rule began to proliferate in the local press, as did new and vocal demands for the end of European privilege: the end of discrimination in the workplace, more government positions for non-Europeans, more Chinese representation in government, and the abolition of prohibitions against Chinese living on Victoria Peak and joining the Hong Kong Club.

Although Hong Kong people naturally demanded retribution against their Japanese abusers and the Chinese and Eurasians who had helped them, Hong Kong's wartime experience never led to the type of bitter recrimination against collaborators that occurred in China and in Europe. For helping the Japanese, some Indian police and prison wardens were sent back to India, and Sikhs were never again recruited for the police force. For the most part, however, the British again found themselves relying on the same people they had counted on before the war. In October 1945, Robert Kotewall was asked to withdraw from public life until his wartime record could be fully cleared. When the colonial civil government was restored the following May, he had to resign his seat on the Executive Council. Kotewall was never allowed to return to public life, Chow Shouson never completely returned, and Li Tse-fong was not reappointed to the Legislative Council. However, the Eurasian Lo Man Kam was able to return to public life because the British believed that he had worked with the Japanese only with great reluctance. (In contrast to his years on the colonial Legislative Council, Lo generally remained silent on the wartime councils. One of the only occasions he spoke was when, asked by the Japanese authorities how they might improve relations between Chinese and Japanese, he replied that the Japanese troops might take the initiative by not relieving themselves in public.) Lo was appointed in 1946 to the Executive Council, where he played a large role, and was subsequently knighted in 1948 for helping to rebuild Hong Kong. Chau Tsun Nin, a prominent lawyer and businessman who had avoided collaborating by taking refuge in neutral Macau, was also appointed to the Legislative and Executive Councils and was made Commander of the British Empire.

Nor did Hong Kong witness the spectacle and trauma associated with the war crimes trials conducted in Europe and in other parts of Asia. Only 21 of the 129 Japanese accused of war crimes and tried in Hong Kong were executed. Lieutenant General Sakai, who had led the invasion in December 1941, was captured in mainland China and executed in Nanjing. Lieutenant General Tanaka Hisakazu, governor of Hong Kong in 1945, was also captured on the mainland and was then tried and executed in Canton. But Governor Isogai Rensuke, who was also tried in Nanjing, served only five years of his life sentence. Nor did the Japanese occupation create the kind of anti-Japanese sentiments that persist to this day in mainland China. Indeed, Japanese businessmen returned quite quickly in the late 1940s, although under the control of American occupation forces.

POSTWAR CHANGES AND THE YOUNG PLAN

The return of Governor Mark Young on May 1, 1946, to the colony that he had surrendered in December 1941 was a symbolic move, designed to emphasize that the Japanese occupation had been only a temporary disruption. But Young quickly showed that he had no desire to set back the clock. Instead, he proposed the most radical constitutional reforms in Hong Kong's history. Young believed that the Chinese of Hong Kong needed more political representation to increase their desire to remain under British rule. Convinced that Hong Kong might eventually become a city-state within the British Empire and Commonwealth, Young called for greater Chinese membership in the Legislative and Executive Councils. He proposed a municipal council, of which two-thirds would be elected mainly by Chinese voters, while letting the colonial government retain control of finance and defense. Young also called for more localization by replacing European government officials with Chinese. Although Young based his plan on the recent constitutional reforms elsewhere in the empire, he was also drawing on an old lesson that the British had learned from the American Revolution and applied to their white subjects in Australia, Canada, New Zealand, and South Africa: cultivate an imperial identity by giving colonial subjects more of a say in government.

Although in July 1947 the British government publicly approved the Young plan in principle, the reforms were doomed from the start. The British government soon sent Alexander Grantham to replace Young, whom it worried was too closely associated with the surrender to the Japanese. Unlike Young, Grantham, who had been in Hong Kong as a cadet during the strike-boycott of 1925–1926, believed that the colony's proximity to China meant that local Chinese could never be molded into loyal British subjects. Grantham agreed that the Legislative Council could be made slightly more representative, but he doubted that Hong Kong could ever have the kind of system that had developed during his governorship in Jamaica, Nigeria, and Fiji. "Hong Kong is different from other colonies," he later wrote, "for Hong Kong can never become independent. Either it remains a British colony, or it is re-absorbed into China as part of the province of Kwangtung [Guangdong]."[13] Nor, Grantham insisted, were Young's reforms even necessary. Grantham, who enjoyed good relations with the British and Chinese merchants of Hong Kong as well as with prominent military and political officials in China, believed that the majority of Hong Kong Chinese preferred British rule and that the British could prevent the Nationalists from trying to recover Hong Kong. He was less optimistic that the British could do the same if the Communists took control of China, but he felt certain that the Communists would not bother Hong Kong as long as they were convinced of the colony's value to them.

The failure of the Young plan cannot, however, be blamed solely on Grantham. Although the new governor was greatly responsible for killing the reforms, they were also hurt by a lack of support from the British government and from Hong Kong's Chinese and expatriate business communities as well as by the changing political situation in China. While the Colonial Office generally supported Young's plan, the Foreign Office worried that introducing democracy would provoke the Chinese government (whether Nationalist or Communist), as would any plans to keep Hong Kong in the British Empire and Commonwealth. Some Hong Kong officials saw the reforms as a threat to their executive authority. Both British and Chinese civil servants and business leaders were afraid that the reforms would enable Chiang Kai-shek's Nationalists to influence local municipal politics. The influx of refugees during the civil war also hurt the plans, because these refugees were more concerned about their immediate livelihood than about constitutional reform. Eager to escape Communist rule, the wave of Chinese refugees who came after the 1949 revolution had even fewer grudges against the colonial government.

The British government's earlier concerns about placating any demands for reform in Hong Kong soon subsided. In December 1948 and again in August 1949, the Labour government, which earlier had declared its commitment to decolonizing the British Empire, affirmed its intention to keep Hong Kong. In June 1949 the predominantly expatriate Hong Kong Reform Club and Kowloon Chamber of Commerce petitioned Grantham for a directly elected Legislative Council, and in July almost 150 Chinese groups, including the Chinese Manufacturers' Union, the Hong Kong Chinese Reform Association, and the Kowloon Chinese Chamber of Commerce, petitioned Grantham for constitutional reforms at the central and municipal levels. After the Communist victory in 1949 and China's subsequent entry into the Korean War in 1950, however, the Foreign Office feared that political reforms would provoke China (as a similar proposal for reform in Gibraltar had provoked Spain).

The Foreign Office approved Grantham's less radical reforms in May 1952, but unofficial members of the legislative and executive councils suddenly opposed any reforms. Four months later, the British cabinet agreed to scrap plans for constitutional reform in Hong Kong. In October, Secretary for the Colonies Oliver Lyttelton told the House of Commons that any constitutional reforms would be confined to the Urban Council and that any significant reform would be "inopportune." Robert Black, who succeeded Grantham as governor in 1958, was also convinced that any political reforms would provoke China. Although historian Steve Tsang has found that none of the declassified British documents for the 1950s and 1960s indicate that leaders of the People's Republic of China (PRC) ever warned the Hong Kong government against any political reforms, British officials frequently used the argument that any democratic reforms would not be tolerated by China to justify Hong Kong's lack of democratization.[14] Thus, writes Leo Goodstadt, who has spent several decades working in and writing on Hong Kong, "an expatriate colonial administration, in collusion with a largely Chinese business elite, frustrated the modest reforms proposed for the territory and ensured the survival of colonial political institutions inherited from the previous century."[15]

The early postwar years nevertheless saw some important changes. Ironically, part of the impulse for these changes came from the Japanese, who in their wartime propaganda had drawn unflattering attention to Hong Kong's problems, most prominently its racial discrimination and legalized opium smoking. "The conquest of December 1941," writes Snow, "had given the old colonial rulers a sort of enforced sabbatical in which to sit back and take stock of their pre-war deficiencies."[16] While some of the old colonials did not necessarily share what became known as "the 1946 outlook," both British government officials and local colonial administrators realized that Hong Kong needed at least minor constitutional changes and that the colony could not return to the prewar days of racial discrimination. Some of these sentiments came from administrators who, like MacDougall and Young, saw British colonialism as an important step toward self-rule. The impulse for change also had a strong pragmatic basis: the British realized that they needed to win over the local Chinese to legitimize and maintain their continued rule in Hong Kong.

In late July 1946, shortly after Young's return, the colonial government repealed the 1904 and 1918 Peak ordinances as well as the ordinance that had reserved part of the island of Cheung Chau for Europeans. Soon wealthy Chinese were moving to the Peak. Racial discrimination was suddenly seen as being out of step with the times. Grantham observed a "marked decline in social snobbishness" and a "greater mixing of the races" compared to when he had been in Hong Kong during the 1920s and 1930s.[17] Whereas visitors from other colonies before the war had frequently commented on the width of the racial divide in Hong Kong, visitors after the war were often surprised to see both Chinese and foreigners using buses and trams. In October, Paul Tsui, the University of Hong Kong graduate who had worked for the BAAG during the war, became the first Chinese cadet officer. The government also banned opium smoking and tripled the minimum daily wage. The Executive Council was expanded to include an equal number of Chinese and European unofficial members.

Yet the magnitude of these changes should not be exaggerated. Many elite clubs remained closed to Chinese and Europeans until the late 1950s. The most important government and commercial positions were still held by Europeans, and the expatriate-dominated Hong Kong General Chamber of Commerce did not get a Chinese chair until the 1980s. The plans for localization made little headway. Instead, government positions were filled with "retreads," expatriate colonial officers brought in from other British colonies. Although many of these new officers were more liberal than the old colonials, the temporary solidarity that had been forged during the war slipped away. Expatriate officials enjoyed higher wages and better terms of employment and promotion as well as superior housing and medical care. Many colonial officials had always doubted the loyalty of the Hong Kong Chinese, but these doubts intensified after the Chinese revolution of 1949, when, writes Goodstadt, "Chinese were viewed as more susceptible to ideological conversion than the English (despite the Soviet spy scandals in the British Foreign Office)."[18] As Chinese refugees flooded in while the civil war escalated, the local demands for reform subsided. Thus, the British could afford to become more confident in retaining Hong Kong without making any significant changes.

In the end, the greatest significance of World War II for Hong Kong was probably economic rather than social or political. On the one hand, the British never regained their prewar hold on Hong Kong's economy. It was the Chinese who, for example, literally rebuilt Hong Kong: in 1946 all of the contractors used by the Public Works Department to rebuild the colony were Chinese. It was also the Chinese who rebuilt the light-industry base they had established before the war. From 1947 to 1949, almost all major firms in Shanghai moved their operations to Hong Kong, which gave the colony larger and more sophisticated factories. Together, local industrialists and these "emigrant entrepreneurs" from Shanghai, as sociologist Wong Siu-lun calls them, built on Hong Kong's earlier industrial base, which had been established in the early 1900s and expanded in the late 1930s when Chinese industrialists had moved to Hong Kong after the Japanese invasion of China.[19]

On the other hand, whereas some British leaders had doubted Hong Kong's economic value, the war helped make Hong Kong an even more important part of the shrinking British Empire. Because the abolition of the foreign concessions in China following the war threatened the economic security that foreigners had enjoyed for so long, many foreign firms soon moved their headquarters from China to Hong Kong. Hong Kong thus became of greater strategic importance than before as the center of British commercial operations in China. With an insurgency in Malaya led by Chinese Communists and the impending Communist victory in China, holding on to Hong Kong also became of great psychological importance. Losing the colony would hurt British prestige and undermine the struggle against Communism in Thailand, Burma, and Malaya. This strategic usefulness was enhanced by the fact that the cost of retaining Hong Kong was extremely low. After 1948, Hong Kong did not require any financial assistance from Britain, although Britain continued to pay for most of the local garrison.

HONG KONG AND THE CHINESE REVOLUTION OF 1949

The reactions in Britain and Hong Kong to the establishment of the PRC in October 1949 were a mixture of anxiety and relief. Most Chinese in Hong Kong were simply glad for the civil war to be over. Chiang Kai-shek's Kuomintang regime, which reestablished the Republic of China on the island of Taiwan, had lost all credibility (although pro-Chiang newspapers in Hong Kong now called for the colony to be restored to the Republic of China). The new PRC government did not seem to directly threaten British commercial interests in China, nor had the Chinese Communists ever cared about recovering Hong Kong. Chairman Mao Zedong, who once referred to Hong Kong as "that wasteland of an island," reportedly told a British journalist in 1946 that neither he nor the CCP was interested in Hong Kong and that as long as the British did not mistreat Chinese in Hong Kong, he would not let the status of Hong Kong harm Sino-British relations. In November 1948, Qiao Mu, head of the local branch of the CCP's New China News Agency, assured the Hong Kong government that a new Communist government would not bother Hong Kong and that it would even allow the colonial government to provide refuge to Nationalist leaders.

Still, the months leading up to the Communist victory had been tense for Sino-British relations and for both the government and the population of Hong Kong. In April 1949, Communist batteries in the lower reaches of the Yangzi River shelled a British warship, HMS *Amethyst*, killing the ship's captain. The *Amethyst* escaped to Hong Kong, where the British community greeted its crew members as heroes and the British press portrayed the escape in gallant terms, but the incident humiliated both the Royal Navy and Britain. Although they doubted that the Communists would try to attack

Hong Kong, the British government began to reinforce Hong Kong's garrison, while the Hong Kong government cracked down on local Communist activities by detaining left-wing journalists and breaking up Communist-run groups. In August 1949, the Legislative Council passed special public security legislation that gave the governor wide powers of censorship and included measures reminiscent of those passed during the Second Opium War: requiring identification cards for all residents over twelve years of age and granting the police wide powers to search private residences and to arrest and deport "undesirables." Although Communist troops stopped at the Hong Kong border on October 17, 1949, after arriving in Canton two days earlier, to many in Hong Kong it had seemed a very close call.

Given that the Communist government of China was dedicated to ending colonialism and imperialism worldwide, why did it tolerate British colonialism in its own backyard? Especially compared with the dramatic and often cataclysmic changes that characterized the first decades of the PRC, the new government's policy toward Hong Kong remained consistently levelheaded and sophisticated. Hong Kong had in fact been an important base for the Communist movement throughout the Chinese civil war. In 1947, the CCP established its Central Hong Kong Bureau (renamed the Central South China Bureau in early 1949). Through the New China News Agency, the CCP spread propaganda within Hong Kong, in China, and among overseas Chinese communities. The CCP trained cadres in the safety of colonial Hong Kong and made an "organized and consistent effort" to recruit members from local schools and factories.[20] When the Communists marched toward victory in 1949, they were more concerned with gaining control of northern China. The Communists reassured the British that they would not try to recover Hong Kong after they took power and ordered their troops not to cause too much trouble as they approached the Hong Kong border.

The Communists' policy toward Hong Kong after their victory in the civil war was equally pragmatic. As Steve Tsang puts it, for the PRC government the Hong Kong issue was "somewhere between foreign policy and domestic policy."[21] Because the British had obtained Hong Kong through the first of the unequal treaties (which the PRC government quickly renounced), Hong Kong was an internal Chinese matter that would eventually be resolved peacefully through diplomacy. Encouraging nationalism in a colony full of anti-Communist refugees would be at best futile and at worst foolhardy, perhaps even pushing local Chinese toward Chiang Kai-shek's regime on Taiwan. (Governor Grantham recalled that the PRC government had a hard time agitating Chinese refugees in Hong Kong, "for the refugees had fled from the communist paradise, and had no love for the government of China.")[22] Even more dangerous, other powers—and the United Nations—might intervene if the Communists tried to foment any anticolonial struggles in Hong Kong. The colony could be of great use to China, just as it had been for more than a century, as a window to the outside world. Remittances from overseas Chinese would provide valuable foreign exchange to help rebuild China's war-torn economy, while the colony would be a base for importing goods that China could not produce.

The Chinese government also realized that Hong Kong might be used to push Britain and the United States apart from each other vis-à-vis their policy in East Asia. Shortly after the outbreak of the Korean War, Premier Zhou Enlai ordered Huang Zuomei, head of the New China News Agency in Hong Kong, to obey the CCP's policy of leaving Hong Kong alone, reminding Huang of Hong Kong's use in overcoming the U.S. and United Nations embargoes and dividing Britain and the United States in their China policies. In 1951, Politburo member Peng Zhen explained that taking Hong Kong would be too difficult and would cause problems in China's international relations. Instead, Peng argued, it would be better to maintain Hong Kong's status quo and to use the colony for rebuilding China's economy. It would be "unwise for us to deal with the problem of Hong Kong rashly and without preparation."[23]

This does not, however, mean that the relationship between Hong Kong and the new China was always a smooth one. Shortly after closing the border with Hong Kong, Guangdong authorities placed loudspeakers at Lo Wu and Man Kam To (the two main crossing points), blasting criticism at the British and Hong Kong governments. PRC border guards taunted their Hong Kong counterparts, threatening to harm their families once the PRC liberated Hong Kong. Colonial authorities worried that the pro-Beijing schools were training students for subversive activities. Formed in the 1950s as part of the Hong Kong police force, the Special Branch kept a close watch on subversive elements in Hong Kong. A failed tramway strike in Hong Kong during December 1949, provoked by authorities in Canton, showed that the new PRC was a force to reckon with. After a fire in November 1951 left some ten thousand people homeless, in March 1952 a violent confrontation occurred between the colonial police and protesting crowds after a comfort mission from Canton was stopped at the border. One protester was shot dead, more than one hundred were arrested, and twelve were deported. After local left-wing newspapers tried to stir up anti-British feelings and some ten thousand sympathizers protested the shooting, the government shut down for six months the pro-Beijing newspaper *Ta Kung Pao*, which had reprinted an article from the *People's Daily* (the CCP's main national newspaper) criticizing the Hong Kong government. In September 1953, Chinese shore batteries fired on a Royal Navy launch on antismuggling patrol in international waters, killing seven and wounding five servicemen.

Such heated incidents, however, were relatively rare. Because Hong Kong depended on PRC goodwill, not to mention food and water from China (the Guangdong government had originally offered to supply Hong Kong with water for free, but the colonial government, worried that it might be used for propaganda, declined the offer), to survive, the colonial government learned to forge a working relationship with the new government across the border. In December 1948, the British Foreign Office had warned that if the Communists won the civil war, Hong Kong would be like "living on the edge of a volcano."[24] Grantham recalled a rather less alarming image of Hong Kong's position at the edge of the PRC. "The attitude of the Chinese authorities towards Hong Kong was a combination of passive hostility with occasional outbursts of active unfriendliness: rather like a pot on the kitchen stove; the pot being Hong Kong. Normally the pot would be kept at the back of the stove gently simmering, but every now and then the cook—the Chinese government—would bring it to the front of the stove when it would boil fiercely. After a while he would move it to the back of the stove again. We never knew when the pot was going to be brought to the boil."[25]

NOTES

1. Tony Banham, *Not the Slightest Chance: The Defence of Hong Kong, 1941* (Hong Kong: Hong Kong University Press, 2003).

2. Ibid., 317–19.

3. "Cultural Activities in the New Hong Kong: A Special Article from the Hong Kong Broadcasting Office," *New Asia*, September 1942, 107–8, reprinted in David Faure, ed., *A Documentary History of Hong Kong: Society* (Hong Kong: Hong Kong University Press, 1997), 225.

4. Philip Snow, *The Fall of Hong Kong: Britain, China, and the Japanese Occupation* (New Haven, CT: Yale University Press, 2003), 133–34.

5. Dorothy Lee, "Release and Rehabilitation," in Sally Blyth and Ian Wotherspoon, *Hong Kong Remembers* (Hong Kong: Oxford University Press, 1996), 27.

6. Snow, *Fall of Hong Kong*, 161–62.

7. Ibid., 130.

8. Ibid., 164–65.

9. Henry J. Lethbridge, "Hong Kong under Japanese Occupation: Changes in Social Structure," in I. C. Jarvie and Joseph Agassi, eds., *Hong Kong: Society in Transition* (London: Routledge and Kegan Paul, 1969), 110–11.

10. G. B. Endacott, *Hong Kong Eclipse*, edited with additional material by Alan Birch (Hong Kong: Oxford University Press, 1978), 238.

11. Snow, *Fall of Hong Kong*, 184.

12. Quoted in May Holdsworth, *Foreign Devils: Expatriates in Hong Kong*, with additional text by Caroline Courtauld (Hong Kong: Oxford University Press, 2002), 44–45.

13. Alexander Grantham, *Via Ports: From Hong Kong to Hong Kong* (Hong Kong: Hong Kong University Press, 1965), 11.

14. Steve Tsang, *Hong Kong: An Appointment with China* (London: Tauris, 1997), 117.

15. Leo Goodstadt, *Uneasy Partners: The Conflict between Public Interest and Private Profit in Hong Kong* (Hong Kong: Hong Kong University Press, 2005), 57.

16. Snow, *Fall of Hong Kong*, 303.

17. Grantham, *Via Ports*, 104.

18. Goodstadt, *Uneasy Partners*, 41.

19. Wong Siu-lun, *Emigrant Entrepreneurs: Shanghai Industrialists in Hong Kong* (Hong Kong: Oxford University Press, 1988).

20. Chan Lau Kit-ching, *From Nothing to Nothing: The Chinese Communist Movement and Hong Kong, 1921–1936* (New York and Hong Kong: St. Martin's/Hong Kong University Press, 1999), 11.

21. Tsang, *Hong Kong*, 69.

22. Grantham, *Via Ports*, 158.

23. Quoted in James Tuck-Hong Tang, *Britain's Encounter with Revolutionary China* (London: Macmillan, 1992), 186.

24. Quoted in James T. H. Tang, "World War to Cold War: Hong Kong's Future and Anglo-Chinese Interactions, 1941–55," in Ming K. Chan, ed., *Precarious Balance: Hong Kong between China and Britain, 1842–1992* (Armonk, NY: Sharpe, 1994), 114.

25. Grantham, *Via Ports*, 179–80.

6

A New Hong Kong

The establishment of the People's Republic of China (PRC) in 1949 gave Hong Kong new prominence, both in the British Empire and across the globe. Despite the Communists' insistence that they had no interest in recovering Hong Kong, many British officials assumed that Hong Kong would eventually have to be surrendered to China. Instead, the Communist revolution brought new labor, capital, and energy to Hong Kong. As Wm. Roger Louis, a leading historian of the British Empire, writes, when the Communists took control of Shanghai, China's economic center, in late 1949, the British realized that "they were witnessing in Hong Kong a demographic as well as an economic revolution that would have profound consequences for the people of the colony and perhaps for the British Empire."[1] From 1946 to the mid-1950s, approximately 1 million people came to Hong Kong from China—an average of almost three hundred people per day. While in May 1950 the colonial government limited the number of Chinese from the mainland, by the end of the year the influx had increased Hong Kong's population to almost 2 million. And although in February 1951 the Chinese government began to control migration to Guangdong, which in turn lowered immigration to Hong Kong, by 1955 the colony's population was around 2.5 million.

THE KOREAN WAR AND THE COLD WAR

With the outbreak of the Korean War in 1950, Hong Kong became a "reluctant Cold Warrior."[2] Needing American help to maintain its world-power status, Britain wanted to show the United States that it was a loyal and reliable ally, but it also had to keep a low profile to avoid provoking the PRC. At the same time, Britain had to protect its interests in China and preserve control over Hong Kong. Britain was less concerned about a direct attack by the PRC than about the prospect of Hong Kong being hurt if hostilities between China and America arose over Indochina, Korea, or Taiwan. The British realized that Hong Kong would be indefensible against an invasion by the PRC—however unlikely—but they were also worried about what they referred to as "the American threat." The United States needed allies to contain China, and Hong Kong was the ideal place for gathering intelligence, spreading propaganda, and organizing covert action against China. But the British worried that working too closely with the United States and allowing it too much leeway in Hong Kong would provoke the PRC into stirring up trouble in Hong Kong or attacking the colony if war broke out with the United States.

Despite America's historical interest in Hong Kong, by World War II the United States had attached little importance to Hong Kong. American exports to Hong Kong were marginal, and the region appeared to have little military value. The establishment of the PRC and the outbreak of the Korean War, however, forced the United States to reconsider Hong Kong's strategic value. And with the escalation of the Cold War, America saw the potential of using existing and former colonies to help contain Communism. With its proximity to China, good British facilities (including signals-intelligence posts), and supply of local Chinese talent, Hong Kong was a perfect base for intelligence gathering and China-watching. In late 1949 the Central Intelligence Agency established a listening post attached to the American consulate. When President Harry Truman closed the American embassy and consulates in China during the winter of 1949–1950, consular and reporting work shifted to Hong Kong. Thus, by the 1950s this consulate had a larger staff than any other American consulate in the world. Hong Kong also played an important role in American psychological warfare against China. The U.S. Information Service in Hong Kong produced anti-Communist magazines, such as *America Today* and *Four Seas*, and a variety of brochures and pamphlets. The colony was a popular rest and recreation destination for the U.S. Navy, as it would be during the Vietnam War. Governor Alexander Grantham recalled how the Chinese government "constantly used this as a propaganda theme; claiming that it proved that Hong Kong was a base for American imperialism, and that Britain was a stooge of the United States."[3]

Ironically, the greatest threat to Hong Kong's economy in the years after the 1949 revolution came not from the Chinese Communists but rather from the United States—the country most determined to contain the spread of Communism. Although Hong Kong drew some economic benefits from supporting British military operations in Korea, the colony's economy suffered from two embargoes: the United Nations (UN) embargo on strategic goods, imposed on China for intervening in the Korean War, and the American embargo on any trade with China. The British government also limited exports to China and Hong Kong, but it was the American embargo inspectors who often took to extremes their orders to ensure that no Chinese goods found their way through Hong Kong into the United States. "The classic example," explained Grantham, "is that of dried ducks. These ducks were processed in Hong Kong and then exported to America. Many of them came from eggs laid in China and brought to Hong Kong to hatch. Were the ducks from these eggs communist ducks or true-blue British ducks? The correspondence on the subject was voluminous before a solution was finally reached. Provided that an inspector was present when the duck was hatched, that he forthwith rubberstamped the duckling's foot, and that on reaching maturity a further marking was put on the duck, then the ducks might be slaughtered, dried and admitted into the United States."[4] Shrimps, notes author Frank Welsh, faced a similar predicament. They "might be caught in the admissible waters of Hong Kong, but had the crustaceans begun their lives there, or were they Communist infiltrators? In the absence of unequivocal evidence all shrimps, therefore, were banned."[5]

As the Cold War tensions escalated, Hong Kong became known as the "Berlin of the East." Created partly by British policymakers to draw international support, this analogy obscured the fact that Hong Kong's survival depended on working out a good relationship with the PRC (especially the authorities in Guangdong) rather than alienating it. The Hong Kong government adopted a very pragmatic policy regarding the PRC during the Korean War and throughout the Cold War. Like the PRC, it simply ignored the issue of Hong Kong's political status. Hong Kong proved of great use to the PRC during the Korean War, when scarce goods such as gas, kerosene, and penicillin were smuggled in during the embargoes, as were remittances from overseas Chinese. Many residents in the New Territories benefited from the embargoes by smuggling goods into China. Cheung Yan Lung, a local community leader, recalled how "whatever could be sold in China was smuggled by truck or ship. On a dark, moonless night the beach at Kat O often resembled how I imagine a smugglers' cove in eighteenth-century England would have looked, with small boats, men with lanterns, and piles of goods!"[6]

Nor did the Berlin of the East analogy necessarily imply agreement between Britain and the United States toward China and Hong Kong. While Britain officially recognized the new PRC on January 6, 1950, America continued to recognize Chiang Kai-shek's government on Taiwan, the Republic of China. An incident of late 1949 shows how the Hong Kong government found itself having to balance its relations with the governments of Britain, China, and the United States. In December, a dispute arose between Britain and China over Chinese state properties and the assets of the China National Aviation Corporation and the Central Air Transport Incorporation (co-owned by American flying ace Claire Chennault, founder of the legendary Flying Tigers in China during World War II), both of which had been transferred to Hong Kong for safety during the civil war. The Nationalist government asked the Hong Kong government to impound the airplanes so they would not be sent to the PRC, where they might be used to invade Taiwan, but before the British government responded, Nationalist agents in Hong Kong bombed seven of the airplanes. To further complicate matters, the American government asked the British embassy in Washington if the Hong Kong government could keep the remaining planes from falling into the hands of the Chinese Communists.

When the Hong Kong chief justice ruled in April 1950 that the airplanes belonged to the new PRC government, the U.S. State Department pressured the British government to intervene. Fully aware of the implications of the issue for Sino-British relations, the British worried that not releasing the airplanes might cause the PRC to organize strikes, riots, and sabotage in Hong Kong or to impose an economic embargo. On the other hand, giving the airplanes to the PRC would hurt relations with the United States. Warning that the airplanes could be used to attack not just Taiwan but Japan and Southeast Asia and accusing Britain of helping the spread of Communism, vocal American senators and congressmen threatened to withhold support for programs that provided economic assistance to Britain. Although the British government tried hard to avoid any appearance of being under American pressure, in June 1952 the Judicial Committee of the Privy Council ruled that the airplanes were the legal property of Central Air Transport but should not be transferred to Taiwan. The airplanes were eventually sold as scrap metals and spare parts by their legal owners.

THE POSTWAR ECONOMIC BOOM

To Hong Kong officials, the American and UN embargoes often seemed to be aimed at hurting Hong Kong's economy, but they were "a boon in disguise."[7] The embargoes forced Hong Kong to shift from entrepôt trade to manufacturing, without which Hong Kong might never have attained its level of economic prosperity after the war. This new emphasis on light industrialization was not the result of any action taken by the colonial government, which in fact continued to view industry with some skepticism while continuing to stress Hong Kong's status as a trading port. Rather, the initiative came from local Chinese entrepreneurs, who realized that while smuggling goods into China under the embargoes could be highly lucrative it was risky and unreliable, and from the influx of Chinese entrepreneurs from the mainland.

The Chinese of Hong Kong, whether long-term residents or recent immigrants, were most responsible for Hong Kong's post-1949 industrial boom, both as producers and consumers. But Hong Kong's colonial status also played an important role in this remarkable economic transformation, as did some of the factors that had shaped Hong Kong's economic development since it became a British colony: its economic and political stability, deep harbor and good port, and steady supply of cheap labor from China. Whereas in 1953 only 30 percent of Hong Kong's exports were produced locally, by 1959 this proportion had risen to 70 percent, with the colony producing and exporting a wide variety of manufactured goods such as textiles and clothing, plastic toys and flowers, flashlights and batteries, and aluminum, enamel, and rattan ware. Nor could this rapid industrialization have occurred without the trading and banking networks built up over the previous century. Chinese industrialists relied heavily on loans from British banks, which enjoyed the favor of the colonial regime. And whereas historians have generally assumed that Hong Kong's rise to a regional financial center began in the late 1960s and early 1970s, economic historian Catherine Schenk argues that this rise actually began in the 1950s, when Hong Kong was "profoundly affected" by its position in the international monetary system and by its colonial status. According to Schenk, the colonial monetary system provided currency stability in the increasingly regulated international system that developed in the postwar period.[8] Hong Kong's status as both a British colony and an Asian entrepôt thus laid the foundation for its emergence as an international financial center, while the political instability in other parts of East Asia increased Hong Kong's economic competitiveness.

COPING IN THE NEW WORLD ORDER

By the late 1950s, Hong Kong had resumed its stature as one of the busiest ports in the world. Its economy had become even more industrialized. However, Hong Kong had lost any real strategic importance for Britain, whose territorial interests in Asia disappeared with the independence of India, Burma, Malaya, and most of the other former British colonies in the region. The Hong Kong garrison was reduced to a minimal level, and the naval dockyard was closed. In October 1957, Prime Minister Harold Macmillan and President Dwight Eisenhower secretly agreed that in return for Britain's promise—at least for the time being—not to push for China's admission to the UN, the United States would help defend Hong Kong in case of an attack by China.

The 1950s were nevertheless critical years for Hong Kong. Many of the refugees from China lived in squatter areas nestled in the hillside, without water or electricity and at the risk of fires and mud slides. Elsie Tu (formerly Elsie Elliot), a British educator, social activist, and former member of the Legislative Council who arrived in Hong Kong in 1951 as a missionary and lived among the squatters, recalls how hard life could be for these refugee families, in which many of the women were embroiderers. Even though they worked "from dawn to dusk," these women "could not earn enough to feed one person. Father had to work at another job, and the children had to earn their coppers if the family was to eat at all. They used only small oil lamps in those huts and could scarcely work after dark, so they would sit at their doorways to catch the last ray of light, straining their eyes over the fine silk strands." Some of the women "were near blind at forty years of age." Even young children "sat for all those hours trying to earn their rice. . . . Most of the children, even the tiniest babies, suffered from enormous boils and skin infections, due to malnutrition and hot, sticky living conditions."[9]

It has become commonplace to assume that the colonial government did not respond to the problem of these squatter areas until a massive fire on December 24, 1953, in Shek Kip Mei, Kowloon, left homeless more than fifty-eight thousand people and prompted the government to construct multistory "resettlement estates." As anthropologist Alan Smart argues, however, the government's response to the Shek Kip Mei disaster did not represent a radical break from earlier policies toward resettlement. Contrary to the "Shek Kip Mei myth," the colonial government had in fact begun substantial efforts to resettle squatters in 1952, mainly because it feared that Hong Kong's vulnerable geopolitical position could be disrupted by civil disturbances following squatter fires and because squatter sites not only posed serious health and safety risks but also threatened government land revenues.[10] Taking a slightly different approach yet also underscoring the strategic purpose of these resettlement efforts, historian David Faure argues that Shek Kip Mei provided an ideal excuse for the colonial government, which, under pressure from the Colonial Office, had wanted to introduce public housing earlier but faced opposition from the Chinese elite.[11] Regardless, the government's public housing scheme developed into a massive resettlement program run by the new Resettlement Department and accompanied by an expansion of education and medical services. The British, Chinese, and American governments all contributed to the housing scheme, once again showing Hong Kong's new geopolitical position.

Although more than 30 percent of Hong Kong's population lived in government housing by the 1960s, these new resettlement policies revealed how Hong Kong remained well behind the rest of the industrialized world in terms of social welfare. The tiny, overcrowded apartments in the new public housing units were often little better than the squatter huts they were designed to replace. Elsie Tu recalls how the rooms in these "rabbit warrens" averaged only 120 square feet for a family of five and 86 square feet for smaller families. Small children "were counted as half persons" and were allocated only 12 square feet each. "A flat consisted of a square or oblong room, with concrete walls, without decoration, and with neither kitchen nor bathroom. Cooking was usually done on the narrow verandahs that surrounded each block, though that was supposed to be illegal. Communal toilets and bathrooms were situated in the centre of each block of flats, along with a washroom for laundering. With no full-size doors, it became a nightmare for women to use the bathrooms, and they usually had to be accompanied by another person, because of the prevalence of 'peeping toms.' The toilets themselves consisted only of a narrow channel that ran through the whole row of toilets. At regular intervals water flowed through the channel to flush it."[12]

The government also continued to rely heavily for social welfare on religious and charitable organizations, such as the Catholic Maryknoll Sisters who, writes historian Cindy Chu, "spearheaded efforts for poor refugee communities"; opened schools, clinics, and youth centers in resettlement estates; and "traveled the hillsides of wooden shacks and cared for the needy."[13] One reason the colonial government did not do more for the refugees from China was that it thought they would return to China once conditions there settled. As G. B. Endacott explained, however, "the unspoken assumption was that Asians, and in particular the Chinese, were not forced to come to Hong Kong, and if they did so that was their own affair and they must accept conditions as they found them."[14] Many colonial officials feared that providing too much social welfare would only attract more refugees from the mainland. Twisted as this logic may seem, it echoed an old concern shared not just by colonial officials and Chinese elites but also by many ordinary Chinese, who often justified conditions in Hong Kong by contrasting them with those on the mainland.

On the political front, the Hong Kong government had to learn how to coexist with both the PRC and the Republic of China on Taiwan. In October 1956, for example, clashes between pro-Beijing and pro-Taipei supporters over a Nationalist flag that had been removed from a resettlement block resulted in riots in Kowloon, leading Nationalist sympathizers to loot stores owned by Communist supporters. When pro-Nationalist mobs attacked and killed Communist sympathizers, the Hong Kong police responded by firing on pro-Nationalist rioters. By the end of two weeks, 59 people were dead, and 443 had been hospitalized.

Hostilities between China and Taiwan often threatened to undermine Hong Kong's stability. The three governments frequently disagreed over fishing rights and territorial waters. Throughout the early 1950s, the Nationalists conducted guerrilla raids on Communist-held coastal islands and searched and harassed foreign vessels, including British freighters. The Hong Kong and British governments were concerned that Nationalist

Young refugee
squatting next to
CARE (Cooperative
for American
Remittances to
Everywhere) boxes,
1958.
Courtesy of the
Prints and
Photographs
Division,
Library of Congress,
Washington, D.C.

blockades, mine-laying, and raids near Hong Kong might convince the PRC that the British were involved in such activities, thus provoking the PRC into attacking Hong Kong. In 1954, Communist Chinese fighter planes shot down a Cathay Pacific airliner, killing eight people. In April 1955, the *Kashmir Princess*, an Indian airliner transporting PRC officials and foreign journalists exploded after taking off for Jakarta from Kai Tak Airport. Blaming the explosion on Taiwan agents, the PRC government demanded that the Hong Kong government capture the agents responsible. In 1956 and 1958, Taiwanese fighter jets landed in Hong Kong after dogfights with Chinese airplanes, causing diplomatic rows involving the governments of China, Taiwan, Britain, and Hong Kong. Although none of these incidents had any long-term effects, they showed the precarious nature of Hong Kong's new geopolitical status.

Culturally, the closing of the border between Hong Kong and China created a sense of isolation for many Chinese in Hong Kong, which the colonial government was quick to exploit through its education policies. In 1952 the Hong Kong Education Department appointed a committee to investigate the place of Chinese history, language, and literature in the Hong

Kong school curriculum. In November 1953, the committee recommended an emphasis on Chinese culture, against the emphasis on nationalism and patriotism in China and Taiwan. This was not an attempt to return to some sort of cultural traditionalism; rather, argues historian Bernard Luk, it was a scheme "for Chinese culture and British colonialism to survive together in the shadow of the Communist threat." Thus, after 1949 "generations of Hong Kong Chinese pupils grew up, learning from the Chinese culture subjects to identify themselves as Chinese but relating that Chineseness to neither contemporary China nor the local Hong Kong landscape. It was a Chinese identity in the abstract, a patriotism of the émigré, probably held all the more absolutely because it was not connected to tangible reality."[15] Although this curriculum helped nurture a sense of Chinese heritage and identity, it also shaped a sense of Hong Kong being at the periphery of both the Chinese and the Western worlds.

THE 1960s

Intrigued by Hong Kong's peripheral quality, British author Ian Fleming described the colony as "the most vivid and exciting city I have ever seen." Offering "modern comfort in a theatrically Oriental setting," Hong Kong was a "gay and splendid colony humming with vitality and progress." Knowing that "six hundred and fifty million Communist Chinese are a few miles away across the frontier seems only to add zest to the excitement at all levels of life in the colony, and from the Governor down, if there is an underlying tension, there is certainly no dismay. Obviously China could take Hong Kong by a snap of its giant fingers, but China has shown no signs of wishing to do so." Fleming concluded that "whatever the future holds, there is no sign that a sinister, doom-fraught count-down is in progress."[16]

Fleming had good reason to be optimistic about Hong Kong. By the early 1960s, the colony had earned an international reputation for its light industry, particularly in electronics such as transistor radios. In 1961 the colony became known across the globe as a meeting place of East and West when Richard Mason's novel *The World of Suzie Wong* was adapted into a film starring William Holden and Hong Kong's own Nancy Kwan. Three years later, the Beatles performed two concerts at the Princess Theatre. The completion in 1963 of the colony's largest reservoir, Shek Pik, on Lantau Island seemed to reaffirm Britain's commitment to holding on to its last Asian colony. And although in the same year the *People's Daily* declared ominously that the question of Hong Kong would be "settled peacefully through negotiations" when conditions were "ripe," three years later the Chinese foreign minister insisted that recovering Taiwan was a priority but that Hong Kong and Macau were not.

Women preparing to string barbed wire along the border to deter refugees from mainland China, 1962. Courtesy of the Prints and Photographs Division, Library of Congress, Washington, D.C.

The Star Ferry Riots of 1966

Beneath this rosy veneer lay serious social tensions. Since 1960, Hong Kong's population had increased from around four million to almost five million. Most of this increase occurred during the catastrophic Great Leap Forward (1958–1961) in China and the subsequent three years of famine. Some 150,000 refugees were estimated to have come in 1962 alone. In May 1962, with help from Chinese border guards, between 60,000 and 100,000 Chinese crossed the border illegally (although some 60,000 of them were arrested and repatriated within a month). Hong Kong police and troops subsequently built a barbwire fence behind the existing British fence. By 1964, almost 500,000 squatters were living in hillside shacks or rooftop huts. With crowded housing, extreme gaps in wealth, poor working conditions, lack of political representation, and the prevalence of government corruption, especially in the police force, it is not surprising that riots would occur in the spring of 1966.

On April 4, a young Chinese man named So Sau-chung protested an increase in fares on the Star Ferry by declaring a hunger strike in front of the

Star Ferry piers, first in Central District, and then in Tsim Sha Tsui, the main tourist district. When the police arrested him for obstruction the next day, other youths rioted and stoned the police. One rioter was killed, and by April 8 more than fourteen hundred youths had been arrested. The cause of the riots does not appear to have been economic. Nor, despite the growth of anticolonial movements around the world, was it particularly anti-British. Rather, the rioters were expressing their social discontent, just as their counterparts were doing in Britain, Europe, and other parts of the world.

After an official inquiry, Elsie Elliot, who was known as an advocate for the poor and for trying to expose police corruption—and whose name the hunger striker had invoked because Elliot had solicited public opinion on whether the fare increases were acceptable—was censured for provoking the demonstrators and making "unsubstantiated" allegations against the police. Although the inquiry commission could offer no other explanation, it insisted that the riots had not been caused by economic, political, or social conditions. Some of the youths admitted to having joined the riots mainly to protest the fare increases, but others claimed to have done so out of the excitement of the moment, for fun, or simply to let off steam. One of the riot leaders later committed suicide; another ended up in a mental hospital. Still, the inquiry commission conceded that overcrowding, the struggle to maintain a living, and "the underlying insecurity of life in the Colony, resulting from international political and economic conditions, create tensions which elsewhere would be more than sufficient cause for frequent disturbances."[17]

The Confrontation of 1967

Whereas the 1966 riots lasted less than a week, a dispute in May 1967 over wages and working hours quickly escalated into more than six months of violence orchestrated by the local branch of the Chinese Communist Party, the Hong Kong and Macau Work Committee. Inspired by the Cultural Revolution in China, where youths known as the Red Guards were heeding Chairman Mao Zedong's call to continue the revolutionary struggle, left-wing activists fought with the colonial police. Although a similar situation had occurred in 1966 in Macau, where Portuguese troops fired on rioting pro-Beijing activists, conditions in Hong Kong became much worse. Rioters burned cars and attacked the police, while local left-wing schools encouraged their students to participate with bombs made in the schools' science laboratories and then planted throughout the colony. By the end of the six months, the official death toll was fifty-one, of which ten were police officers. At least eight hundred people were injured in the riots and more than three hundred others were wounded by bombs. More than five thousand people were arrested and jailed, often without trial, while many others were secretly deported. Sino-British relations reached their lowest point in the history of the new PRC.

Hong Kong had never experienced anything like the Confrontation (as colonial officials called it) of 1967, but the disturbances, like the Star Ferry riots the previous year, revealed many of the conditions in Hong Kong that provided a favorable environment for civil unrest. Lower labor costs in Taiwan and South Korea had encouraged fears of unemployment and dislocation, half of the population was under age twenty-one, and only 13 percent of youths fifteen to nineteen years old were in school. Some 12 percent of these students were enrolled in pro-Beijing schools, where they were inspired by the Cultural Revolution and by the anti-imperialist movements around the world.

On May Day, traditionally a day for workers' celebrations and demonstrations, three labor strikes began. The disputes had not been resolved by the end of the week, and on May 6 one of the strikes, at the Hong Kong Artificial Flower Works in San Po Kong, Kowloon, turned violent as nonstriking workers and, subsequently, the police were brought in. As John Cooper, a Briton who was living in Hong Kong at the time and wrote one of the most thorough accounts of the disturbances, stated, San Po Kong had "all the natural advantages" for civil unrest. "Street upon street of tall dilapidated buildings vied with each other for the limited space available, hundreds upon hundreds of hostile citizens lived out their lives in human rabbit warrens, plenty of workers were available to start a riot, plenty of workers' organisations existed to support it and plenty of students would come along to give it political backing."[18]

In such a conducive environment, by the morning of May 11 the strike in San Po Kong had turned political, with posters condemning the "British authorities of Hong Kong" and workers waving Mao's "Little Red Book," chanting revolutionary slogans, and singing revolutionary songs. By afternoon, demonstrators were banging on the factory gates, and the police were called in. That evening, the demonstrators, now joined by crowds of youths, started pelting the police with stones and bottles. The police, who had been trained to handle riots since the 1956 anti-Communist riots and who had sharpened their antiriot training after the 1966 Star Ferry riots and the hostilities in Macau, responded with clubs and tear gas. As the unrest spread to the nearby Tung Tau Resettlement Estate, the entire area was placed under a curfew. The next morning, drivers and conductors for the Kowloon Motor Bus Company were chanting Mao's sayings at the bus terminal at the Star Ferry in Tsim Sha Tsui and affixing anti-imperialist stickers to their buses. Two youths in Red Guard uniforms, both claiming to be from Canton, were shouting Communist slogans outside a school in Mongkok. The next day, posters were calling "Down with David Trench," while crowds were building roadblocks and barricades and were setting cars and buses on fire.

By the middle of May, the unrest had spread throughout Kowloon and to Hong Kong Island. Angry demonstrators plastered posters on the gates and

Protesters outside Government House, summer 1967. Photo courtesy of Tim Ko.

walls to Government House demanding to see the governor and also demanding that their arrested comrades be released. The demonstrators marched through Central District, defacing buildings, attacking a BBC television team from Britain, and demanding that the Hilton Hotel take down its British and American flags. With all sorts of rumors flying about—water and electricity were going to be stopped, for example, and there would be a general strike—prices soared. To boost morale, the government had to issue a statement and radio broadcast that the rumors were unfounded. Still, from late May into early June, strikes broke out in transport services, food production, and retail sectors; textile mills; and some government departments.

Although many accounts of the 1967 disturbances portray them as being instigated almost solely by local Communists and Red Guards from Guangdong, the Anti-British Struggle Committee enjoyed strong support in China, both—at least in the early stages—from the central government and from the population at large. Like the leftist radicals in Hong Kong, the PRC government insisted that the struggle in Hong Kong was part of the worldwide fight against colonialism and imperialism. In mid-May, the PRC vice minister for foreign affairs, Luo Guibo, presented Donald Hopson, British chargé d'affaires in Beijing, with a formal protest and list of demands: accept all of the workers' demands, free all arrested people, end all "fascist measures," apologize to victims and compensate them, and guarantee that there would be no more similar incidents. Luo condemned the British "atrocities" and "sanguinary oppression" as part of the British government's "collusion with American imperialism against China" and accused the British of letting the United States use Hong Kong as "a base for aggression against Vietnam." Crowds marched outside Hopson's office, shouting slogans, waving flags and placards, and burning effigies of Prime Minister Harold Wilson.

On May 17, one million protesters marched past the British office in Beijing armed with posters demanding that the British leave Hong Kong and vowing to "Hang Wilson." The PRC state radio declared that the British atrocities in Hong Kong were a carefully orchestrated part of Britain's collusion with the United States against China. (The United States saw the matter as being between China and Britain and did not interfere, particularly since no American citizens were involved.) A mass rally on May 18 at the sports stadium in Beijing attracted one hundred thousand people. Dignitaries in attendance included Premier Zhou Enlai, Foreign Minister Chen Yi, and Public Security Minister Xie Fuzhi, who accused the Hong Kong government of conspiring with Chiang Kai-shek to destabilize the PRC. In Shanghai, protesters broke into and destroyed the home of Peter Hewitt, the British diplomatic representative. They defaced a picture of Queen Elizabeth and tried to make Hewitt bow before a picture of Mao. When Hewitt refused, the protesters forced him to march around his house, and they harassed his wife and children.

Although the British government had initially declined to comment on Beijing's list of demands, on May 18 it issued a statement supporting the Hong Kong government for fulfilling its "inescapable duty to maintain law and order as impartially and fairly as possible for the benefit of all in Hong Kong" and insisting that labor and management should be able to resolve the cause of this disturbance—a "comparatively small industrial conflict"— "in reason and goodwill." The British also sent three officials from the Commonwealth Office and the Foreign Office on a one-week mission to investigate the situation. On June 2, Judith Hart, minister of state for Commonwealth affairs, defended the Hong Kong government in the House of Commons but promised that she would inquire into Hong Kong's labor laws and mechanisms for resolving labor disputes. Even after a *People's Daily* editorial on June 3 beckoned Hong Kong Chinese to "launch a vigorous struggle against the wicked British imperialists," the British government confirmed that it would still try to help China get a seat in the UN. On June 22, the House of Lords debated the Hong Kong situation, calling for Britain to maintain the security of Hong Kong but to try to improve labor conditions.

The leftists also had an arsenal of propaganda equipment in Hong Kong: approximately ten left-wing newspapers; the New China News Agency, which directed the propaganda campaign and sent exaggerated reports of local support to newspapers in China; loudspeakers placed outside buildings such as the Bank of China; posters demanding "Blood for Blood," "Stew the White-Skinned Pig," "Fry the Yellow Running Dogs," "Down with British Imperialism," and "Hang David Trench"; and effigies of the governor and other local British and Chinese leaders, often decorated with real or simulated bombs to discourage the police from removing them. Left-wing newspapers saw the Hong Kong police as trying to protect management from the legitimate complaints and grievances of workers. The New China News Agency denounced Governor Trench for not meeting petitioners and for making Government House "a place to condemn the British paper tiger and a big classroom for the creative study and application of the invincible thoughts of Mao Zedong." On May 29, the agency accused the British of using the aircraft carrier HMS *Bulwark*, supposedly in Hong Kong on a routing training exercise, to intimidate the Chinese of Hong Kong. (Trench had in fact requested the British Admiralty to dispatch the vessel as a show of force.)

The colonial government responded with its own extensive counterpropaganda campaign, whose organizer, Jimmy McGregor, received frequent death threats and was condemned by the leftists as a "vagabond and a criminal," the "governor's jackal," and a "wolf whining in the night." Under the Emergency Regulations Ordinance, the police were allowed to detain suspected activists without trial. In mid-May, the colonial government banned loudspeaker broadcasts such as those coming from the Bank of China. Governor Trench appeared on television and encouraged the public to stand tall during the disturbances. On June 1, the government prohibited inflammatory posters and specified punishments for anyone who produced, distributed, or displayed such posters. The PRC government and the local branch of the New China News Agency condemned the ban as a "political provocation" and "fascist decree."

Having served in other colonies, some British police commanders knew the danger of responding to such movements with force, especially with China so close. The situation was particularly delicate in the New Territories, where the border between Hong Kong and China was often relatively porous. On the morning of July 8, villagers from the Chinese part of Sha Tau Kok, a border village divided into Chinese and British sectors, attacked a police post with stones, bottles, bombs, and, later, automatic weapons. A violent clash had already occurred in the same village on June 24, but five policemen were killed in this second attack. With more than eighty of their policemen holed up in the police post but anxious not to provoke China, Hong Kong authorities had to await approval from London before sending in the military. This clash at Sha Tau Kok, along with reports of several thousand people in uniform moving toward the Man Kam To bridge, a major border-crossing point, sent the colony into panic. From July 9 to July 11, violent clashes occurred between rioters and policemen throughout Hong Kong Island, with one policeman left dead. On July 12, the government imposed curfews in Hong Kong and Kowloon.

The deaths of six policemen in one weekend shocked the colony. They also made the police take a much more active, less restrained approach to dealing with the leftists, raiding (often working closely with local military regiments and battalions) suspected centers of Communist activities and seizing weapons, bombs, and Communist literature. As the police changed their tactics in mid-July, so did the leftists, who started bombing police stations and other government buildings. By late July, the targets of the bombings expanded to theaters, parks, markets, and other public places. Buses and taxis were set on fire, and bombs—real or fake—were planted nearly everywhere. On July 20, the government put into effect nine emergency regulations enacted in 1949, most giving the police wider powers of search and arrest. The editors, publishers, and printers of three leftist newspapers were charged and convicted of false reporting.

When in August the leftists shifted from riots to attacking people who opposed them and planting bombs, the police stepped up their crackdowns. The most sensational raid was on August 4, when more than one thousand policemen and soldiers, supported by three helicopters from HMS *Hermes*, launched an attack from the ground and the air on three leftist strongholds, one of which was booby-trapped and contained bomb-making equipment. The leftists then turned to planting bombs where children could easily find them. In one incident, a bomber's children—whom the bomber had taken with him while planting bombs—were killed when the bombs exploded prematurely. On August 20, two children in North Point on Hong Kong Island were killed by a bomb planted in a ball. On August 24, the leftists attacked the car of Lam Bun, a popular radio commentator who had criticized their activities. After setting Lam's car on fire, they poured gasoline on Lam and his cousin and set them on fire. The leftists had already been sending threatening letters to Chinese business and community leaders; now they issued lists of other so-called traitors to be executed.

The PRC government was concerned about the heavy-handed police response to the rioters and was particularly disturbed by signs of military activity in Hong Kong, such as visiting British warships. It was most bothered, however, by the "barbaric" and "fascist" arrest and confinement of left-wing reporters. When the Hong Kong police arrested Xue Ping of the New China News Agency, on July 21 the Chinese government placed Reuter's correspondent Anthony Grey under house arrest in Beijing. (He was not released until October 1969, well after the disturbances had ended.) When Hong Kong police raided pro-Beijing shops, closed down newspapers, and arrested supporters, on August 22 Red Guards set fire to the British mission in Beijing and physically assaulted Hopson and two women in the mission until Chinese soldiers intervened and escorted the diplomats to safety. After the PRC government prevented British diplomatic and commercial personnel from leaving China, the British and Chinese governments suspended some of each other's diplomatic privileges. When Chinese diplomats got into a scuffle with British civilians in London on August 29, the police had to intervene. This prompted more angry responses from China. Protesting that the British had instructed their police to beat the Chinese diplomats, the PRC government canceled all exit permits for Britons in China. Red Guards demonstrated again outside the British mission in Beijing.

By September, the local leftists had begun to lose the support of Beijing and seemed to be fighting a lost cause. The police had closed down many of the leftists' headquarters, and the colonial government agreed to show leniency to strikers who promised not to strike again. The leftists appeared to be divided, with one side preferring less violence and the other wanting to continue the attacks. Relations between China and Britain had improved. Toward the end of September, the British ambassador to the UN reported that despite China's recent behavior, Britain still believed that it should be admitted to the UN. On October 1, China's national day, the PRC followed its annual tradition of honoring its agreement to provide water to Hong Kong twenty-four hours a day (the water supply had been reduced during the disturbances).

PRC leaders ultimately helped keep the movement from becoming too powerful by rerouting supplies after Red Guards disrupted supplies to Hong Kong and resisting calls from the Red Guards to overthrow Hong Kong's capitalist and colonial systems. Having monitored events closely from the outset, the PRC government became increasingly critical of the leftists' tactics. It did not approve of how certain prominent leftists in Hong Kong were known to live extravagantly. (One leading Communist had arrived at the Government House protests in his chauffeur-driven Mercedes-Benz.) The PRC government also became upset when it realized that the Hong Kong leftists were sending inflated or even fabricated accounts of police atrocities and were exaggerating local support for the leftists. One leader of the Anti-British Struggle Committee embarrassed the leftists and the PRC by defecting to Taiwan. Jiang Qing, Chairman Mao's wife, complained that a cash gift to the committee should have been used instead to promote Red Guard activities in the colony's schools. A lavish dinner party held by the committee in honor of October 1 also drew widespread criticism from the PRC government and the mainland press.

Conflicts still occurred, however, both in the urban areas of Hong Kong and Kowloon and along the Chinese border. In late September, two Hong Kong Chinese police constables were abducted, to be released only in late November in return for five mainlanders arrested by the Hong Kong police. In mid-October a British police officer was abducted, although he managed to escape back into Hong Kong a month later (leading some observers to suspect that he had been released in a prisoner exchange). The arrival on October 13 of Lord Shepherd, British minister of state for Commonwealth affairs, prompted a new wave of violence. Still, bomb reports were down by December, and the unrest had generally fizzled out by January 1968.

It is not hard to see why the leftists never found widespread local support for their cause, especially among a population that included so many people who had fled the Communist government in China and who viewed the Cultural Revolution with horror and revulsion. Although some young people participated because of the way they had been treated by the police in the 1966 riots, the leftists failed to obtain widespread support from students. The Federation of Students called for an end to the violence, and the University of Hong Kong Students' Union sent the government a message of support. Many community organizations, professional associations, and schools expressed their support, while scores of local people joined the Hong Kong Auxiliary Police Force. Whereas the left-wing Chinese press supported the disturbances as the natural, heroic, patriotic reactions of an oppressed people, other Chinese newspapers called for people to stay out of the disturbances. Letters to the editor in both Chinese and English newspapers often called for the government to take stronger measures but also appealed for an end to the disturbances and suggested ways of conciliation. The disruption pushed many people to support the colonial government, while the leftists' violent tactics made the police look like heroes—even when they attacked rioters with tear gas and clubs and arrested and imprisoned teenagers.

(The fact that an American television station caught on film a group of young protesters "bloodying" their heads with Mercurochrome just before the police in antiriot gear approached them did not endear the leftists to the population at large.) For its loyal service, in 1969 Queen Elizabeth renamed the police force the Royal Hong Kong Police Force.

The 1967 disturbances had several important effects on Hong Kong. Although the local Communist movement did not recover until the 1980s, the government's treatment of the rioters strengthened the pro-Beijing convictions of people such as Tsang Yok Sing, whose teenage brother and sister had been arrested and imprisoned—he for printing and distributing leaflets, she simply for misbehaving at school. Tsang recalls many of the rioters as being "simple workers who had been oppressed all their lives" and the government as responding to the riots in a "very high-handed, colonial manner." Tsang was shunned at his university after the riots, but he found "lots of warm friendship, comradeship, and sympathy in the leftist circle."[19] He later became principal at one of Hong Kong's leftist Chinese schools and in 1992 founded the pro-Beijing Democratic Alliance for Betterment of Hong Kong. His brother, Tsang Tak Sing, worked for one of the pro-Beijing daily newspapers in Hong Kong.

For the majority of Hong Kong people, however, the disturbances gave the government new popularity and legitimacy. The 1967 riots seemed to be proof that life in Hong Kong was better than on the mainland and that the people in Hong Kong had little to gain from any sort of anti-British campaign. David Faure, who was then a student at the University of Hong Kong, writes that "the riots of 1967 were the first taste of open action directed against an established government, but for many, the demonstration, the bombs, and the occasional riot, confirmed what they were learning in the press of the excesses of the Cultural Revolution."[20] Forced to choose between the PRC and Hong Kong, most people in Hong Kong identified with the colonial regime as their government. At the same time, they increasingly saw themselves as members of a special community, separate both from the colonial government and from their compatriots on the mainland.

The disturbances also prompted demands in Britain and Hong Kong for the colonial government to improve labor relations, foster a sense of belonging, improve communication between government and people, and expand education—not in the least so that youths would not be so vulnerable to political indoctrination. The local press expressed concern that the Emergency Regulations might be continued and criticism of the Labour Department for not being able to intervene in labor disputes. Questions arose about how to deal with the arrested leftists: many residents wanted the death penalty for those involved in the bombings, but others argued that many of the activists were young and had been misguided by committee leaders who had walked away scot-free. Some of the convicted defendants received very stiff punishments. For example, a fourteen-year-old boy received four years for carrying a bomb, and a fifty-four-year-old man was given five years for participating in a riot in Sha Tau Kok.

Governor Trench's administration had shown that it would not tolerate such disturbances, but it also realized that it needed to "close the gap" between government and people. This resulted in several administrative changes designed to reduce the political alienation of Hong Kong's population and to help prevent further disturbances. The City District Officer system, based on the District Officer program used in the New Territories since the early 1900s, appointed district officers to mediate between government and people. These officers were to "assist those suffering from a sense of grievance to present their cases coherently and, when necessary, to act as their advocate."[21] Public relations within government departments were improved and various advisory committees expanded, while unofficial members of the Legislative and Executive Councils were given larger roles. By renaming the position of Secretary for Chinese Affairs as the Secretary for Home Affairs in 1969, the government admitted that the overwhelming majority of Hong Kong's population could not be treated as a distinct group. The government also made plans for compulsory free public education and more social welfare and labor legislation (for example, in 1970 a mandatory weekly day off was finally introduced). Although many of these reforms would not be implemented until the early 1970s under Trench's successor, Murray MacLehose, "1967 marked a crucial turning point in the development of the colonial regime's irreversible awareness of and irrevocable commitment to a more conscientious and responsive social policy with greater care and concern for the grass-roots community."[22] Hong Kong would not experience serious civil unrest again until January 1984, when taxi drivers rioted briefly in Mongkok, in Kowloon.

However, the 1967 disturbances effectively shelved Trench's plans for constitutional reforms. After talk in Britain about expanding political representation in Hong Kong, in 1964 Trench, who had arrived that year intent on political reform, had established a committee to consider the possibility of an elected Legislative Council. But in 1967 the British government announced that because of Hong Kong's unique geographic and political status, an elected council would be out of the question, especially given the turbulent conditions in China and the tense Sino-British relations during the Cultural Revolution. The buzzword now was "consultation," using advisory committees rather than votes to reach a consensus. Justifying Hong Kong's lack of democracy, Trench argued in 1969 that "there is no one brand of politics, or one line of policies, which is right for all places at all stages of development."[23]

Nor should the government's attempts to "close the gap" be exaggerated. Although proposals were offered for an ombudsman post that would investigate complaints against maladministration, such a post—the commissioner for administrative complaints—would not materialize until 1989. When the government introduced the Official Language Ordinance in 1974 making Chinese an official language, it did so mainly in response to demands from local activists. Government policy papers and internal documents continued to be written completely in English for another twenty years, while laws were not issued in Chinese until 1989. As late as 1995, English was still the only language in the higher courts, and Chinese defendants still received summonses in English.

BUILDING THE WELFARE STATE

Until the early 1970s, the Hong Kong government had tried to spend as little as possible on social services. As a 1965 government white paper put it, "The economic well-being of any community demands that as far as possible every resident contributes to, rather than draws upon, its resources." Contrary to the common view of Hong Kong as a laissez-faire capitalist paradise, however, the government played an increasingly critical role in Hong Kong's economy in the 1960s and 1970s. The 1967 disturbances convinced senior officials in Britain and Hong Kong that they would have to improve social conditions if they intended to maintain British rule in Hong Kong, especially given the anti-imperialist rhetoric coming from China during the Cultural Revolution, from other British colonies, and even from within Britain. The Star Ferry riots had revealed the discontent generated by social and economic conditions, while the disturbances of 1967 had shown how this discontent could fuel political tensions.

The main engineer of the Hong Kong government's new "'positive non-intervention' policy" was John Cowperthwaite, financial secretary from 1961 to 1971. Unlike his contemporaries in Britain, Cowperthwaite believed that the economy was best left to businessmen and that government should intervene as little as possible. Still, he felt that government had an obligation to provide public works, public education, medical services, and housing to those truly in need. During his tenure, real wages rose by 50 percent, and the percentage of impoverished families dropped from around 50 percent to around 15 percent. Nevertheless, Cowperthwaite helped to delay the offering of free and compulsory primary education and to thwart a plan for expanded welfare reform, including workers' retirement and insurance. Living conditions in the new resettlement estates could be dismal (with fifty residents sharing one communal bathroom). Although Queen Mary Hospital, opened in 1963, was the largest hospital in the Commonwealth, clinics and hospitals remained overcrowded, with patients sometimes even sharing a bed. Many children had no formal education, and compulsory free education was not introduced until 1971 for the primary level and 1978 for the secondary level.

Given the problems and conditions of the 1960s, many people in Hong Kong found the administration of Murray MacLehose "almost too good to be true."[24] The first Hong Kong governor to be chosen from among career diplomats in the Foreign Office rather than from the colonial service, MacLehose had been consul in Hankou after World War II and then ambassador to Saigon and Copenhagen; he had also been political advisor to Governor Robert Black in the early 1960s. MacLehose tried hard to evince a noncolonial image—walking to the Legislative Council chambers from Government House rather than taking the governor's limousine, meeting and talking to ordinary people, and wearing short-sleeved, open-necked shirts while strolling through local neighborhoods. Elsie Tu recalls MacLehose as a "different kind of Governor, being a diplomat, not a colonial official of the old school that cared little about the rights of the local people in the colonies they ruled."[25]

Unlike his predecessors, MacLehose found the concept of welfare appealing, as long as it was economically feasible and not abused. His administration saw a massive expansion of public housing, free comprehensive primary education, public assistance, transport, labor legislation, and social welfare. MacLehose was a master at publicizing his programs with bold promises. He claimed, for example, that his Ten Years Housing Scheme would end squatter areas and eliminate overcrowding. Ambitious as this claim was, other reforms, especially in education and health, gave his administration a good image. By 1983, more than 40 percent of Hong Kong's population lived in government housing, mainly large complexes of high-rise blocks. MacLehose's government also began a complex of new towns, or satellite towns, in the New Territories. Intended to be self-contained communities rather than simply residential units, each town would include schools, shops, restaurants, and recreation areas as well as space for industry. Under MacLehose, the civil service expanded by more than 70 percent, from almost 102,000 in 1973 to almost 174,000 in 1983. Faced with widespread environmental degradation, in 1976 MacLehose's government established a network of country parks. (Hong Kong's longest hiking route, the MacLehose Trail, is named after the governor.)

MacLehose clearly represented a departure from the old colonial-style governor. Many of his reforms, however, had been conceived earlier under Trench, partly as a response to the unrest in 1966 and 1967. MacLehose's reforms also benefited greatly from Hong Kong's changing economic and geopolitical status. When he arrived in November 1971, Hong Kong had already recovered from the 1967 disturbances. Prime Minister Harold Wilson's Labour government was more concerned with social issues and workers' rights than was the Conservative Party, which had ruled Britain in the

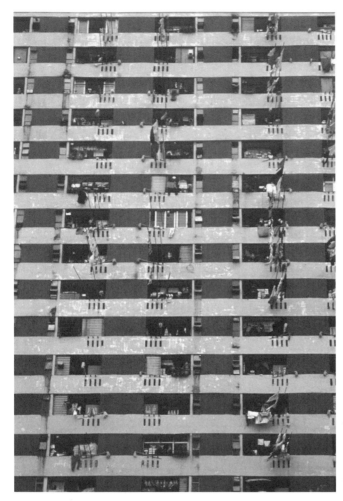

Apartment block in low-cost public housing estate, circa 1985. Courtesy of Alamy Stock Photography.

late 1950s and early 1960s. Philip Haddon-Cave, who succeeded Cowperthwaite under MacLehose, subtly departed from his predecessor's conservative economic policy. From 1970 to 1972, government expenditures increased by more than 50 percent, setting a pattern that steadily spiraled upward. In 1970–1971, social welfare spending was HK$40 million; it was more than $2.5 billion in 1986–1987 and more than $15 billion in 1996–1997.

MacLehose also happened to be in Hong Kong during a period of remarkable economic growth. By the late 1960s, Hong Kong had all the ingredients for a successful economy: strong trade networks and a solid industrial base, a modern international banking system, good public services, and a relatively educated workforce. Its large population, increased by the number of immigrants from China, meant more producers and consumers. The colony's gross domestic product grew at an average of 10 percent per year from the 1960s through the 1970s and then by five times from the early 1970s to the early 1980s. Hong Kong's economy benefited immensely from the growth of real estate development, led mainly by Chinese entrepreneurs such as Li Ka-shing, an immigrant from Guangdong who had begun his career in plastics and property, as well as from a large influx of foreign investment, especially from Japan and the United States. By the late 1970s, Chinese firms had begun to eclipse the old British hongs, and Chinese entrepreneurs had founded three new stock exchanges to compete with the European-dominated Hong Kong Stock Exchange founded in the 1880s (the four stock markets merged in 1986). In 1979, Y. K. Pao, a shipping magnate who had started his business in the 1950s with only one small vessel, bought out the Hong Kong and Kowloon Wharf and Godown Company, a subsidiary of Jardine and Matheson founded in 1889. In 1980, Li Ka-shing acquired Hutchison-Whampoa, a local British giant originally established in the 1870s in docks and shipping.

Furthermore, MacLehose was the first postwar governor who did not have to worry about tensions with China. Britain and China had begun negotiations for normalizing relations during Prime Minister Edward Heath's administration. Relations between Britain and China became even better after China began its open door policy in the late 1970s and started to play a larger role in Hong Kong's economy. Whereas in 1972 the United States and Britain were Hong Kong's first and second most important markets, by 1986 China had become its second-largest market (the United States was still the largest, while Britain had dropped to fourth place). In 1972, Japan and China were Hong Kong's top two sources of imports; Britain was number four. By 1981, China had overtaken Japan as Hong Kong's largest source of imports. By 1986, Britain had dropped to Hong Kong's seventh-largest source of imports. In overall terms, by 1986 Hong Kong was doing more business with China than with any other country.

MacLehose has often been criticized—as he was during his tenure—for not introducing political reforms. Indeed, Hong Kong's constitutional structure saw little change. Until 1981, the Urban Council was the only council that was elected. MacLehose rejected suggestions from senior officials to change the shape of the Legislative Council. Almost half of the members of the Legislative Council were government officials, and the unofficial members represented a tiny portion of the population. The Executive Council consisted mainly of senior government officials and appointees who represented business interests, especially those of the old British firms. As journalist Richard Hughes cheerfully put it, "there is no nonsense about democracy in Hong Kong. Administration and legislation are conducted along unashamed colonial lines."[26] However, during Mac-Lehose's tenure some Legislative Council members were appointed from the lower classes, while in 1976 he gave the unofficial Legislative Council members a majority simply by not appointing the full quota of official members. The District Administration Scheme, introduced in 1981, aimed to provide an effective forum for public consultation and participation in administration at the district level. Although the District Boards introduced during MacLehose's tenure were only partly elected and had no authority to pass legislation or make policies, they nevertheless played an advisory role.

MacLehose's reforms should not, however, overshadow some of the less impressive aspects of his tenure. Despite his efforts to improve relations between government and people, the colonial government frequently spied on reformist and pressure groups such as the Hong Kong Observers, the Education Action Group, the Christian Industrial Committee, and the Society for Community Organisation, and it bugged the telephones of political and social activists, often trying to intimidate them by denouncing them as radical leftists. Expatriates held more than half of the senior posts in the civil service until the mid-1980s, often justifying the reluctance to hire local Chinese on the grounds that they did not have the right character, aptitude, outlook, or interest in public affairs. As Leo Goodstadt writes, the "separation of government from the people was aggravated by the restricted role of local Chinese men and women in the government and the way that the most senior and sensitive posts in the Civil Service were monopolized by expatriates until the final decade of British rule."[27]

Nor should the remarkable improvements in living standards during the 1970s and 1980s obscure some of the tragedies and disappointments. In June 1972, for example, more than 250 people were killed in landslides after some forty inches of rain fell in four days. After the Communist victory and unification of Vietnam in 1975, some 70,000 Vietnamese boat people came to Hong Kong as refugees. Captured brilliantly by local director Ann Hui in a 1982 film, *Boat People*, their plight drew some sympathy from Hong Kong people, but their presence also provoked resentment and hostility, especially as these refugees strained already tight social services and housing facilities. In July 1982, large numbers of Vietnamese refugees were held in closed camps run by the Correctional Services and designed as deterrents to more refugees. Despite efforts to resettle the refugees in host countries or persuade them to return voluntarily to Vietnam, the camps remained until 1992. Well into the late 1980s, Hong Kong still had many homeless people, not to mention some 400,000 squatters living in huts in the hillsides. During Chinese New Year in the winter of 1986, a huge fire in Chu Ku Tsai village, New Territories, left 2,000 people homeless.

NOTES

1. Wm. Roger Louis, "Hong Kong: The Critical Phase, 1945–1949," *American Historical Review* 102(4) (October 1997): 1056.

2. Chi-kwan Mark, *Hong Kong and the Cold War: Anglo-American Relations, 1949–1957* (Oxford, UK: Clarendon, 2004), 6.

3. Alexander Grantham, *Via Ports: From Hong Kong to Hong Kong* (Hong Kong: Hong Kong University Press, 1965), 169.

4. Ibid., 166.

5. Frank Welsh, *A Borrowed Place: The History of Hong Kong* (New York: Kodansha, 1993), 450–51.

6. Cheung Yan Lung, "Rural Politics," in Sally Blyth and Ian Wotherspoon, *Hong Kong Remembers* (Hong Kong: Oxford University Press, 1996), 38.

7. Michael Yahuda, *Hong Kong: China's Challenge* (London: Routledge, 1996), 23.

8. Catherine R. Schenk, *Hong Kong As an International Financial Centre: Emergence and Development, 1945–65* (London: Routledge, 2001), 8.

9. Elsie Tu, *Colonial Hong Kong in the Eyes of Elsie Tu* (Hong Kong: Hong Kong University Press, 2003), 62–63.

10. Alan Smart, *The Shek Kip Mei Myth: Squatters, Fires and Colonial Rule in Hong Kong, 1950–1963* (Hong Kong: Hong Kong University Press, 2006).

11. David Faure, *Colonialism and the Hong Kong Mentality* (Hong Kong: Centre of Asian Studies, University of Hong Kong, 2003), 31–32.

12. Tu, *Colonial Hong Kong*, 45.

13. Cindy Yik-yi Chu, *The Maryknoll Sisters in Hong Kong, 1921–1969: In Love with the Chinese* (New York: Palgrave Macmillan, 2004), 6.

14. G. B. Endacott, *Hong Kong Eclipse*, ed. Alan Birch (Hong Kong: Oxford University Press, 1978), 320.

15. Bernard Hung-kay Luk, "Chinese Culture in the Hong Kong Curriculum: Heritage and Colonialism," *Comparative Education Review* 35(4) (November 1991): 667–68.

16. Ian Fleming, *Thrilling Cities* (London: Glidrose, 1963), reprinted in John Miller and Kirsten Miller, *Hong Kong: Chronicles Abroad* (San Francisco: Chronicle Books, 1994), 101–3.

17. Quoted in John D. Young, "The Building Years: Maintaining a China-Hong Kong-Britain Equilibrium, 1950–71," in Ming K. Chan, ed., *Precarious Balance: Hong Kong between China and Britain, 1842–1992* (Armonk, NY: Sharpe, 1994), 138.

18. John Cooper, *Colony in Conflict: The Hong Kong Disturbances, May 1967–January 1968* (Hong Kong: Swindon, 1970), 10.

19. Tsang Yok Sing, "Coming of Age in '67," in Blyth and Wotherspoon, *Hong Kong Remembers*, 98.

20. Faure, *Colonialism and the Hong Kong Mentality*, 75–76.

21. "The City District Officer Scheme: A Report to the Governor, 24 January 1969," *City District Officer Scheme: Report by the Secretary for Chinese Affairs* (Hong Kong: Government Printer, 1969), reprinted in Steve Tsang, ed., *A Documentary History of Hong Kong: Government and Politics* (Hong Kong: Hong Kong University Press, 1995), 218.

22. Ming K. Chan, "Labour vs. Crown: Aspects of Society-State Interactions in the Hong Kong Labour Movement before World War II," in Elizabeth Sinn, ed., *Between East and West: Aspects of Social and Political Development in Hong Kong* (Hong Kong: Centre of Asian Studies, University of Hong Kong, 1990), 142. This article is also reprinted in David Faure, ed., *Hong Kong: A Reader in Social History* (Hong Kong: Oxford University Press, 2003), 575–95.

23. Quoted in John Rear, "One Brand of Politics," in Keith Hopkins, ed., *Hong Kong: The Industrial Colony* (Hong Kong: Oxford University Press, 1971), 55.

24. David Faure, ed., *A Documentary History of Hong Kong: Society* (Hong Kong: Hong Kong University Press, 1997), 111.

25. Tu, *Colonial Hong Kong*, 120.

26. Richard Hughes, *Borrowed Place—Borrowed Time: Hong Kong and Its Many Faces*, 2nd rev. ed. (London: André Deutsch, 1976), 35.

27. Leo Goodstadt, *Uneasy Partners: The Conflict between Public Interest and Private Profit in Hong Kong* (Hong Kong: Hong Kong University Press, 2005), 38.

7

Becoming Hong Kongese

The social, economic, and political changes of the 1950s, 1960s, and 1970s had important consequences for the growth of a distinctively Hong Kong identity. Most scholars argue that this identity did not emerge until after the Communist revolution of 1949. According to this argument, because most Chinese in Hong Kong before 1949 were sojourners, they identified primarily with China. However, because most people born in Hong Kong after 1950 had little experience of China and were born to parents who had fled from there, they were less likely to identify with the People's Republic of China (PRC), especially with its Communist government. Governor Alexander Grantham wrote in 1962 that whereas in the past the "majority of Chinese" had "little loyalty to Hong Kong," the "picture is changing since China went communist, as few Chinese in Hong Kong now intend to return to the country of their birth. They are becoming permanent citizens."[1] Especially during the Great Leap Forward and the Cultural Revolution, Hong Kong people contrasted the political stability and economic freedom in Hong Kong with the repression and chaos in China. Thus, during the 1960s and 1970s more locally born Chinese started to see Hong Kong as their home.

A sense of local identity had in fact emerged by the late 1800s, when many wealthy Chinese in Hong Kong came to see themselves as permanent residents and as a special kind of Chinese, separate from their counterparts on the mainland. This sense of belonging became even stronger after the 1911 republican revolution and the revolutionary nationalism of the 1920s, especially during the general strike of 1925–1926. However, it was during the 1960s and 1970s that other parts of the population also began to identify more closely with Hong Kong. This was not a matter of a Hong Kong identity trickling down from the top. Rather, this sense of belonging was shaped by several factors, among them Hong Kong's rising economic prosperity, its closer ties with China, and the efforts of the colonial government to foster a sense of local identity. Perhaps what most shaped this sense of Hong Kong identity, however, was the realization in the early 1980s that Hong Kong would revert to Chinese sovereignty in 1997.

ECONOMIC, SOCIAL, AND CULTURAL DEVELOPMENTS

This sense of Hong Kong identity had strong economic roots. In 1973, Hong Kong's gross domestic product (GDP) had risen by 117 percent since 1968. By the 1970s, more people could afford to buy apartments and to invest in Hong Kong's economy. More money and time for leisure meant new opportunities for traveling abroad, which enabled them to compare Hong Kong with other parts of the world. With the increased economic prosperity came a rising interest in culture, from Cantonese opera to the annual Hong Kong Arts Festival, featuring orchestras from Europe and performing arts from across the globe. In the late 1970s and 1980s, the government spent more on promoting the arts, shown in the establishment of the Arts Centre in 1979, the Academy for the Performing Arts in 1984, and the Hong Kong Museum of Art in 1985.

Hong Kong's rapid economic development from the early 1970s to the 1980s also led to the rise of a local popular culture expressed in film, music, and television shows. The year 1974 saw the creation of Canto-pop, sentimental love songs with Cantonese lyrics backed by Western-style pop music. The explosion of the local film industry in the late 1960s and early 1970s led by the Shaw Brothers Studios (established in 1961 by Run Run Shaw, who made his film fortune in Singapore) and Golden Harvest Studios (cofounded by ex-Shaw executive Raymond Chow) was embodied in the short but dynamic career of Bruce Lee, whose 1972 film *The Way of the Dragon* both popularized kung fu and put Hong Kong on the cinematic map. (Lee died in 1973 from a cerebral hemorrhage.) The first Jackie Chan movie, *Snake in the Eagle's Shadow* (1978) was a big hit. In 1983 Tsui Hark's *Zu Warrior from the Magic Mountain* became a landmark in special effects for Hong Kong film. In the late 1980s, Wong Kar-wai, who made his directorial debut with *As Tears Go By* (1988), created a new form of expressionistic, melodramatic cinema, while John Woo's *A Better Tomorrow* (1986) pioneered a genre of police-and-gangster cinema that would later inspire Hollywood filmmakers. It also became clear that Hong Kong had some cultural, social, and economic influence on China. In the 1980s, for example, Hong Kong film, pop songs, and radio and television programs became popular in Guangdong, often to the dismay of local authorities who worried about this so-called spiritual pollution. Hong Kong's Cantonese language had long possessed its own idiosyncrasies, but these differences became even more pronounced in the 1970s and 1980s, as words from Hong Kong Cantonese, such as *dik-see* (taxi) and *see-daw* (store), began to creep into the Guangdong vocabulary.

Many local people became proud of Hong Kong's hybrid status: its blend of Chinese and Western culture and its emphasis on both traditional Chinese values such as family and education and on modern Western values such as economic freedom and the rule of law. With the establishment of Hong Kong Polytechnic and Chinese University (an amalgamation of three separate schools, New Asia College, Chung Chi College, and United College) in the New Territories, Hong Kong's population was becoming more educated. By the 1970s, many educated people were taking jobs locally instead of going overseas. Hong Kong had also become more cosmopolitan rather than just Chinese and British. American popular culture, which had been introduced mainly during the 1950s, became even more influential during the 1960s and 1970s, partly through the large numbers of American military personnel who came to Hong Kong during the Vietnam War but mostly through the media. Hollywood films had always had a widespread influence on Hong Kong, but in the 1960s and 1970s a generation of Hong Kong people grew up watching American television programs dubbed into Cantonese. The first McDonald's restaurant opened in 1975 in Causeway Bay on Hong Kong Island; by the late 1990s, Hong Kong would have some one hundred McDonald's restaurants, including four of the world's busiest branches. And even while some local activists protested Japan's claims to the Diaoyutai (Senkaku) Islands, eight uninhabited islands located in the East China Sea and claimed by both China and Japan, from the 1970s on things Japanese became more popular, especially as the younger generation had no memory of World War II. Japanese department stores were popular shopping venues, while children enjoyed watching dubbed Japanese cartoons and science fiction television programs.

From the late 1970s on, Hong Kong and Guangdong became increasingly reintegrated in a symbiotic relationship shaped by Guangdong's inexpensive labor and land and Hong Kong's capital and extensive international connections. Hong Kong's business knowledge and connections in the capitalist world helped China's economic reforms through investment, finance, and trade. Hong Kong investors poured money into Guangdong and began to open factories there, especially in the Shenzhen Special Economic Zone established in 1982. By the late 1980s, more than three million mainlanders were working for Hong Kong firms in Guangdong. China's economic reforms thus helped transform Hong Kong from a manufacturing base for light industrial goods such as electronics into a leading financial and service center. Whereas in the late 1970s the service sector made up less than 65 percent of Hong Kong's GDP, by the mid-1990s it accounted for almost 85 percent. By the mid-1990s, some 90 percent of Hong Kong factories had moved to China, with manufacturing counting for less than 10 percent of Hong Kong's GDP. (This transfer of production to China had a significant socioeconomic impact on Hong Kong. The biggest devaluation of skills was for blue-collar women workers, since men were more able to find work as foremen across the border. Coupled with the emphasis on academic credentials for good jobs in the service sector, this increased income inequalities in Hong Kong.)

As China became more open to the outside world in the late 1970s and early 1980s, visits to the PRC showed Hong Kong people how different Hong Kong was from the mainland. Between 1978 and 1987, Hong Kong residents made more than 30 million trips to Guangdong. Whereas in the past traveling to China meant a long train ride, by the 1980s Hong Kong people could take hydrofoils, direct buses, and airplanes into Guangdong. By 1987, more than 170,000 PRC residents had visited Hong Kong, mainly to see relatives there. Although the new contacts with China made some Hong Kong people feel that they were part of China, they also made many feel that they were a special, even different, kind of Chinese. People came to realize that they could be culturally Chinese without accepting the PRC regime. A 1985 survey showed that three-fifths of Hong Kong's Chinese population preferred to see themselves as Hong Kongese rather than Chinese. In the 1980s, local academics started to write about Hong Kong's historical contributions to modern China.

This sense of Hong Kong identity could also be seen in the way activist discourse and campaigns shifted from Chinese nationalism to local community affairs. In the early 1970s, the focus of activism was often on Chinese affairs. For example, college students in Hong Kong started to take a greater interest in Chinese politics and to show their pride in China, which after decades of opposition from the United States had finally been admitted to the United Nations (UN). In 1971, students held an unauthorized demonstration in Victoria Park to protest Japan's refusal to surrender its claims to the Diaoyutai Islands. University student federations organized trips to China in 1971 and 1972 and a series of "China Week" exhibitions in 1973 and were instrumental in the campaign to make Chinese an official language. As Hong Kong's economy improved and its population became more educated, however, activist groups such as the People's Council on Public Housing Policy, the Society for Community Organisation, the Christian Industrial Committee, the Hong Kong Professional Teachers' Union, and the Hong Kong Social Workers General Union demanded more from the government. Thus, in 1976 they organized protests against rent increases in public housing. In 1977 they demanded more participation in public housing policy. In 1980 they organized a protest against increases in bus fares. Many of these groups were organized by the former student activists who had taken such a strong interest in Chinese affairs.

Developments in communications and transportation also helped people to think of themselves as being from one place, Hong Kong, rather than from Hong Kong Island, Kowloon, or the New Territories. The opening of the first cross-harbor tunnel in 1972 brought Hong Kong Island and Kowloon much closer together, as did the Mass Transit Railway (MTR), begun in 1975 and completed by the late 1980s. Fast, clean, and efficient, the mostly underground MTR meets with the Kowloon-Canton Railway, linking Hong Kong, Kowloon, and the New Territories. Until the 1950s, the New Territories had remained very much its own part of Hong Kong. Society revolved mainly around agriculture and markets, which were both commercial sites and social gatherings. There were few schools or medical facilities. By the end of the 1960s, however, the pace of life was changing rapidly. The shift in the New Territories during the 1950s from agriculture to industry coincided with Britain's postwar economic regeneration. Because until 1962 anyone born in the British Commonwealth could settle in Britain, New Territories residents began a pattern of chain migration to Britain, leading to the rise of Chinese restaurants and Hong Kong Chinese communities there and stimulating the New Territories economy through money remitted by these emigrants. After the government decided in 1972 to develop the New Territories to relieve overcrowding in Hong Kong and Kowloon, the "new town" projects helped change the character of the New Territories by bringing in residents from other parts of the colony and blurring the line between rural and urban.

From a colonial perspective, Hong Kong had also become its own place with its own administrative identity, enjoying a wide degree of political and economic autonomy. After the budget surplus of the 1947–1948 fiscal year, Britain surrendered its tight budgetary supervision over Hong Kong. By the early 1950s, the British government had given Hong Kong a considerable level of administrative and financial autonomy. After the British government stopped reviewing Hong Kong's annual budget in the late 1950s during the tenure of Governor Robert Black, the colony became free to set its own tax policies and forge its own housing and social welfare programs. In the 1960s and 1970s the colonial administration won the right to set its own commercial policies and exchange rate and to handle its own foreign reserves. While this autonomy frequently enabled the colonial government to evade the British government's orders and guidelines for decolonization and political reform, it enabled Hong Kong to function as its own administrative and economic entity. The colony participated independently in a variety of international organizations and maintained trade development offices in all major cities. (The British government retained the right, however, to overrule in matters such as capital punishment, as it did in 1973 when Murray MacLehose refused to pardon an offender sentenced to death. Hong Kong's last execution occurred in 1966, although capital punishment remained on the books until 1991.) The British government had historically shown little interest in Hong Kong, and as Britain's diplomatic and economic relations with China took precedence over its concerns about Hong Kong, colonial officials and British businessmen found themselves increasingly both isolated from the British government and defensive about Hong Kong's status.

IDENTITY THROUGH CREDIBILITY:
THE FIGHT AGAINST CORRUPTION

As it had in earlier decades, the colonial government played an important role in shaping this sense of Hong Kong identity. In the 1970s, for example, the government responded to the increased interest in Chinese affairs by trying to cultivate a Hong Kong identity through such events as the Hong Kong Festival and the Keep Hong Kong Clean Campaign and by encouraging consumerism as a contrast to the Socialism in China. This local identity was reinforced by the government's toughened policies toward Chinese illegal immigrants, often smuggled into Hong Kong by boat owners known as snake heads. In October 1980, Governor MacLehose announced that the government's "touch base" policy would be ended. Whereas since 1950 the government had allowed illegal immigrants who had joined their families or found gainful employment to stay in Hong Kong, captured illegal immigrants would now be repatriated. The old policy, the governor explained, had become a "tragic charade" in which the illegal immigrants had "little to lose and everything to gain by running the gauntlet of Chinese and Hong Kong forces." Reflecting popular local sentiments, MacLehose argued that these illegal immigrants strained housing, medical facilities, education, and social welfare and were responsible for crime "out of all proportion to their numbers."[2] These crackdowns on illegal immigrants clearly distinguished Hong Kong Chinese, reminding them that they had special rights and privileges unavailable to Chinese on the mainland.

The colonial government's efforts to create a local identity could not have succeeded had it not achieved a remarkable level of political credibility by tackling one of Hong Kong's most serious problems: corruption. More than any of his other reforms, Governor MacLehose is best known for his fight against government corruption. According to Elsie Tu, who spent decades uncovering government corruption and other abuses, MacLehose "would not close his eyes to corruption as his predecessors had." Having tried for so long to show how corruption was "making a mockery of the rule of law" but succeeding in gaining "only trouble" for herself, Tu concludes that "without Governor MacLehose it is certain that corruption would have continued, because the law enforcement body, the police, were themselves corrupt, making it impossible to take legal action against that heinous crime that was destroying our community."[3] Leo Goodstadt, who has spent many years working in Hong Kong and writing about the region, is less impressed by MacLehose's efforts to end corruption. According to Goodstadt, the governor refused to listen to senior police officers who tried to complain about police corruption because he "did not want integrity to become a public issue for fear of tarnishing the new, positive image he was anxious to create for the colonial administration."[4]

Despite their differing attitudes toward MacLehose, these two veterans of Hong Kong's political scene help us understand why corruption was such a problem in Hong Kong and why controlling it ultimately became such a test of the government's credibility. Colonial officials often blamed the prevalence of corruption on the Chinese community, insisting that corruption was so deeply ingrained in Chinese culture that it could never be curbed, let alone eradicated, and that "the British themselves were largely untainted."[5] But the number of expatriates later convicted of corruption once the government finally tried to tackle the problem proves that there was nothing particularly Chinese about corruption. For Tu, the root of the evil lay in the lack of representation in the legislature, which created "many opportunities for corruption and malpractice in the civil service."[6] Similarly, Goodstadt blames the problem on the "uneasy partnership" between the colonial government and the local British and Chinese business elite, which "created an environment in which the dishonest and the venal found it easy to flourish in both the public and private sectors."[7]

It is somewhat difficult to blame the prevalence of corruption entirely on colonialism and the lack of political representation, for democratic governments can also be corrupt. Regardless, corruption had been a way of life since the founding of colonial Hong Kong but became especially prevalent and highly institutionalized after World War II. Still, most colonial authorities assumed that it was confined mainly to low-ranking Chinese officials and police officers. Despite evidence of extensive corruption in the mid-1950s that led to the formation of the Advisory Committee on Corruption in 1958, Goodstadt argues that Governor Grantham's measures to tackle the problem were "feeble" and "merely token measures."[8] Corruption became a serious political issue after the Star Ferry riots of 1966. Although the colonial government downplayed the situation in the official published report, senior officials privately were more concerned and sent a mission to Singapore to study how that former British colony had cracked down on corruption. But even though the 1966 riots had raised concerns about corruption in the police force and other parts of government, the police force's performance in the 1967 disturbances improved its reputation "dramatically" and made the Hong Kong public ready to "overlook conduct that would have been unacceptable in less troubled times."[9]

By the early 1970s, corruption permeated the Hong Kong government, from senior officials down to police officers who were deeply involved in syndicated corruption and firemen who refused to turn on their hoses until they received their "water money." But even when the "general public was bitterly resentful about the endless extortion it experienced in its daily contacts with government departments," writes Goodstadt, colonial officials "dismissed its complaints as malicious or exaggerated."[10] The case of Peter Godber, however, embarrassed the government in such a way that MacLehose could no longer ignore the problem. In April 1973, the commissioner of police learned that Godber, a chief superintendent of police who had been decorated for his courage in the 1967 riots and had been promoted to second-in-command of the Kowloon police in 1971, was sending large sums of money outside of Hong Kong. An investigation by the Anti-Corruption Branch of the Criminal Investigation Department revealed that Godber's resources were six times his salary from the previous twenty years. But Godber was able to use his government connections to evade security checks at the airport and escape, first to Singapore and then to Britain, where he knew he could not be extradited to Hong Kong. The scandal was widely publicized in the local and British media. Local activists quickly organized a "Fight Corruption, Catch Godber" campaign, which further humiliated the government by holding large public demonstrations against corruption.

After Godber's highly publicized escape, MacLehose appointed High Court judge Alistair Blair-Kerr to run an inquiry. Blair-Kerr's report "portrayed a deeply-corrupt police force and a government riddled with dishonesty in almost every department."[11] In 1974, MacLehose established the Independent Commission against Corruption (ICAC) led by Jack Cater, who had first come to Hong Kong right after World War II in the interim military administration and then returned in 1967 as defense secretary, and John Prendergast, an intelligence officer who had previously served in Palestine, the Gold Coast, Egypt, Kenya, Cyprus, and Aden. Cater "launched a campaign against corruption of almost evangelical fervour."[12] Although the commission was initially greeted with cynicism, its success in extraditing Godber in 1975 showed that it meant business. Godber, notes Tu, "had given the game away, served a prison term, and unintentionally set the wheels of justice against corruption in motion."[13]

The ICAC now faced another problem. So many police officers were arrested that police morale plummeted, and lower-ranking officers complained that the ICAC was using convicted policemen and other criminals to obtain evidence. In October 1977, several thousand police officers marched on the police commissioner's office. Some of the protesting officers then marched on the ICAC headquarters, breaking into the building and injuring several ICAC officers. Fearing that the police might go on strike and plunge the colony into anarchy, on November 5 MacLehose issued a partial amnesty for corruption committed before January 1, 1977, except for extremely grave cases. Although many people were shocked and dismayed that the governor would yield, there would have been no way to replace Hong Kong's large police force on such short notice without calling in the military. As MacLehose later recalled, "it would have been feasible to go on prosecuting people for offences committed long ago, but the risk of such prosecutions had resulted in an alliance between the formerly corrupt and the presently corrupt which was the heart of the near mutiny of the police. The amnesty split off these two rather different elements and simplified the ICAC's ability to press on with the prosecution of current corruption."[14]

The 1977 crisis carved a deep rift between the police and the ICAC that would not be bridged until the mid-1980s. The ICAC also lost a considerable degree of face, although it was eventually able to regain public confidence. Other problems remained unresolved. For example, the ICAC often seemed less willing to prosecute British civil servants. It also lacked control over triad gangs, who often served as middlemen for corrupt civil servants, especially among the police force. As Goodstadt argues, "criminal proceedings against police officers and the more flamboyant nature of police corruption distracted public attention from the far more lucrative and better-organized conspiracies in the business world." Corruption was especially rife in the property and construction businesses. With fire and safety restrictions to be avoided, "scandals in the property sector and the construction industry plagued the rest of British rule and continued under the post-colonial administration." And although the ICAC exposed "a small number of senior officials and some minor business and professional persons," some government officials "continued to maintain close social connections with business and professional circles they were supposed to oversee, unintimidated by the ICAC's public criticisms of such behaviour."[15]

Given Hong Kong's deep-rooted and widespread corruption, however, the establishment of the ICAC and the fight against corruption in the 1970s was a remarkable feat. "Almost overnight," writes Goodstadt, "the principle of honest administration had become part of the civil service culture. The community now looked to a professional organization . . . to police the colonial administration and enforce zero tolerance of corruption." The establishment of the ICAC did more than help the government tackle corruption. As Goodstadt argues, it "generated invaluable political dividends for British rule." The Hong Kong public "became convinced almost at once that, at last, the British had established an agency to which it could complain, fearlessly and effectively, about abuse of office, dereliction of duty, and the unlawful exactions of officialdom. At a stroke, the ICAC encountered deep-rooted cynicism about the colonial administration and its sense of duty towards the population at large. In a colonial and non-democratic political environment, that change of image was an invaluable source of credibility."[16]

NEGOTIATING HONG KONG'S FUTURE

Looming over the changes and developments in the 1970s was the question of Hong Kong's future political status. Since coming to power in 1949, the Chinese government had generally left Hong Kong alone, rarely even discussing its political status. Hong Kong had played an important role in the Chinese economy in the 1960s and 1970s. After the disastrous Great Leap Forward and through the Cultural Revolution, foreign currency acquired through colonial Hong Kong financed much of the PRC's imports. In the 1960s, the PRC earned almost half of its hard currency from selling food and water to Hong Kong. Journalist Richard Hughes described Hong Kong as "China's only rewarding bridgehead with the rest of the world and China's most convenient springboard for export dumping forays into South East Asia." Through Hong Kong, the PRC was flooding markets with bicycles, canned goods, clothing, radios, and sewing machines that cost half as much as their Japanese equivalents. In Hong Kong, the PRC government ran more than fifty department stores, the Bank of China and eight smaller banks, two insurance companies, three financial syndicates, and "a Maoist flush of shoe stores, publishing houses and restaurants."[17] Whereas Hong Kong was better known as a British and American listening post on China, it served a similar function for Chinese Communist Party cadres and activists, who used the colony to stay in touch with the outside world. Not surprisingly, PRC leaders realized Hong Kong's economic and political value and were eager to continue the pragmatic relationship with the colonial administration that had been built in the 1950s.

After the PRC was finally admitted to the UN in November 1971, however, in March 1972 Huang Hua, China's ambassador to the UN, clarified Hong Kong's political status as "a Chinese territory under British administration" and asked that Hong Kong and Macau be removed from the UN's list of colonial territories. Huang insisted that Hong Kong was an internal Chinese matter, to be solved by the Chinese government "in an appropriate way when conditions are ripe." When on November 2, 1972, the UN General Assembly removed Hong Kong and Macau from its list of colonial territories, Britain, which had not objected to Huang's declaration, ended its practice of sending annual reports on Hong Kong to the UN secretary-general. In a language shift designed to reflect this change and to suit both the British and the Chinese governments, Hong Kong changed from a Crown Colony to a Dependent Territory (although the word "Colony" remained on banknotes until 1985), while the colonial secretary became the chief secretary. As a gesture of goodwill to the PRC government, in 1973 the British government persuaded the Hong Kong government to release the last of the prisoners from the 1967 riots.

Not only had Huang Hua insisted that Hong Kong's future political status would be determined by China rather than Britain, he had also implied that the people of Hong Kong would not have a role in this process. But many people in Hong Kong took Huang's declaration as little more than official rhetoric, assuming that the PRC would continue its traditional practice of leaving Hong Kong alone. The economic boom of the 1970s led some people in Hong Kong to hope that China would simply let Hong Kong be, especially since it had so much to gain from the colony's continued economic prosperity. And when the PRC government turned down Portugal's offer in 1974 to return Macau, many people in Hong Kong took this as a sign of hope that China might be willing to do the same for Hong Kong. When Queen Elizabeth visited Hong Kong in May 1975 as the first reigning British sovereign to do so, she was welcomed by thousands of well-wishers. In September 1978, a senior official at the Hong Kong branch of the New China News Agency admitted that the 1967 riots were a mistake and that China should learn from Hong Kong and from other industrializing countries.

Some Hong Kong investors, however, grew concerned about taking out new leases since the government could not grant any leases beyond the 1997 deadline. In 1976, Jimmy McGregor, director of the Hong Kong General Chamber of Commerce, warned that investors would need assurances from the PRC government before making long-term investments in Hong Kong. When in March 1979 the PRC government invited MacLehose to Beijing on an official visit, the governor saw the first official visit to the PRC by a sitting governor as a chance to discuss the expiration of the New Territories lease. In his meeting with new Chinese leader Deng Xiaoping, MacLehose suggested that the Legislative Council unilaterally set aside the 1997 deadline without making any permanent claims to the territory. Although Deng rejected this suggestion, MacLehose returned to Hong Kong relieved and optimistic. Choosing his words carefully, he explained to the Hong Kong public that while Deng had maintained that China would eventually resolve the Hong Kong issue, he had also assured the governor that Hong Kong investors could "set their hearts at ease." MacLehose did not tell the Hong Kong public that Deng had rejected the proposal to set aside the 1997 deadline.

No one knows exactly when the PRC government decided that it would retake Hong Kong. Journalist Kevin Rafferty believes that Deng told MacLehose during his trip to Beijing that China would recover Hong Kong in 1997. Rafferty notes that the passing of the British Nationality (Hong Kong) Act of 1981, which demoted more than 2.5 million Hong Kong Chinese entitled to carry British passports to "British Dependent Territory citizens" and excluded them from right of abode in Britain, implies that the British government knew that 1997 would see the end of British Hong Kong.[18] Although the un-official members of the Legislative and Executive Councils had wanted to send a delegation to London to lobby the British Parliament against voting for the bill, MacLehose told them to cancel the trip. (The unofficial members may well have succeeded, for the bill passed by only three votes.)

In any case, MacLehose's visit to Beijing created a temporary sense of re-lief in Hong Kong. The stock market and property markets rose, and foreign banks and businesses poured into Hong Kong even while land in Hong Kong became the most expensive in the world. Hong Kong people were im-pressed by China's economic modernization and Deng's policy of opening China to the outside world. This optimism began to wane by 1982. British prime minister Margaret Thatcher was planning a trip to Asia in September that would include China, where she would surely have to broach the sub-ject of Hong Kong. There were other ominous signs. The Chinese National People's Congress, the PRC's highest legislative body, had drafted provi-sions for a Special Administration Region (SAR) the previous year. In Jan-uary 1982, Chinese premier Zhao Ziyang told British lord privy seal Humphrey Atkins that the PRC had already made provisions for Hong Kong after 1997. In July, senior PRC official Peng Zhen spoke of the reuni-fication of Hong Kong, Macau, and Taiwan as SARs. Although some schol-ars believe that Thatcher never actually thought a settlement might be reached for retaining Hong Kong, when the prime minister arrived in Bei-jing on September 22, fresh from Britain's victory against Argentina in the Falkland Islands, she at least appeared as if she thought she had a chance to keep Hong Kong because of the treaties ceding Hong Kong and Kowloon. Thatcher insisted that the Sino-British treaties could only be altered, not abrogated, and that Britain had a moral obligation to the people of Hong Kong, but PRC officials declared that the treaties were unequal and had been signed with the long-defunct Qing government.

By the time Thatcher left Beijing, it was clear that China would try to re-cover Hong Kong in 1997. Deng Xiaoping did, however, assure Thatcher that Hong Kong people could rule Hong Kong after China resumed control. Shortly thereafter, prominent Hong Kong people were invited to visit Bei-jing, where they were welcomed by PRC leaders. Still, public confidence in Hong Kong's post-1997 future dropped so far that it caused panic in Hong Kong's financial markets and a collapse in the property market. The sharp decrease in investor confidence led to Hong Kong's slowest growth in GDP since 1975. In September 1983, the plunging Hong Kong dollar was pegged to the American dollar, which restored some self-assurance. But much of this confidence was undermined in March 1984 when one of the oldest and largest British firms in Hong Kong, Jardine and Matheson, which only one year earlier the PRC government had praised for helping to develop China's international trade, declared that it would move its legal domicile from

Hong Kong to Bermuda in order to protect its ability to function under English law after 1997.

For China, recovering Hong Kong was a way to end the unequal treaties and to reclaim face and honor. For Deng Xiaoping in particular, who saw Hong Kong as part of a larger reunification that included Taiwan and Macau, it was a way to show Taiwan that the one country, two systems model—originally meant to apply to Taiwan rather than Hong Kong—could work. As China's economy became more open in the late 1980s, it became more plausible to think of Hong Kong as part of China rather than as a source of spiritual pollution. Whereas earlier Chinese leaders had been content to benefit from Hong Kong being under British rule, Deng, who took a deep personal interest and leadership role in the recovery of Hong Kong, now believed that the PRC could have sovereignty over Hong Kong and could benefit from it economically (hence his call for mainland industries to invest in Hong Kong). And the fact that the PRC had tolerated Hong Kong's colonial status for so long meant that it would inherit a much richer prize in 1997.

Could the British have played their cards any differently? The suggestion from some quarters in Britain to return the New Territories but retain Hong Kong Island and Kowloon would have neither worked nor satisfied the Chinese government. The British might have argued that by international law the 1842 and 1860 treaties were still valid. But by now Britain, which had long ceased to be an imperial power, was neither interested in nor capable of defending Hong Kong from China, where it had larger diplomatic and commercial interests to pursue. By the early 1960s, British investment in Hong Kong had dropped to less than half of what it had been in the early 1930s. In 1967 the British Treasury concluded that Hong Kong was no longer an economic asset for Britain. Nor could Britain have resisted China militarily. British planners had realized by the late 1950s that Hong Kong could not be defended from an attack by China. The Naval Dockyard was closed down in 1958, and shortly afterward the local garrison was pared down to the minimum needed for internal security. In 1968 the British government announced that it would withdraw all British troops east of Suez by the end of 1971. In the same year, the Colonial Office became part of the Commonwealth Office, which in 1971 was subsumed by the Foreign and Commonwealth Office. From then on, British strategy was simply to hold off for as long as possible any PRC attempts to recover Hong Kong.

THE SINO-BRITISH NEGOTIATIONS AND THE JOINT DECLARATION

MacLehose's successor, Edward Youde, arrived in Hong Kong in May 1982 during a period of great anxiety. According to an opinion poll conducted in

May and June, the majority of Hong Kong's population preferred the continuation of British rule, even though the British Nationality Act of 1981 had provoked a sense of betrayal. The British government nevertheless saw in Youde someone who could work out a suitable agreement with the PRC. A career diplomat who had once been ambassador to Beijing and was fluent in Mandarin, Youde had negotiated with the Chinese Communists in 1949 for the release of the HMS *Amethyst*.

The Sino-British negotiations on Hong Kong's future took two years. The first round of negotiations, from October 1982 to June 1983, were conducted mainly between the British ambassador to China, Richard Evans, and the Chinese foreign ministry. The chief bone of contention was China's demand that the British acknowledge Chinese sovereignty over Hong Kong, which Britain refused. Only after Margaret Thatcher conceded that Hong Kong would revert to Chinese sovereignty, on the condition that the people of Hong Kong accept the reversion, did the negotiations move on to the second stage. Another problem was that the two sides had very different views of what the final product would look like. As David Wilson, former political advisor to the Hong Kong government (he had accompanied MacLehose to Bejing in 1979) and member of the British negotiating team, recalled, "We had wanted to write a book—which would have looked rather like the *Encyclopaedia Britannica*—while the Chinese wanted about two or three sides of A4 paper."[19]

The second phase of negotiations began in July 1983. The Chinese negotiating team was led by Vice Foreign Minister Yao Gang, who was later replaced by Assistant Foreign Minister Zhou Nan. The British side was led by former ambassador to China Percy Cradock, although he was replaced by Ambassador Richard Evans in late 1983. Governor Youde participated in the negotiations, but the Chinese insisted that he be present only as a member of the British delegation; the official PRC line was that the negotiations were solely between Britain and China, which represented the people of Hong Kong. Although public opinion in Hong Kong overwhelmingly opposed a return to Chinese rule (a point that Xu Jiatun, the PRC's de facto representative in Hong Kong as director of the New China News Agency local branch, realized all too well), Deng Xiaoping believed otherwise. In late 1983, Deng warned that unless the negotiations were completed by October 1 (the PRC's national day) in 1984, the Chinese would make a unilateral declaration.

The main obstacle to the second phase of negotiations was Britain's hope to continue administering Hong Kong after 1997, even under Chinese sovereignty. Cradock later claimed that Deng Xiaoping was determined to recover Hong Kong fully, "even if it meant taking it back as a barren rock."[20] As it became clear that the Chinese were insistent on recovering Hong Kong, in late 1983 the British shifted their emphasis to maintaining stability in Hong Kong after the transfer to Chinese sovereignty, and in April 1984 Foreign Secretary Geoffrey Howe regretfully informed the Legislative Council that it would be unrealistic to continue British rule after 1997. Another obstacle arose when the Chinese suggested appointing a joint commission to manage the transition. Convinced that this arrangement would fail, Governor Youde instead suggested a Sino-British Joint Liaison Group that would be strictly consultative. (This Joint Liaison Group was established in Hong Kong shortly after the end of the negotiations; the British side of the group was led by David Wilson, who would return to Hong Kong as governor in 1987.)

Signed by Thatcher and Premier Zhao Ziyang on December 19, 1984, and ratified on May 28, 1985, the Sino-British Joint Declaration laid out the main terms of the agreement regarding Hong Kong's future political status. All of Hong Kong would revert to Chinese rule on July 1, 1997. Britain would administer Hong Kong until then and would help maintain its economic prosperity and social stability; the PRC would cooperate in this process. Hong Kong would become an SAR with a high level of autonomy, except in defense and foreign affairs. Hong Kong's social and economic systems would remain unchanged, as would most of its current laws. The Hong Kong government would retain control over trade policies and trading agreements. Hong Kong would remain a free port, with no taxes paid to China. The rights and freedoms of speech, assembly, and religion would be preserved. Troops of the Chinese People's Liberation Army troops stationed in Hong Kong would not interfere in internal SAR affairs. This one country, two systems arrangement—which Thatcher described as "an ingenious idea" and Deng Xiaoping called "a product of dialectical Marxism and historical materialism"—would last for fifty years after 1997.

Local reactions to the Joint Declaration were mixed. Opinion polls showed that most people preferred that Hong Kong remain a British colony, but most people had come to accept that this was not a reality. Although some feared the prospect of living under Chinese rule, they were glad that a deal had finally been struck. While most Chinese leaders had pushed the British to try to hold on to Hong Kong, they quickly turned their attention to China once the deal was finished. Some took Chinese citizenship and gave up their British awards and titles, but this was not always enough for Beijing. In June 1984, Q. W. Lee, Lydia Dunn, and Sze-yuen Chung—all senior members of the Executive Council—were invited to visit Beijing. The leader of the delegation, Chung, who had been knighted twice by the British and had originally argued for continued British administration of Hong Kong, was chastised by Deng Xiaoping for questioning China's ability to adhere to the one country, two systems model.

For the PRC government, the Joint Declaration was a way to prepare Hong Kong for reunification as smoothly as possible and to assure Hong Kong people that their way of life would not change. Still, many people in Hong Kong were frustrated, and they resented the way that the negotiations had been conducted, without their having any say in the process. These feelings were captured brilliantly by Zunzi, a political cartoonist for a leading local Chinese newspaper, in a cartoon depicting Thatcher and Deng Xiaoping as parents and Hong Kong as a girl about to marry a roll of paper held by an anonymous, headless man. The roll of paper represented the Joint Declaration, with the cartoon suggesting that Hong Kong's return to China was like a traditional Chinese arranged marriage in which the bride had no say. This sense of frustration and resentment helps explain the blossoming of new political groups in the early 1980s, such as the Hong Kong Prospect Institute, the New Hong Kong Society, Meeting Point, the Hong Kong Forum, the Hong Kong Affairs Society, the Hong Kong People's Association, the Association for Democracy and Justice, and the Hong Kong Policy Viewers. Although they represented a spectrum of political opinions, these groups had several common traits. They were generally organized by former student activists who were now service professionals with strong links to the grassroots through their jobs. Strongly committed to nationalism, democracy, and welfare capitalism, these groups used legal channels such as public seminars, news conferences, and position papers to broadcast their goals.

For the British, the Joint Declaration was an attempt to protect Hong Kong after 1997 and to withdraw with dignity and without appearing as if they had surrendered Hong Kong and betrayed its people. (Cradock called the declaration "as comprehensive protection as could be devised and agreed.")[21] This helps explain why the British made minor and belated attempts to introduce democracy to Hong Kong during the Sino-British negotiations, not only to protect Hong Kong under Chinese rule but also to make the transfer to Chinese rule more palatable to the British Parliament. In July 1984 the Hong Kong government published a consultation green paper on political reform, explaining its intention to "develop progressively a system of government the authority for which is firmly rooted in Hong Kong, which is able to represent authoritatively the views of the people of Hong Kong, and which is more directly accountable to the people of Hong Kong." The plans for reform included an indirectly elected part of the Legislative Council. Although the government did not commit to direct elections, in November 1984 it published a policy white paper conceding that "the bulk of public response from all sources suggested a cautious approach with a gradual start by introducing a very small number of directly elected members in 1988 and building up to a significant number of directly elected members by 1997."

The PRC proceeded with the Joint Declaration without complaint. But in 1985 Xu Jiatun, the PRC's representative in Hong Kong, accused the British of violating the Joint Declaration and trying to run Hong Kong after 1997. As a compromise, the British agreed on no major reforms until after the promulgation of the Basic Law in 1990. Although in 1985 the Legislative Council was expanded by twenty-four elected members (and then to twenty-six in 1988), elected members still accounted for only 40 percent of the total membership. None were directly elected; rather, half were selected by functional constituencies, while the other half came from twelve electoral colleges whose members were from the lower councils. On September 26, 1985, the first indirect elections were held for twelve functional constituency seats and twelve district seats for the Legislative Council (consisting of fifty-seven seats). Until then, the last significant constitutional development had been in 1896, when two unofficial members were added to the Executive Council. Although both the Legislative Council and the Executive Council had increased in size and Chinese members had been added to each, the overall structure of the government had not changed, nor had the relationships among the governor, the two councils, and the civil service.

JITTERY CITY

Designed by renowned British architect Norman Foster, the new headquarters of the Hong Kong and Shanghai Bank—long a symbol of Hong Kong's colonial status—was the world's most expensive building when it was completed in 1985. Bank and government officials hoped that the new building would convey confidence in Hong Kong's future. And although many foreign firms left Hong Kong in anticipation of the 1997 transition, even more came to take advantage of the economic opportunities provided by Hong Kong's reintegration with China. The Hong Kong government appeared to have survived the Sino-British negotiations remarkably well. In surveys taken in 1985, less than 32 percent of respondents said that they trusted the PRC government, while more than 73 percent said that they trusted the Hong Kong government.

In May 1986, however, the cover of the locally based *Far Eastern Economic Review* described Hong Kong as a "jittery city." After the nuclear catastrophe at Chernobyl in the Soviet Union in April of that year, people in Hong Kong became concerned about China's plans to build a nuclear power station at Daya (Bias) Bay, about thirty miles northeast of Hong Kong. The site had been chosen in 1982, and while the British, Chinese, and Hong Kong governments all supported the project, which was to be built by a French company, pressure groups such as the Joint Organization for the Concern of Nuclear Energy and the Friends of the Earth lobbied hard against it. After the Chernobyl disaster, surveys showed that 77 percent of Hong Kong people opposed the project. More than one million Hong Kong people signed a petition against it (although most people lost interest once the Chinese government decided to go ahead with the plan).

This sense of fear and uncertainty was intensified when on December 5, 1986, Governor Youde died of a heart attack in his sleep at the British embassy in Beijing, becoming the first Hong Kong governor to die in office.

When his body was returned to Hong Kong for the funeral and cremation, huge crowds came out to pay their respects to the governor who had fought for Hong Kong in the Sino-British negotiations even while not being allowed to represent Hong Kong officially. The late governor was replaced temporarily by Chief Secretary David Akers-Jones, who served as acting governor from December 1986 until April 1987, when David Wilson, the former political advisor and China scholar, arrived in Hong Kong to take governorship.

While some people in Hong Kong reacted to this uncertainty by taking a stronger interest in local politics, others responded by voting with their feet. People had been emigrating from Hong Kong (mainly to Australia, Britain, Canada, and the United States) before and throughout the Sino-British negotiations, but the scale and intensity of emigration increased dramatically after the Joint Declaration, when Hong Kong saw a "gathering wave of emigration."[22] Whereas some twenty thousand people left every year from 1980 to 1986, according to government figures the number rose to almost thirty thousand in 1987 and forty thousand in 1989. These figures are even more significant given that they represent only the people who were actually able to find host countries willing to accept them rather than those who wanted or tried to emigrate. Although Governor Wilson denied that Hong Kong was experiencing a brain drain, most of these emigrants were educated, bilingual, middle-class professionals with British passports who, denied the right of abode in Britain after the 1981 British Nationality Act, looked elsewhere for havens before the transition to Chinese sovereignty in 1997.

Desperate to maintain public confidence, in May 1987 the Hong Kong government published a consultation green paper on representative government and established a survey office to track public opinion. The green paper invited the Hong Kong public to choose from four options, including direct elections to the Legislative Council. However, the options were presented in such a way that the issue of direct elections was obscured (the paper did not simply ask whether respondents favored direct elections). When in October the survey office released its findings showing that the majority of the population did not favor direct elections, even though independent surveys showed that the overwhelming majority of people in Hong Kong favored direct elections in 1988, the local reaction was "extremely hostile."[23] Critics accused the government of manipulating the survey to postpone democratic reform. Martin Lee, a lawyer and Legislative Council member, led the Delegation for Democracy and flew to London in January 1988 in an unsuccessful bid to persuade British government officials and members of Parliament to support direct elections. In February 1988, the Hong Kong government published a policy white paper, which explained that because there was no "clear consensus," direct elections would be postponed until 1991. Instead, indirect elections were held in September 1988 for twenty-six seats in the fifty-seven-member Legislative Council. The Hong Kong and

British governments had caved to pressure from the Chinese government not to introduce democratic reforms by claiming that the people of Hong Kong did not want them—and the people of Hong Kong knew it, which made them view all three governments negatively.

THE BASIC LAW

Almost immediately after the Joint Declaration had been ratified, the Chinese side began to work on drafting the Basic Law. While it was supposed to codify the guarantees made by China in the Joint Declaration, the Basic Law was also a chance to ensure that any political changes in Hong Kong before 1997 would comply with what China had in mind for Hong Kong after 1997. But the drafting of the Basic Law also showed the inherent weaknesses in the Joint Declaration—many of them areas that had been left vague because the Sino-British negotiators had been unable to agree. These vague areas for the most part enabled Britain and China to interpret the terms of the declaration in their own ways. As political scientist James Tang argues, the Joint Declaration did not settle the Sino-British differences; rather, it became "the source of these differences."[24]

The main bone of contention was the pace and scope of institutional change in Hong Kong before 1997. The Joint Declaration specified that the "current" institutions of Hong Kong were to remain unchanged for fifty years, but it gave no definition of "current." The Chinese government argued that Hong Kong should return to China as it stood in 1984, when the joint agreement was signed, but the British and Hong Kong governments insisted that Hong Kong could not be frozen in time for thirteen years. The Chinese government viewed any efforts to introduce political, institutional, or legislative changes as attempts to maintain a British presence after 1997. Britain and China had agreed that by 1997 the Legislative Council would be "constituted by elections," but Britain and China interpreted this differently. The Chinese government firmly opposed any suggestions of universal suffrage, especially since the British had waited so long in their rule even to consider this. In 1985 Xu Jiatun declared that "consultation" constituted a form of election. Although the British had insisted that the Joint Declaration should specify that Hong Kong's legislature would be "constituted by election," the Chinese later claimed that they were unaware of the ramifications of the British definition of the term "election." However, the British had proposed modest reforms in 1984, even before the end of the Sino-British negotiations, including indirect elections to the Legislative Council in 1985 (although these elections did not take place).

The Basic Law took almost five years to draft. On July 1, 1985, the National People's Congress established the Hong Kong Basic Law Drafting

Committee, which consisted of 59 appointed members (36 from the main-land and 23 from Hong Kong) and held its first plenum that week in Beijing. On September 18, the Basic Law Consultative Committee was established in Hong Kong, consisting of 180 appointed members, all local residents. In early 1986, Timothy Renton, the British Foreign Office minister for Hong Kong, announced his government's policy of convergence, meaning that Britain would consult with China on all matters pertinent to the 1997 tran-sition and that no political reforms would be made until after the publica-tion of the Basic Law in 1990. In fact, Britain and China had made a secret agreement in late 1985 to delay any major constitutional reforms until 1991. Although Britain later argued that this arrangement forced the Chinese gov-ernment to agree to more extensive political reforms in 1991 than it would have otherwise allowed, the policy of convergence was seen by many people in Hong Kong as a capitulation to the Chinese government and seriously hurt the Hong Kong government's image. The policy of convergence received symbolic approval when Queen Elizabeth visited Beijing, Shanghai, Guangzhou, and, finally Hong Kong in October 1986.

Released in late April 1988 for a five-month public consultation, the first draft of the Basic Law provoked a storm of criticism in Hong Kong. Almost seventy-five thousand submissions were received over the consultation pe-riod. The amended second draft, released in late February 1989, also received a great deal of criticism during the eight-month consultation period, mainly from liberal groups but even from moderate and conservative groups, for not allowing more room for representative government. The drafting process was also disrupted after the student protests in Beijing that culminated in the Tiananmen Square Massacre in June 1989. Two members of the drafting com-mittee—Louis Cha, a publisher, and Peter Kwong, the Anglican bishop—re-signed after the PRC government imposed martial law on May 20. The PRC excluded from the drafting committee Martin Lee and Szeto Wah, the two most vocal advocates of democratization on the committee and the founders of the Hong Kong Alliance in Support of the Patriotic Democratic Movement in China.

The British government tried to persuade the PRC to modify some of the clauses, including those enabling the PRC to station troops in Hong Kong and to declare a state of emergency, but instead the PRC added a new clause: Ar-ticle 23, which allowed the future HKSAR to prohibit subversion against the PRC government. After meeting in January to amend the law, in February 1990 the drafting committee held its ninth and final plenum in Beijing, where it adopted its final draft. In accordance with a secret deal made by British and Chinese officials in January-February in Beijing, the new final draft included an amendment calling for eighteen directly elected Legislative Council seats in 1991 and twenty in 1995. The British government later justi-fied this secret deal by insisting that the compromise ensured that the Chinese would allow the new constitutional arrangement to last beyond 1997. On April 4, 1990, the National People's Congress formally enacted the Basic Law, which was then promulgated by the PRC government.

Most people in Hong Kong understood that while the Basic Law was the PRC government's attempt to show Hong Kong people that it was sincere about the one country, two systems model, it was also the government's way to show that it was in charge of Hong Kong's post-1997 future. As Hong Kong's miniconstitution, the Basic Law promises a "high level of autonomy." It makes Beijing responsible for Hong Kong's foreign policy and defense but allows Hong Kong to participate independently in international organizations such as the World Trade Organization and the Olympics. Although both the Joint Declaration and the Basic Law guarantee that Hong Kong's legal and judicial systems will not be changed, the Standing Committee of the National People's Congress has the ultimate authority to interpret and amend the Basic Law and to revoke any Hong Kong law that it feels violates the Basic Law.

THE END OF THE KOWLOON WALLED CITY

The tensions permeating the Sino-British negotiations and the drafting of the Basic Law would escalate after the Tiananmen Square Massacre in June 1989 as Hong Kong's countdown toward the reversion to Chinese sovereignty drew the attention of the world. Yet given the violence and warfare that often plagued the end of European rule in other colonies, the end of British rule in Hong Kong was a remarkably calm and orderly process. Scarcely noticed outside of Hong Kong, one event neatly characterized the end of British rule in Hong Kong. In January 1987, with the support of the PRC government, the Hong Kong government announced that the Kowloon Walled City would be demolished and turned into a public park before 1997. Excluded from the 1898 lease of the New Territories but subsequently claimed by Britain after Qing troops helped villagers resist British rule in the New Territories, this small area became an independent enclave where the British generally took a hands-off approach. Although the Walled City had almost disappeared by the eve of World War II, it was revived after the war and after the 1949 revolution. As author Jan Morris puts it, the area "felt like an enclave within the city, extra-territorial and even slightly unreal."[25]

By the 1960s, the Walled City had grown into a hodgepodge of ramshackle buildings crammed so closely together that daylight could almost not come through. There was no formal sewage system, and electricity was tapped illegally through a mesh of wires that frequently led to fires. The area, writes Morris, was "a frightful slum. No four-wheeled vehicle could enter it—there were no streets wide enough—and its buildings, rising sometimes to ten or twelve storeys, were so inextricably packed together that they seemed to form one congealed mass of masonry, sealed together by overlapping structures, ladders, walk-ways, pipes and cables, and ventilated only by foetid air-shafts. . . . A maze of dark alleys pierced the mass from one side to the other. Virtually no daylight reached them. Looped electric cables festooned their low ceilings, dripping alarmingly with moisture."[26]

Like Hong Kong itself, the Walled City became a city of contradictions and nuances. An internationally notorious center for drugs, gambling, and prostitution, it was also home to a close-knit community of more than thirty thousand residents with a strong sense of collective identity who lived among the shops, small factories and workshops, brothels, massage parlors, gambling dens, and unlicensed doctors and dentists. Although the Walled City was often managed and policed by powerful triad societies—leading critics to contrast its lawlessness and crime with the law and order in the rest of Hong Kong—by the early 1980s the crime rates appeared to be no higher than in the surrounding region. The PRC government had remained consistently ambivalent about the Walled City, never surrendering its claim to jurisdiction over the area yet never making too much of a commotion about it since that might suggest recognition of British jurisdiction over the rest of the region. Thus, concludes Morris, the Walled City "remained a strange reminder of China's stage in Hong Kong, and of the subtle, patient, cat-and-mouse way in which the Chinese viewed the progress of the colony."[27]

In accordance with the 1987 agreement, in 1994 the Walled City was razed and turned into a classical Chinese garden that was officially opened in December 1995 by Hong Kong's last colonial governor, Chris Patten. Just as the Joint Declaration put an end to Hong Kong's uncertain political status, the decision to raze the Walled City signaled that China would regain full sovereignty over the region after 1997. As historian Seth Harter argues, recreating a classical Chinese garden where the Walled City once stood consciously stresses Hong Kong's original Chineseness rather than the East-West hybridity that has defined much of Hong Kong's history since the arrival of the British. The style of the garden comes from the early Qing era, the "highpoint" of pre–Opium War Chinese cultural and economic development and territorial integrity, a period in which China was "virtually unmolested by European colonialism" and during which imperial control over Guangdong and the Hong Kong region reached its zenith. Just as the Joint Declaration reunites long-lost Hong Kong with the rest of China, this "purely Chinese" garden unites Hong Kong's precolonial past with its postcolonial present and future.[28]

NOTES

1. Alexander Grantham, *Via Ports: From Hong Kong to Hong Kong* (Hong Kong: Hong Kong University Press, 1965), 112.

2. *Hong Kong Hansard: Reports of the Meetings of the Legislative Council of Hong Kong,* October 23, 1980, 103–5, reprinted in Steve Tsang, ed., *A Documentary History of Hong Kong: Government and Politics* (Hong Kong: Hong Kong University Press, 1995), 287–88.

3. Elsie Tu, *Colonial Hong Kong in the Eyes of Elsie Tu* (Hong Kong: Hong Kong University Press, 2003), 8, 15, 63.

4. Leo Goodstadt, *Uneasy Partners: The Conflict between Public Interest and Private Profit in Hong Kong* (Hong Kong: Hong Kong University Press, 2005), 145.

5. Ibid., 13.

6. Tu, *Colonial Hong Kong,* 134.

7. Goodstadt, *Uneasy Partners,* 139.

8. Ibid., 143.

9. Ibid., 147.

10. Ibid., 31.

11. Ibid., 141.

12. Ibid.

13. Tu, *Colonial Hong Kong,* 117.

14. Lord MacLehose, "Social and Economic Changes," in Sally Blyth and Ian Wotherspoon, *Hong Kong Remembers* (Hong Kong: Oxford University Press, 1996), 125.

15. Goodstadt, *Uneasy Partners,* 140, 148, 151.

16. Ibid., 146, 156.

17. Richard Hughes, *Borrowed Place—Borrowed Time: Hong Kong and Its Many Faces,* 2nd rev. ed. (London: André Deutsch, 1976), 41–42.

18. Kevin Rafferty, *City on the Rocks: Hong Kong's Uncertain Future* (London: Viking, 1989), 389.

19. Lord Wilson, "Learning to Live with China," in Blyth and Wotherspoon, *Hong Kong Remembers,* 179.

20. Quoted in Michael Yahuda, *Hong Kong: China's Challenge* (London: Routledge, 1996), 21.

21. Percy Cradock, *Experiences of China* (London: John Murray, 1994), 209.

22. Wong Siu-lun, "Deciding to Stay, Deciding to Move, Deciding Not to Decide," in Gary G. Hamilton, ed., *Cosmopolitan Capitalists: Hong Kong and the Chinese Diaspora at the End of the 20th Century* (Seattle: University of Washington Press, 1999), 136.

23. Goodstadt, *Uneasy Partners,* 84.

24. James T. H. Tang, "Hong Kong's Transition to Chinese Rule: The Fate of the Joint Declaration," in Judith M. Brown and Rosemary Foot, eds., *Hong Kong's Transitions, 1842–1997* (London: Macmillan, 1997), 150.

25. Jan Morris, *Hong Kong: Epilogue to an Empire* (New York: Vintage, 1997), 264.

26. Ibid.

27. Ibid., 265.

28. Seth Harter, "Hong Kong's Dirty Little Secret: Clearing the Walled City of Kowloon," *Journal of Urban History* 27(1) (November 2000): 104–5.

8

The Countdown to 1997

By the late 1980s, most people in Hong Kong had reluctantly accepted the inevitability of Hong Kong's reversion to Chinese sovereignty in 1997. According to a 1988 poll, more than half of the respondents believed that reversion to Chinese rule would hurt civil rights and individual liberty. Almost half said that they trusted the Hong Kong government, about 30 percent said that they trusted the British government, but only about 20 percent said that they trusted the Chinese government. More than 70 percent wanted the Hong Kong government to be democratic (although only 25 percent supported the creation of political parties). The events in Beijing during the spring of 1989, however, caused many people in Hong Kong to lose all faith in the Chinese government and to "consciously . . . reevaluate their identities and their options for the future."[1]

After the death on April 15, 1989, of former Chinese Communist Party (CCP) general secretary Hu Yaobang, who had been sacked for failing to end student demonstrations in 1986, university students in Beijing organized a series of prodemocracy demonstrations. By May 4, the seventieth anniversary of the May Fourth Movement, the demonstrations had attracted the world's attention. On May 13, the students occupied Tiananmen Square, where they began a hunger strike protesting government corruption and demanding democratic reforms. In Hong Kong, the demonstrations in Beijing were hopeful signs that China was on the verge of becoming more democratic. However, when Premier Li Peng imposed martial law on May 20, more than five hundred thousand Hong Kong people braved a typhoon and marched in the streets to show their support for the demonstrators.

Some marched to show their Chinese patriotism. Others were frustrated that Hong Kong people had been left out of the Sino-British negotiations and the Joint Declaration. Leaders of the local democracy movement organized the Hong Kong Alliance in Support of the Patriotic Democratic Movement in China, which quickly raised money, mainly through a huge pop concert, to send blankets, sleeping bags, and tents for the students in Beijing. The demonstrations in Beijing also convinced many people of the need to accelerate Hong Kong's own democratization. On May 24, the official members of the Executive and Legislative Councils unanimously agreed that 50 percent of Hong Kong's legislature should be directly elected by 1995 and 100 percent by 2003. Even conservative businesspeople who had normally opposed the introduction of democracy in Hong Kong started to express their support for the students and to hope that political reform in China might accelerate democratization in Hong Kong.

TIANANMEN SQUARE: REACTIONS AND IMPLICATIONS

The Tiananmen Square Massacre on June 4 "sent the whole colony into mourning."[2] Like the millions of people across the world who saw images of the massacre on television, people in Hong Kong were shocked, disgusted, and horrified. They also worried that something similar could happen in Hong Kong after 1997. In the largest public demonstration in Hong Kong's history, almost one million people—many of them dressed in the traditional Chinese mourning colors of black and white or wearing black armbands—marched in the streets to support the fallen demonstrators and to condemn the PRC leadership. The protests brought out all elements of Hong Kong's population, including otherwise apolitical businesspeople, pro-Beijing trade unionists, and employees of the Bank of China and pro-Beijing newspapers. The cenotaph in Central District honoring Hong Kong's war dead was covered with flowers and black flags. Many people donated blood. Others tried to force a run on local PRC banks by withdrawing all their deposits. The Alliance in Support of the Patriotic Democratic Movement in China received more than thirty million Hong Kong dollars in donations to support prodemocracy activities in the PRC.

Tiananmen Square changed local attitudes toward the 1997 transition and the Chinese government. Older Chinese who had left the mainland before or after the Communists took over in 1949 had often kept their negative views of the PRC. But many younger people had been convinced that the Chinese government had changed, especially after Deng Xiaoping's reforms in the late 1970s. Tiananmen Square, however, caused many Hong Kong people to lose all faith in the PRC government and in Hong Kong's future. This was reflected in how the stock market dropped by 25 percent and property values sank while applications for immigration visas soared, and in surveys later that year that showed how confidence in the PRC not to make changes after 1997 had plummeted. Democratic Party leader Martin Lee compared handing over Hong Kong people to China with surrendering Jews to Adolf Hitler's Germany. Lydia Dunn, a prominent businesswoman and member of the Executive Council, asked how the British could in good conscience surrender "British citizens to a regime that did not hesitate to use its tanks and forces on its own people."

The initial British reaction to the Tiananmen Square Massacre was shock. Prime Minister Margaret Thatcher expressed "utter revulsion and outrage" at the killings, promising to help assuage the concerns of Hong Kong people by relaxing British immigration laws. In July 1989, the British government unilaterally suspended the Sino-British Joint Liaison Group meetings scheduled for that summer. Nevertheless, the British insisted that the 1984 Joint Declaration remained in force and that Beijing had pledged to keep Hong Kong autonomous for fifty years. And there was little the British government could do. When Thatcher raised the Hong Kong situation that summer at several international forums, the *People's Daily* accused the British of trying to use international support to keep China from recovering Hong Kong. The British did, however, take several measures designed to appease the international community and to restore confidence in Hong Kong: a nationality plan that would encourage people to stay in Hong Kong, the acceleration of representative government, and a Bill of Rights that would continue after 1997.

British officials, Hong Kong government officials, and local business leaders realized that a sudden exodus from Hong Kong could have catastrophic results. The Legislative and Executive Councils thus launched the "Hong Kong is Our Home" campaign, asking the British government to give full British citizenship, with right of abode, to the 3.25 million British subjects in Hong Kong and to help the rest find homes elsewhere, the idea being to keep people in Hong Kong by giving them the option to leave if conditions soured after 1997. Not surprising given the rising unemployment rate in Britain, Thatcher's government rejected this request, which the Chinese government would have considered an insult to its guarantees in the Joint Declaration. In July 1989, Foreign Secretary Geoffrey Howe visited Hong Kong, where he discounted the possibility of granting full citizenship. Instead, the British government reluctantly agreed to Governor David Wilson's request to grant British citizenship to fifty thousand qualified people in important positions and their direct dependents for up to a total 225,000 Hong Kong residents.

Announced in December 1989, the British Nationality (Hong Kong) Act offered full British nationality to fifty thousand such people and their families. (With two-thirds from the private sector and one-third from the public sector, the number of people to be granted British citizenship was a compromise between the Foreign Office, which wanted as many as possible, and the Home Office, which wanted as few as possible.) The Chinese government accused the British of violating the Joint Declaration and the Basic Law, insisting that it would not recognize these people as British citizens after 1997. As it turned out, the nationality package drew considerably fewer applicants than the British and Hong Kong governments had expected, mainly because most people realized that the scheme was devised to convince them to stay in Hong Kong and because the PRC insisted that it would not honor the consular protection rights of the new passports.

The Bill of Rights, enacted in June 1991, was another part of the British government's attempt to restore confidence in Hong Kong. The Chinese government opposed the bill from the outset, insisting that it violated the law and the spirit of the Joint Declaration and that the Basic Law already provided sufficient protection. Local jurists disagreed, however, and in October 1989 Governor Wilson announced that the government would introduce a new Bill of Rights that would enshrine the provisions of the International Covenant on Civil and Political Rights; the International Covenant on Economic, Social, and Cultural Rights; and the International Labour Conventions. The Chinese understandably took the bill as an insult. Not only did it question the sincerity of their promise to maintain Hong Kong's existing economic and political systems, but the British had waited until the last decade of their rule in Hong Kong to introduce such a bill. PRC officials now claimed the right to review and repeal all Hong Kong laws (including the Bill of Rights) that violated the Basic Law.

Although the Chinese government was eager to restore confidence in Hong Kong after the Tiananmen Square Massacre and reiterated its promise that Hong Kong would not change after 1997, it condemned Hong Kong people for sending money to the striking students and accused them of helping the students try to overthrow the Chinese government. Some PRC officials even referred to the Tiananmen Square demonstrations as a joint U.S.–Hong Kong plot. The Chinese government also purged several local Communist groups that had supported the demonstrators and had participated in the Hong Kong protests. On July 11, 1989, new CCP general secretary Jiang Zemin cautioned that "the well water does not interfere with the river water," implying that since China would not try to introduce Socialism into Hong Kong after 1997, Hong Kong should not try to force democracy and capitalism into China, and warning Hong Kong people not to interfere in mainland politics. On July 21, the *People's Daily* condemned Martin Lee and Szeto Wah, the two founders of the Alliance in Support of the Patriotic Democratic Movement in China, for directing "subversive activities" against the Chinese government. The Chinese government excluded Lee and Szeto from the Basic Law Drafting Committee (although this gave the two men even more support in Hong Kong) and urged the Hong Kong government to ban the alliance. Although the Hong Kong government argued that such alliances were perfectly legal in Hong Kong, on October 23

William Ehrman, Hong Kong's political advisor, assured Ji Shaoxiang, head of the New China News Agency Hong Kong branch's foreign affairs department, that the Hong Kong government had "no intention of allowing Hong Kong to be used as a base for subversive activities" against China.

THE AIRPORT CONTROVERSY

The Tiananmen Square Massacre undermined the already tenuous trust between the British and Chinese governments and harmed Sino-British relations for the next few years. It also created an atmosphere of distrust and suspicion between the Hong Kong and Chinese governments. In the fall of 1989, for example, a dispute arose over the case of Yang Yang, a Chinese swimmer who had sought asylum in Hong Kong and claimed to be a member of a prodemocracy organization in China. When the Hong Kong government refused the Chinese government's demand to repatriate Yang, the Chinese government refused to accept Chinese illegal immigrants arrested in Hong Kong. This caused great anxiety in both Hong Kong, where many people feared that the news would encourage an influx of illegal immigrants, and in Guangdong, where officials worried that their province would be overrun by unemployed people from all over China en route to Hong Kong.

The Yang incident faded from importance by late October, but tensions between the Hong Kong and Chinese governments were inflamed that month when Governor Wilson announced a plan to build a new airport and container port at Chek Lap Kok, off of Lantau Island. The existing airport at Kai Tak in Kowloon could not be expanded, and Hong Kong had recently passed Rotterdam to become the world's busiest container port. The Port and Airport Development Strategy (PADS) project would cost almost HK$130 billion and would take until 2006 to complete, although the first stage (the airport) would be completed by 1997. Wilson later denied such assertions, but many observers saw the project as an attempt to restore public confidence in Hong Kong's future, especially since Wilson announced the project the same month that he initiated the process for drafting the Bill of Rights.

In the wake of the Tiananmen Square Massacre, the PADS project almost immediately became a source of contention between Britain and China. Insisting that it was supposed to be consulted on all policies that would affect post-1997 Hong Kong, the Chinese government saw the project as a clever scheme to make it pay for any construction not completed by 1997. As Jiang Zemin put it, "You invite the guests, but I pay the bill." On April 27, 1990, Guo Fengmin, the new Chinese head of the Joint Liaison Group, insisted that China be consulted on all major decisions. In August Ji Pengfei, director of the Chinese State Council's Hong Kong and Macau Affairs Office, asked Britain to send a delegation to Beijing to discuss the airport project. The British government, which saw the airport as an internal economic issue that required no approval from either the British or the Chinese governments, accused China of withholding support as a way to force Britain to curb democratization in Hong Kong. Still, in September 1990 Lord Caithness, British minister for Hong Kong, suddenly visited Hong Kong and declared that Beijing should be consulted on the airport project and ordered the Hong Kong government to provide information about the project to Chinese officials.

Even before the PRC airport delegation arrived, however, in October the Hong Kong government announced that the first stage of the project, the construction of the Lantau Bridge, would proceed as scheduled with public money. After the Chinese government refused to endorse the project, Governor Wilson visited Beijing in January 1991 to discuss the airport project. Wilson now stressed that the Hong Kong government was ready to be flexible and agreed on the need to consult China on any such projects transcending July 1997. In April, British foreign secretary Douglas Hurd—the most senior British official to visit China after the Tiananmen Square Massacre—went to Beijing to discuss the airport project. Finally, in June, Percy Cradock, foreign policy advisor to Prime Minister John Major, led a secret mission to Beijing to discuss the airport issue. Meanwhile, Governor Wilson visited London, where he met with Major and other senior British officials.

After more than a year and a half, an elaborate compromise was finally reached. On June 30, 1991, Cradock initialed a memorandum of understanding with the Chinese, and on July 4 Wilson announced a Sino-British accord on the airport project: Hong Kong would pay for the first part of the project, a PRC official would participate in the planning and construction, British and Chinese foreign ministers would meet twice a year, and Prime Minister Major would visit China as a gesture of respect (making him the first major Western leader to visit China after the Tiananmen Square Massacre). On September 3, 1991, Major went to Beijing, where he signed the Memorandum of Understanding with Premier Li Peng. Although the memorandum eased tensions between Britain and China, many people in Hong Kong considered it an unnecessary concession that would give China excessive influence over Hong Kong's finances before 1997.

COPING WITH 1997

The people of Hong Kong had no say in the compromises between Britain and China following the Tiananmen Square Massacre. One proposal, which the PRC government would have never accepted but which revealed the sense of frustration and helplessness in Hong Kong, called for urging China to lease the region to the United Nations for one hundred years. Some observers even posited a connection between this sense of malaise and Hong Kong's rising divorce rate, which doubled from 1983 to 1992. And even if they did not worry about a brutal crackdown such as that at Tiananmen Square, many people justifiably worried that PRC officials simply did not understand Hong Kong well enough. In 1988, Xu Jiatun, then sitting director of the Hong Kong branch of the New China News Agency, admitted that had he not lived and worked in Hong Kong for four years, he would have had the same ignorant views of capitalism as his comrades on the mainland. In March 1995, Li Ruihan, a member of the Standing Committee of the Chinese Politburo, admitted that Chinese leaders lacked an understanding of what had made Hong Kong so successful. Li compared the recovery of Hong Kong with a story about a woman who had agreed to sell a hundred-year-old teapot that was famous for the tea it dispensed. Not realizing that the tea's flavor derived from the residue that had built up inside, she scrubbed and polished the teapot. When the purchaser came to claim his teapot, he declared it worthless. As Li explained, "if you don't understand something, you are unaware of what makes it valuable and it will be difficult to keep it intact."[3]

The crackdown at Tiananmen Square and the uncertainty surrounding 1997 created such a panic that many Hong Kong people responded with two main strategies: by voting with their feet and by voting with the ballot. Emigration was part of a longer-term pattern rather than just a reaction to the Tiananmen Square Massacre, but the number of emigrants rose dramatically from 40,000 in 1989 to 65,000 in 1990, cresting at 66,000 in 1992. From 1984 to the eve of the transition, around 10 percent of Hong Kong's population left—mainly for Australia, Canada, and the United States but also to Britain, New Zealand, and Singapore. (When the Singapore government announced after the Tiananmen Square Massacre that it would allow 25,000 Hong Kong families to immigrate over the next five to eight years, more than 10,000 people showed up the next day at the Singapore consulate.) By the early 1990s, there were approximately 58,000 Hong Kong–born people in Australia, 500,000 in Canada, and 147,000 in the United States—mostly concentrated in large cities such as Sydney, San Francisco, Los Angeles, New York, Vancouver, and Toronto. And even though various British immigration acts from the 1960s to the 1980s slowed immigration to Britain, by the mid-1990s Chinese comprised the third-largest ethnic group in Britain.

Although many emigrants returned after obtaining foreign citizenship, this mass emigration both expanded Hong Kong communities overseas and created two new types of family structures: astronaut households and parachute kids. Also a Cantonese pun meaning a man with an absentee wife, the term "astronauts" refers to fathers who have moved their families but who continue to shuttle back and forth for business between Hong Kong and their new adoptive countries; parachute kids are the offspring of parents who have returned to Hong Kong but who leave their children overseas for safety. Scholars have suggested that both arrangements complicate the idea of where home actually lies and demonstrate a reluctance to sever completely all ties with Hong Kong. Perhaps the economic factor is even more important: these families quickly learned that they could not make as much money in their new adoptive countries as they could in Hong Kong.

Even while the Tiananmen Square Massacre drove many people out of Hong Kong, it created a political awakening by bringing more people into local politics. Although this new interest in politics was based on concern for the crackdown in Beijing, it also reflected fears about what the PRC authorities could do in Hong Kong after 1997. According to a poll in February 1994, 58 percent of respondents were satisfied with the performance of the Hong Kong government, but only 29 percent were satisfied with the performance of the PRC government in China. As sociologist Alvin So explains, the Tiananmen Square Massacre "led to an explosion in Hong Kong's civil society." All sorts of new civic organizations were founded, and student movements were revived. After the Tiananmen Square Massacre, "the terms *democracy* and *democrats* became hegemonic in Hong Kong's political discourse," as even conservative businesspeople and pro-Beijing leftists changed their minds about democratization.[4] The Tiananmen Square Massacre also helped strengthen the existing sense of Hong Kong identity. It reminded many people that although they were ethnically Chinese, they did not identify with the Communist government of China. "Hong Kong people," argue political scientists Lynn White and Li Cheng, "became more fully Chinese in that year, even while their disaffection with the Chinese government soared and while they looked internationally for safe havens they might later need."[5]

After the Tiananmen Square Massacre, the British were under great local and international pressure to speed up Hong Kong's democratization. But China opposed the recommendation by the official members of the Executive and Legislative Councils for 50 percent of Hong Kong's legislature to be directly elected by 1995 and 100 percent by 2003. In January 1990, Governor Wilson convinced Premier Li Peng and other Chinese officials in Beijing that not increasing the number of directly elected Legislative Council members in 1991 would undermine public confidence in both the Hong Kong government and in Beijing's post-1997 political plans. As a compromise, the British agreed to allow eighteen directly elected Legislative Council seats in 1991, while China would allow twenty directly elected seats in the HKSAR council in 1997, twenty-four in 1999, and thirty by 2003. In March 1991, more than 424,000 (32.5 percent of the electorate) voted in the District Board elections. In May, more than 393,000 (23 percent of the electorate) voted in the Urban Council and Regional Council elections. Although less than 40 percent (some 750,000 people) of registered voters turned out, the first direct elections to the Legislative Council, held in September 1991, showed many Hong Kong people's feelings toward the PRC government. The most important issue was the candidates' reaction to the Tiananmen Square Massacre. Prodemocracy candidates won as handily as all the pro-Beijing candidates lost. The United Democrats—formed in 1990 and led by Martin Lee, Szeto Wah, Yeung Sum (a professor of social work), Ng Sung-man (a doctor), Lee Wing-tat (a teacher), Siu Yin-ying (a union leader), and Ng Ming-yum (an educator)—won twelve of the eighteen seats.

The September 1991 elections were so humiliating to China that Lu Ping, director of the Hong Kong and Macau Affairs Office of the PRC State Council, warned Governor Wilson not to appoint Martin Lee or Szeto Wah to the Executive Council. Adding insult to injury, on October 1, the PRC's National Day, most of the directly elected legislative councilors protested against China's treatment of political prisoners. Although in March 1992 Lu Ping encouraged Hong Kong people to become involved in local party politics, in June Guo Fengmin, the Chinese head of the Joint Liaison Group, opposed the possibility of Martin Lee being appointed to the Executive Council. Wilson insisted that such appointments were the prerogative of the governor alone, but in deference to China none of the United Democrat leaders was invited to join the Executive Council.

THE LAST IMPERIALIST: CHRIS PATTEN'S REFORMS

Into this politically and emotionally charged atmosphere stepped the last colonial governor of Hong Kong, Chris Patten. Nicknamed "the last imperialist" because he had been sent to manage Britain's withdrawal from its final major colony, Patten, when he arrived in the summer of 1992, made it clear from the start that he would be a different governor. Not only did he dispense with the traditional governor's uniform and regalia, but he was also the first Hong Kong governor to be a political appointee, having been given the post of governor by his friend John Major for helping the Conservative Party win the 1992 elections as chairman of the party (although he had lost his own seat in the House of Commons).

As a political appointee, Patten had more political clout than earlier governors. In early October 1992 he announced a range of proposals for political reforms in 1994/1995 that would widen the electoral base of the functional constituencies and strengthen representation in the Legislative Council. The reforms would include raising the number of directly elected Legislative Council seats from eighteen to twenty (in accordance with the Basic Law), eliminating all appointed seats to the Municipal Councils and District Boards, widening the electoral base of the twenty-one functional constituencies by replacing corporate voting with individual voting and adding nine new functional constituencies, combining multiple-seat geographic constituencies into single-seat constituencies, and reducing the voting age from twenty-one to eighteen (as in Britain and China).

Given how long and hard the British had argued against political reform in Hong Kong, many critics—and not just in the PRC government—argued that Patten arrived in Hong Kong with a mandate from the British government to engineer an honorable withdrawal from Hong Kong, to curb anti-British feeling stemming from the uncertainty after the Tiananmen Square Massacre, and to help maintain British influence after 1997. But Patten's proposed reforms also reflected the desires of many liberal politicians in Hong Kong. In May 1992, Martin Lee and Yeung Sum, chairman and vice chairman of the United Democrats, went to Britain, where they met with John Major and governor-designate Patten to discuss the possibility of increasing the number of directly elected seats in the 1995 election. As Patten put it, he was trying to work within the "grey areas" in the Basic Law, giving Hong Kong people as much control over their own affairs as possible while ensuring certainty about Hong Kong's post-1997 future. "The reality," argues Leo Goodstadt, "was that, by the late 1990s, it was obvious that without an expansion of the public's participation in the process of government, the credibility of Hong Kong's political institutions could not be maintained and there would be a crisis of governability."[6]

Patten's reforms were not as radical as he made them seem, for less than one-third of the Legislative Council would be elected directly. But the reforms exceeded what China had in mind and broke with the (albeit rather new) practice of consulting with China over any political arrangements that would affect post-1997 Hong Kong. The Chinese government, which distrusted Patten from the start, claimed that his proposals violated the Joint Declaration, the Basic Law, and the understanding between the British foreign secretary and the Chinese foreign minister in 1990. Patten's reforms made him very popular in Hong Kong, however, especially among ordinary people. Although Beijing demanded that Patten be replaced, the British knew that doing so would hurt their prestige, not just in Hong Kong but also among the international community. In March 1993, China agreed to negotiate with Britain over electoral arrangements for the 1994/1995 elections. The Chinese were willing to lower the voting age but not to end the practice of appointing members to the Municipal Councils and District Boards, insisting that this should be a matter for the post-1997 government to decide. The Chinese also wanted the continuation of corporate voting, since they wanted business and financial interests to be represented in the Legislative Council. The Chinese accepted proposals for a single-seat, single-vote for the Municipal Councils and the District Boards, but they wanted to postpone plans for the Legislative Council.

Despite seventeen rounds of negotiations, the two sides failed to reach an agreement. After publishing the negotiations in a parliamentary white paper and insisting that their proposals were what Hong Kong people wanted, in November 1993 the British pushed through a modified version of Patten's proposal, giving the PRC only a few days' notice while hoping to continue the negotiations. The PRC ended the negotiations and announced its "second stove" (the Chinese terms for setting up a new household) policy, insisting that all of Patten's reforms would be replaced by new institutions after 1997. The PRC also preemptively formed the Preliminary Working Committee to look into appointing the HKSAR Preparatory Committee to handle arrangements for Hong Kong after July 1, 1997. Led by Vice Premier and Foreign Minister Qian Qichen, all fifty-seven members of the Preliminary Working Committee either were from the PRC political machinery or were Hong Kong residents known for opposing Patten's proposals. The Chinese charged the British with being insincere and violating the Sino-British agreements and understandings, blaming them for the collapse of the negotiations. With the support of the Legislative Council, which voted 32 to 24 in late June 1994 in favor of his proposals, Patten then decided to proceed unilaterally with his proposals for District Board and Municipal Council elections in 1994 and elections for the Legislative Council in 1995. Beijing responded by declaring that the last Legislative Council elected under Patten's reforms would be dissolved after the 1997 transition and replaced by the Provisional Legislative Council appointed by a four hundred-member selection committee. This dashed any hopes for a through train of legislators who would serve through the transition until mid-1999.

Overlooking the earlier tensions after the Tiananmen Square Massacre and over the airport project, many critics blamed Patten for ending a decade of Sino-British understanding. Patten's supporters, however, insisted that Beijing was simply using his reforms to enhance its control over Hong Kong before the transition. Both sides underestimated the complexity of Patten's dilemma: he wanted to make the British look good and obtain the support of Hong Kong people by introducing democracy and to come off better than Wilson (who was seen by many in Hong Kong and Britain as having been too willing to give in to the PRC), all while trying to keep on good terms with the PRC government, which refused to believe that Patten could be sincere about political reform. To make things worse for Patten, London suddenly tried to patch things up with Beijing in 1995 by withdrawing support for his reforms.

Regardless, Patten's proposals led to years of friction and mistrust between Beijing and London, with each side insisting that it had adhered to both the Joint Declaration and the Basic Law. Because Beijing was afraid that the Hong Kong democracy movement would revive the democracy movement on the mainland, it took a much stronger stance against Hong Kong's democratic reforms than it had before the Tiananmen Square demonstrations. Some Chinese officials saw Patten's proposal not only as a violation of the Joint Declaration and the Basic Law but also as an attempt to maintain British influence and even to help destabilize China by introducing democratization. China also accused Britain of violating certain secret agreements that the British claimed they had never made. Beijing came up with an anti-imperialist discourse not seen since the days of the Cultural Revolution, including colorful names for Patten—such as "liar," "serpent," "prostitute," "two-headed snake," "sinner of the millennium," and "tango dancer"—for introducing democracy only after 150 years of colonialism and for violating the Joint Declaration and the Basic Law. It also supported the Democratic Alliance for Betterment of Hong Kong, a local grassroots political group that had been established soon after Patten arrived in Hong Kong in 1992.

Although Sino-British relations improved somewhat after 1995, with agreements on the Court of Final Appeal and the new airport project, they were far from smooth. After Qian Qichen visited Britain in October 1995, the British and Chinese foreign ministers agreed to work together on matters dealing with Hong Kong. Patten pledged to help the Preparatory Committee and whoever was appointed to be the HKSAR's chief executive. Lu Ping, director of the PRC's Hong Kong and Macau Affairs Office, visited Hong Kong in March 1996, while Anson Chan, Hong Kong's chief secretary, went to Beijing the following month. However, the two sides could not agree on arrangements for the handover ceremony in July 1997. The Hong Kong government was reluctant to transfer certain information about government departments to the PRC. It also steadfastly opposed the establishment of the provisional legislature, insisting that Hong Kong could not have two legislative bodies at once.

When Beijing and London began working together directly to plan for the 1997 transition, Chris Patten became gradually marginalized. (Percy Cradock called this the "spectacle of the incredible shrinking governor.") Nevertheless, his reforms had several important effects in Hong Kong. They benefited the prodemocracy forces since the Democrats controlled almost half of the Legislative Council seats after 1995. Patten's proposals led to conflict between Britain and China, but they also represented the desires of many Hong Kong people, which could be seen in the results of the Legislative Council elections of 1995. In September, 36 percent of Hong Kong's registered voters turned out, many of them voting against candidates seen as being pro-Beijing, such as the Democratic Alliance for Betterment of Hong Kong. Pro-Beijing candidates won only sixteen out of sixty seats. Martin Lee's Democratic Party, despite its electoral successes, did not win power, but prodemocracy candidates such as Lee, Szeto Wah, Lau Chin-shek, and Emily Lau became the most popular members of the Legislative Council.

On the one hand, Patten's reforms increased political participation through regular channels so dramatically that "voting had become a socially acceptable behavior."[7] On the other hand, the reforms promoted a contested democracy since Beijing, irate at Patten for violating the Joint Declaration, appointed prominent businesspeople as local advisors to the Preliminary Working Committee. In late January 1996, Beijing established the Hong Kong Preparatory Committee, as stipulated in the Basic Law. Led by Vice Premier and Foreign Minister Qian Qichen, the committee consisted of 150 members (56 from the mainland and 94 from Hong Kong). Many of the Hong Kong members were businessmen known for being pro-Beijing; 28 came from political parties or political groups such as the New Hong Kong Alliance, the Hong Kong Progressive Alliance, the Democratic Alliance for Betterment of Hong Kong, the Liberal Democratic Foundation, and the Association for Democracy and People's Livelihood. Most of the Hong Kong people were members of the Chinese People's Political Consultative Conference (the PRC's main political advisory board) and the National People's Congress. The most glaring absence was that of the Democratic Party, even though it was the largest political party in the Legislative Council: Martin Lee's criticism of Beijing and support for Patten's reforms led Beijing to exclude his party from the committee.

In November 1996, the Preparatory Committee formed a four hundred-member Selection Committee to pick the HKSAR's first chief executive and the Provisional Legislative Council. This committee was also overwhelmingly big business (including heavyweights such as Li Ka-shing, Walter Kwok, Gordon Wu, Stanley Ho, and Lee Shau-kee). In December, the Selection Committee created an unelected provisional legislature for after June 30, 1997, drawing protests from both the Hong Kong and British governments. The Preparatory Committee tried to make this provisional body look like a Hong Kong Legislative Council: more than half of the sixty members were on the pre-existing Legislative Council (four members of the Association for Democracy and People's Livelihood were included, although no one from Martin Lee's Democratic Party was). However, ten of the defeated pro-PRC candidates from the 1995 elections were appointed to the provisional council, while 85 percent of the appointees were on the Selection Committee. When a Hong Kong member of the Preparatory Committee voted against establishing the provisional legislature, Chinese officials declared that he would be barred from that committee as well as from the committee for selecting the chief executive of post-1997 Hong Kong.

Patten's reforms may have also prompted Beijing to take a tougher approach to Hong Kong and to show that it would not tolerate criticism and dissent. In August 1994, the Chinese government closed down the Beijing branch of Giordano, a chain of clothing stores owned by colorful Hong Kong entrepreneur Jimmy Lai. Also the founder of *Next Magazine*, Hong Kong's best-selling weekly, Lai had routinely criticized the PRC leadership, even calling Premier Li Peng "a turtle's egg with a zero IQ" and "a national shame." The reforms also fueled the general sense of uncertainty that pervaded Hong Kong in the mid-1990s. There was a serious concern about whether upper-level civil servants would be able to keep their posts after 1997, especially those who had supported Patten's proposals. And rather than helping Britain make an honorable withdrawal from Hong Kong, the reforms drew attention to its historical failures. In October 1996, for example, Lee Cheuk-yan, a Legislative Council member known for his anti-Beijing views, criticized the British for waiting so long to introduce democracy.

THE RACE FOR HKSAR CHIEF EXECUTIVE

With the Provisional Legislative Council selected, in December 1996 Premier Li Peng appointed Tung Chee-hwa, a former shipping magnate, as the chief executive who would run Hong Kong after the transition. The selection process for chief executive had not been democratic, but it was designed to involve the entire Hong Kong community, with the candidates meeting all the main political parties and interest groups. Interviews with the Selection Committee were broadcast on television and viewed widely. The campaign also showed how many of the same elites who had previously urged the British to try to hold on to Hong Kong changed their allegiance after the Joint Declaration in 1984. T. S. Lo (son of Eurasian lawyer Lo Man Kam), who started going by his Chinese name, Lo Tak-shing, took a PRC passport in the early 1990s and gave up his British citizenship and his title of Commander of the British Empire. When Lo, whose popularity rating was only around 1 percent, withdrew, Simon Li, former justice and director of the Bank of East Asia (and nephew of Li Tse-fong, whom we met in chapter 5), entered the race. Li supported the Provisional Legislative Council and tightening public security to maintain Hong Kong's stability and prosperity. Chief Justice Ti-liang Yang, who gave up his British knighthood, warned against challenging the PRC's supremacy. Peter Woo, son-in-law of late shipping tycoon Y. K. Pao, checked with Beijing before announcing his intention to run.

The selection of Tung, who won 80 percent of the votes, surprised no one. Many pundits had considered his selection a done deal when Chinese president and CCP general secretary Jiang Zemin singled him out for an exceptionally cordial handshake at an earlier meeting in Beijing. While many critics, particularly in the Western media, scoffed at Tung's lack of political experience and dismissed him as a Beijing lackey, some Chinese leaders and pro-Beijing forces in Hong Kong were concerned about his political reliability (he had old family connections with Taiwan). The American press in particular dismissed him as Beijing's man, but, as local journalist Frank Ching argued on the eve of the handover, all colonial governors had been appointed by London, without any consultation with Hong Kong people; at least Tung's appointment involved some consultation with Hong Kong people.[8]

Born in Shanghai, Tung was educated there and in Hong Kong and Britain and worked in the United States in the 1960s. Although his father had been driven out of China after the 1949 revolution and went to Hong Kong, where he built a shipping empire that his son would inherit, he sent his son to a pro-Beijing school in Hong Kong. The younger Tung had old ties to the PRC government, for the Bank of China had helped rescue his firm, Orient Overseas, from bankruptcy in the 1980s. He had been a member of the Consultative Committee for the Basic Law Drafting Committee and had been nominated to the Chinese People's Political Consultative Committee by the Hong Kong and Macau Affairs Office and by the New China News Agency local branch. He also had considerable business and political experience in Hong Kong. Although he was not widely known until the campaign in late 1996, he was among the first group of Hong Kong advisors chosen by Beijing in 1992 and became a member of Patten's Executive Council the same year after the PRC government recommended Tung indirectly (although he ultimately resigned from this position to avoid any conflict of interest with his position on the Preparatory Committee).

Shortly after his selection as chief executive and while Patten was still governor, Tung appointed his Executive Council designed to satisfy both Hong Kong people and PRC interests, partly by retaining two members of Patten's Executive Council. By not including any of the Democrats on his council, however, Tung prompted complaints that the new Executive Council was no different from the old colonial one. He also drew fire for supporting Chinese proposals to limit political expression in Hong Kong. Frequently emphasizing social order when talking about civil liberties, Tung consistently defended his attitudes toward public demonstrations and protests in Hong Kong by invoking his memories of protests in the United States, where he "saw what happened with the slow erosion of authority" as "society became less orderly than is desirable." Throughout his campaign for chief executive, he had insisted that Hong Kong people cared more about housing and education than about politics and protests. He had warned that freedom of expression might have to be sacrificed in order to prevent international forces from interfering in the handover. He was also criticized for opposing foreign donations to local political parties, even though he had donated heavily to the British Conservative Party in the 1992 general election.

THE COUNTDOWN ENDS

At 8:00 P.M. on June 30, 1997, the most expensive fireworks display in all of history exploded over Hong Kong's Victoria Harbour. Shortly afterward, as four thousand guests sat down to an elegant banquet at the newly built harbor-front Convention Centre in Wanchai, troops of the People's Liberation Army (PLA) crossed the border to assume their positions in the Hong Kong garrison. Led by Charles, Prince of Wales and heir to the British throne, the British delegation to the handover ceremony included Prime Minister Tony Blair, Foreign Secretary Robin Cook, Governor Chris Patten, and General Charles Guthrie, chief of the British General Staff. On the Chinese side sat President Jiang Zemin (Deng Xiaoping had died earlier that year), Premier Li Peng, Vice Premier and Foreign Minister Qian Qichen, PLA chief and vice chairman of the Central Military Commission General Zhang Wannian, and Tung Chee-hwa. Among the guests were representatives from all over the world. In what a Guangzhou newspaper described as "the battle of the century for the Chinese and foreign media," thousands of journalists came to cover this historic occasion and the festivities surrounding it. Accompanied by renowned French-born, Chinese American cellist Yo-Yo Ma and a children's choir from the mainland, the Hong Kong Philharmonic played *Symphony 1997*, written specially for the handover by mainland composer Tan Dun.

After the colonial Hong Kong flag was lowered at 11:30 P.M., Prince Charles began his speech, much of which dealt with the guarantees enshrined in the 1984 Sino-British Declaration. The prince explained that Hong Kong's "dynamism and stability" had made its economy "the envy of the world" and had shown how "East and West can live and work together." The "solemn pledges made before the world in the 1984 Joint Declaration," declared Prince Charles, would "guarantee the continuity of Hong Kong's way of life." He promised that Britain would "maintain its unwavering support for the Joint Declaration." As midnight and the end of British rule drew near, the prince promised the people of Hong Kong that "we shall not forget you, and we shall watch with the closest interest as you embark on this new era of your remarkable history."[9]

At midnight, July 1, the British flag was lowered and the Chinese flag raised, accompanied by the new flag of the Hong Kong SAR, emblazoned with a bauhinia flower, the official symbol of the new SAR. Approximately half a mile away, the camp commander of the British Forces headquarters in Hong Kong turned over the building to the PLA. President Jiang Zemin, the first PRC leader to visit Hong Kong, declared that July 1, 1997, would "go down in the annals of history as a day that merits eternal memory." Jiang explained that the "return of Hong Kong to the motherland after going through a century of vicissitudes indicates that from now on, the Hong Kong compatriots have become true masters of this Chinese land and that Hong Kong has now entered a new era of development." He promised that the PRC government would "unswervingly" abide by the one country, two systems concept.[10]

In his inaugural speech, Tung Chee-hwa, the first Chinese to administer Hong Kong in more than 150 years, declared that "for the first time in history, we, the people of Hong Kong, will be master of our own destiny." Stressing how "Hong Kong and China are whole again," Tung reassured his new constituency and the world that "we value this empowerment and we will exercise our powers prudently and responsibly."[11] Shortly after the handover ceremony, the British delegation left the former colony on the Royal Yacht *Britannia* and on HMS *Chatham*. As Patten and his family waved farewell to the crowds assembled at the dock, the Royal Marines band played "Rule Britannia" and "Land of Hope and Glory." In a display of military might not seen since the celebrations for Queen Elizabeth's coronation in 1953, early in the morning of July 1 four thousand troops and twenty personnel carriers of the PLA crossed the border. Other troops arrived by helicopters and naval ships.

Like any historical event, the handover meant something different to the various parties involved. For Britain, it marked the end of what had once been the world's greatest empire, by now limited mainly to Gibraltar and a dozen or so small islands scattered across the oceans of the world. "Under menacing monsoon skies," the BBC television news reported on June 30, "Hong Kong woke up to its final day of British rule and to an appointment with uncertain destiny."[12] In a rain-drenched, emotional ceremony held on June 30 at the former British naval base, Patten declared the day a "cause for celebration not for sorrow." Emphasizing Hong Kong's "promise" and "unshakeable destiny," he insisted that "the story of this great city is about the years before this night and the years of success that will surely follow it."[13] Royal Marines bandsmen in white tropical uniforms lined up with kilted pipers from the Black Watch and the Scottish Division and with musicians from the Gurkhas and the Scots Guards for one final tattoo. Thousands of spectators watched members of the British Army, the Royal Air Force, and the Royal Navy march before Prince Charles, Patten, and other British representatives. As the rain came down, the Union Jack was lowered. Conspicuously missing from this ceremony was Tung Chee-hwa, who was greeting President Jiang Zemin. Tung had insisted before the ceremony that his absence should not be considered a slight to the British, but it nonetheless symbolized Hong Kong's new political status. And instead of driving three times round the driveway of Government House—an old tradition signifying that a colonial governor would return—this time Patten's limousine did not make a third circuit.

Yet the handover had also brought Britain a new sense of prestige and respect. In the years counting down to 1997, the British, who had not introduced political representation until late in their rule in Hong Kong, were magically transformed—particularly in the Western media—into stalwarts of democratic reform, especially compared to the PRC regime. Any concerns

Governor Chris Patten receiving the British and Hong Kong colonial flags, June 30, 1997. Photo courtesy of Tim Ko.

about the colonial government's history of racial discrimination and lack of political representation were lost in the self-congratulatory assurances that had Hong Kong not become such a prosperous place under the British, the PRC might never have wanted it back in the first place. The BBC report praised Hong Kong as "Britain's legacy, a free market low-tax paradise, the perfect marriage of Chinese energy and benign British administration."[14] Mike Chinoy, Hong Kong bureau chief for news network CNN, noted that American news coverage of the PLA troops marching into Hong Kong "really gave the impression that the butchers of Beijing were arriving," ignoring the "thousands of happy residents in the New Territories who welcomed the PLA."[15]

A huge diplomatic, national, and psychological victory over the unequal treaties imposed by the Western powers in the mid-1800s, the recovery of Hong Kong was a major event in modern Chinese history. Newspapers and posters throughout China celebrated the end of "a century of shame." The front page of the July 1 edition of the *China Daily*, the PRC's official international English-language newspaper, read "Home at Last," with the handover photo cropped so that it centered on the Chinese delegation and omitted Patten. In a ninety-seven-page special issue that the *Guangzhou Daily* promised would become a collector's item, the newspaper declared that the handover was "time for the Chinese nation to wash away one hundred years of shame and feel proud and elated!" The newspaper predicted that July 1 would "draw attention from all over the world, and be inscribed in history books forever."

The historic nature and political urgency of the transition was inscribed in the Hong Kong Clock, a gigantic clock installed by the PRC government in 1994 at the entrance to the Museum of Revolutionary History, in the middle of Tiananmen Square, to count down the days, hours, minutes, and seconds to the return of Hong Kong. This placement of the clock, argued China scholar Michael Yahuda in 1996, "was done as a public reminder to the people of Hong Kong that they were due to be embraced by the motherland under the leadership of the Chinese Communist Party before too long." Yet the clock was also ticking for Beijing, for by placing the clock in "a place of such symbolic meaning," the PRC government "elevated the significance of the transfer to a matter of national pride and significance." Not only was the clock a warning to the people of Hong Kong that their time under colonial rule was almost up, it became "a graphic reminder that the resumption of sovereignty and taking this new step towards national reunification involved matters of the highest prestige that the new leaders would have to manage well and manage soon."[16] As art historian Wu Hung wrote in spring 1997, the clock was "a political statement as well as Beijing's threatening gesture to Hong Kong." A "political timer," the clock warned people in Hong Kong against using democracy as a pretext for trying to subvert Communism in China and "sharply demarcated" Hong Kong's "two alternative identities"—a "foreign colony" or an "integral part of the socialist motherland"—denying it the possibility of a third, alternative identity of its own.[17]

Although most people in China had not paid much attention to Hong Kong until then, the final countdown to 1997 was observed with great enthusiasm, including with multiepisodic television documentaries on Hong Kong. In Beijing, more than twelve hundred miles away, some one hundred thousand carefully chosen guests watched President Jiang's handover speech on gigantic television screens in Tiananmen Square. As the Hong Kong Clock counted down to zero, crowds cheered and fireworks exploded over the square, accompanied by patriotic songs and a traditional lion dance. A poster printed for the occasion showed a smiling Deng Xiaoping, architect of the one country, two systems concept, flanked by the Great Wall of China and Tiananmen Square as he hovered approvingly above Hong Kong's spectacular harbor and skyline. Another poster showed a mainland Chinese mother clasping her small son, who in turn held up the flag of the new Hong Kong SAR. In the background were representatives of China's various ethnic minority groups, all joining together to welcome Hong Kong and to celebrate its new political status.

For Hong Kong people, the handover represented a mixture of pride, apprehension, and nostalgia. As the impending transition to Chinese sovereignty approached, many local artists became more concerned with expressing their local identity and their concern with Hong Kong's uncertain future. One artist, Ho Siu Kee, produced a video performance of a man trying to walk on two balls, suggesting the difficulty of maintaining a balance under the one country, two systems. Another artist, Phoebe Man, produced a satirical mixed-media piece consisting of large Chinese characters repeating the sentence "I am very excited about the '97 return of Hong Kong." For many other artists, the handover prompted a sense of nostalgia and retrospection, captured in their depictions of certain historical places or moments. Particularly in the immediate months leading up to the transition, this sense of nostalgia extended beyond the artistic community. In March 1997, the Hong Kong government issued its last set of stamps bearing the portrait of Queen Elizabeth. More than eleven thousand stamp collectors, many of whom had waited overnight, descended on the General Post Office; an elderly collector collapsed and died in the frenzy. During the weekend of March 8–9—the last weekend during which the grounds of Government House, the governor's official residence, were opened to the public—some one hundred thousand visitors took advantage of this historic occasion.

The different attitudes toward the handover were also manifested in feelings toward emigration, which were shaped by both culture and class. Two years after the handover, sociologist Wong Siu-lun identified four main sets of attitudes toward the reversion to Chinese sovereignty. "Loyalists," who were born in China and came to Hong Kong later in life and who generally hailed from the lower classes, saw the reversion as good for Hong Kong's and China's economies and as a means of reuniting families that had been divided since the 1949 revolution. Born to lower- and working-class families and raised in Hong Kong, "locals" were younger people who had few family ties to China. Politically neutral but attached to the Hong Kong lifestyle of personal freedom and self-expression, they were "firmly attached to Hong Kong" and prepared to "accept the changeover without fanfare." Mostly from working classes, "waverers," who wanted to emigrate but were unable to find countries to accept them, preferred British rule to Chinese rule but were waiting to see what would happen. "Cosmopolitans," usually born in Hong Kong to upper- or middle-class political refugee families that had left China after 1949 and who opposed reunification and preferred British rule, had been planning for 1997 years in advance and already had family ties in the West.[18]

In March 1996, many people had seized one last opportunity to secure their post-1997 future by lining up outside the Hong Kong Immigration Department to apply for naturalization as British Dependent Territory Citizens. Although this Dependent Territory citizenship would expire on June

30, 1997, naturalization would qualify them for a British National (Overseas) passport. These passports do not grant their holders the right to live in Britain, but they enable them to travel without visas to many countries. In 1990 more than three million Hong Kong people held such passports. The Hong Kong government had announced in 1993 that no more applications for naturalization would be accepted after March 31, 1996, and although few people initially accepted the government's offer, by late March so many applicants lined up outside the Immigration Department that the department had to stay open twenty-four hours a day. When the department closed at one minute before midnight on March 31, more than fifty-four thousand people had applied for naturalization. This last day became a public spectacle, especially when a group of rowdy young men had the misfortune of cutting in front of an elderly man who happened to be an expert in martial arts.

By early 1997, however, confidence in Hong Kong's future had increased dramatically. A February survey conducted by the Hong Kong Transition Project at Hong Kong Baptist University found that more than 60 percent of respondents were "optimistic" or "very optimistic" about Hong Kong's future, compared with only 6 percent who were "pessimistic." Moreover, more than 60 percent (as opposed to around 40 percent in February 1993) preferred reunification with China rather than remaining a British colony or becoming independent. Satisfaction with the Chinese government had risen to its highest level (38 percent), although this was only slightly greater than half of the approval rating of the Hong Kong government (73 percent). A survey taken in February 1997 by the *Ming Pao*, a prominent Chinese-language newspaper, showed that the public confidence indicator was as high as it had been before the Tiananmen Square Massacre. Whereas a government survey of November 1994 showed that only 56 percent of the respondents had confidence in Hong Kong's post-1997 future, a similar survey in April 1997 showed that almost 75 percent of the respondents believed that Hong Kong would remain stable and prosperous after the transition.

Much of this (albeit guarded) confidence and optimism stemmed from Hong Kong and China's growing economic interdependence and from China's economic development, which by the late 1980s had helped make Hong Kong the world's third-largest financial center (after London and New York). According to government reports, in 1996 every day more than 26,000 cars, 20 trains, 72 airplanes, and 800 ships traveled between Hong Kong and China. Whereas only 362 Chinese oceangoing ships had arrived in Hong Kong in 1979, almost 20,000 such ships arrived in the first half of 1997. Encouraged by the PRC government after the Tiananmen Square Massacre, in the early 1990s Hong Kong manufacturers relocated even more of their production to Guangdong (in 1979 Hong Kong had almost

900,000 manufacturing employees; by 1997 this number had dropped to around 380,000). Large Hong Kong firms invested in mainland real estate and infrastructure, starting in the Pearl River Delta region but soon spreading throughout China. On the eve of the transition, more than 97,000 Hong Kong residents were working in China.

The largest investor in China, Hong Kong now handled half of China's exports and almost 60 percent of its total foreign investment and provided one-third of its foreign exchange reserves. And whereas in 1986 China was the third-largest investor in Hong Kong (after the United States and Japan), by 1994 it was investing more than twice as much as the United States and Japan combined. More than seventeen hundred Chinese companies were registered in Hong Kong, where Chinese enterprises hired more than fifty thousand people. The increasing commercial importance of China was also reflected in Hong Kong's shifting physical landscape. In March 1990, the Bank of China moved to its new headquarters, a seventy-story aluminum-and-glass tower in the Central District designed by renowned Chinese American architect I. M. Pei. Not only did the Bank of China building, then the world's fifth-tallest building, tower over Hong Kong's main colonial bank, the Hong Kong and Shanghai Bank, but it also cost half as much to build.

Whereas Hong Kong people still harbored reservations about China and its lack of political change, as has so often been the case in modern Chinese history there was nothing like the threat of Japanese nationalism to inspire a sense of Chinese nationalism and patriotism. In the summer of 1996, a Japanese right-wing group placed a lighthouse and a Japanese flag on two of the contested Diaoyutai (Senkaku) Islands. When the local Chinese press declared that the Diaoyutai Islands had fallen, Hong Kong people organized marches and demonstrations and protested outside the Japanese consulate. A group from Hong Kong and Taiwan sent two expeditions to the islands. The first expedition ended tragically on September 26 when its leader, the colorful Hong Kong activist David Chan, drowned while trying to swim ashore, but the second expedition managed to evade a Japanese naval blockade and plant the PRC and Taiwan flags on one of the islands. Whereas some observers saw this "Defend the Diaoyutai" campaign simply as a media attempt to stir up anti-Japanese feelings, others saw it as a way for Hong Kong people to show their Chineseness.

What had not changed significantly was the concern among many parts of the Hong Kong population that the PRC government would try to interfere in Hong Kong affairs after 1997. In January 1997, the Preparatory Committee chose the new provisional legislature, apportioning approximately half the seats to existing Legislative Council members and some of the remaining half to pro-PRC candidates who had lost in the 1995 Legislative Council elections. In the same month, the legal subgroup of the

The Bank of China (left) towering over the Hong Kong and Shanghai Bank (right), circa 2000. Courtesy of Alamy Stock Photography.

Preparatory Committee proposed to repeal or amend more than 10 percent of Hong Kong's 240 existing laws. The February 1997 survey conducted by the Hong Kong Transition Project found that many people were still worried about losing their personal freedom after 1997. In April 1997, the legal subgroup of the Preparatory Committee announced two new post-handover HKSAR ordinances, one requiring demonstrations to have police approval, another requiring local groups to obtain permission for associating with foreign organizations. These measures were widely seen as Beijing's attempts to limit Hong Kong's freedoms. Only half an hour after the handover, members of the Democratic Party, realizing that they would lose access to the building at midnight, staged a peaceful demonstration and an appeal for democracy at the Legislative Council building that put them in the international media. Party leader Martin Lee delivered his own handover speech, calling for the "freedom we are entitled to under the Joint Declaration" and warning that "if there is no democracy there will be no rule of law; if there is no freedom, human rights will not be respected."

The handover had an international impact that stretched far beyond Hong Kong. While many Chinese all over the world celebrated, many others, especially those in cities with large Hong Kong Chinese communities, watched in anxiety as the British flag was lowered. Depending on their views toward reunification with the mainland, for people in Taiwan the handover was either a source of inspiration or a chilling warning of what could happen to them next. In East and Southeast Asia, the handover represented the end of colonialism. Even as their own nations' relations with China improved, many people in these regions saw Hong Kong's transition to Chinese sovereignty as an ominous sign of China's expanding power and a potential threat to their own security. Others feared that Chinese rule would make doing business in Hong Kong more difficult by increasing corruption and curtailing political freedoms. The handover was also watched closely by many Japanese, for whom Hong Kong was the most popular tourist destination; they also worried that Hong Kong was to be surrendered to an authoritarian state and were concerned about China's growing wealth and power in Asia. This explains why on the eve of the handover there were twice as many Japanese journalists as mainland Chinese or British journalists in Hong Kong and why only the local media was larger than the Japanese press corps.

The handover also had important implications for relations between China and the United States. In 1992 the U.S. Congress enacted the United States–Hong Kong Policy Act, which stipulates that the United States would continue to treat Hong Kong as a separate territory after 1997 as long as the president considers Hong Kong "sufficiently autonomous." Also known as the McConnell Act after its author, Republican senator Mitch McConnell from Kentucky, the act called for bilateral ties with Hong Kong and for the American secretary of state to make regular reports, which in the early 1990s expressed support for democratic reform and freedom of expression. While Washington frequently reminded Beijing of its promise to uphold the one country, two systems concept after 1997, Beijing just as frequently reminded Washington that Hong Kong's status was a Chinese matter.

Given all the suspicions and mistrust, why did the transfer of sovereignty proceed as smoothly as it did? At the most basic level, Britain was a lame duck and in no position to try to keep Hong Kong, the Chinese government realized that Hong Kong needed to remain prosperous and knew that the handover was being watched all over the world, and the people of Hong Kong could do little to change the course of history. Even as 1997 represented the end of what PRC leaders frequently referred to as China's "century of humiliation," it represented a new beginning for the PRC as the nation entered an era of rapid economic development, less social control, and improved relations with the rest of the world. The handover was a chance to prove to the world, especially to Taiwan, that China was sincere about the one country, two systems model. The situation was more complicated, however, and involved changing conditions and attitudes in both China and Hong Kong.

Beijing had adopted a new, more conciliatory policy as the handover approached. Hong Kong people's confidence in China was so low in late 1995 that Larry Yung, son of Chinese vice president Rong Yiren, warned that attempts by mainland officials to interfere in Hong Kong's affairs after 1997 could "kill Hong Kong." Subsequently, the PRC government began to take a more reassuring stance. The vice director of the New China News Agency local branch compared Hong Kong's economy to a big cake, insisting that Chinese enterprises were in Hong Kong "not to divide the cake" but to make it "bigger and bigger, sweeter and sweeter." Both Lu Ping, director of the Hong Kong and Macau Affairs Office, and Premier Li Peng, reviled by so many in Hong Kong for his role in the crackdown in Tiananmen Square, declared that the CCP would not send a party secretary to supervise Hong Kong's chief executive. In April 1996, the PRC government invited Anson Chan, who in November 1993 had become the first ethnic Chinese and first female chief secretary of Hong Kong, to Beijing, where Vice Premier Qian Qichen praised Hong Kong's civil servants and urged them to stay in Hong Kong after 1997. Nor did Chinese officials criticize the large number of Hong Kong people applying for British Dependent Territory Citizenship who, if accepted for naturalization, would have to swear allegiance to Queen Elizabeth. The Chinese insisted that the elections for Hong Kong's first chief executive would be open and fair and that the candidate had to be someone acceptable to the people of Hong Kong.

In what Alvin So calls an "antagonistic alliance," Beijing, the new HKSAR government, and the Democratic Party reached a "democratic compromise" just before July 1, even as they continued to disagree on ideological and policy issues.[19] This understanding was based on an agreement to include all the major parties in the post-1997 elections and on a consensus on the need for continued economic prosperity and political stability. On the eve of the 1997 transition, the three biggest political parties in Hong Kong were the Democratic Party, the Democratic Alliance for Betterment of Hong Kong, and the Liberal Party. Headed by Martin Lee, the Democratic Party was prodemocratic and anti-Communist but not opposed to reunification with China (its early slogan was "democratic reunification"). Its leaders were mostly middle-class professionals critical of the crackdown in Tiananmen Square, but the party also enjoyed strong support from lower classes because of its welfare policies. Led by Tsang Yok Sing, principal of a pro-Chinese patriotic school, the pro-Beijing Democratic Alliance for Betterment of Hong Kong had strong connections to working-class unions. Despite their different political attitudes toward China, the Democratic Party and the Democratic Alliance for Betterment of Hong Kong were for the most part in agreement regarding policies toward education, housing, health care, education, labor, and welfare. The Liberal Party consisted mainly of businesspeople and professionals. Whereas it had maintained a good relationship with Patten even while maintaining its commitment to reunification with China, it shifted its allegiance toward Beijing as 1997 approached.

1997 IN WORLD HISTORY

Several features made Hong Kong's transition to Chinese rule in 1997 so distinctive in world history. Not only was it the last significant British colony to decolonize, it was also the most economically successful of British colonies. As Goodstadt writes, Hong Kong's "record of sustained and self-generated growth seemed to redeem the reputation of both colonialism and capitalism. The last remnant of the British Empire in Asia had made itself the equal of First World cities against considerable political and economic odds."[20] The transition was prearranged in a way that distinguished it, for example, from the independence of India in 1947 or the fall of the Berlin Wall in 1989. Nor would the handover lead to independence, as it did in most other European colonies in the decades after World War II. Indeed, to some observers Hong Kong was not being decolonized; rather, it was being recolonized, with the metropole simply shifting from London to Beijing. The most pressing question for the majority of the people in Hong Kong, however, was not how this transition figured in world history but instead whether Hong Kong would indeed be able to keep its distinctive way of life after 1997 under the one country, two systems model.

NOTES

1. Lynn White and Li Cheng, "China Coast Identities: Regional, National, and Global," in Lowell Dittmer and Samuel S. Kim, eds., *China's Quest for National Identity* (Ithaca, NY: Cornell University Press, 1993), 180.

2. Kevin Rafferty, *City on the Rocks: Hong Kong's Uncertain Future* (London: Viking, 1989), 7.

3. Quoted in Michael Yahuda, *Hong Kong: China's Challenge* (London: Routledge, 1996), 56.

4. Alvin Y. So, *Hong Kong's Embattled Democracy: A Societal Analysis* (Baltimore: Johns Hopkins University Press, 1999), 159, 176.

5. White and Li, "China Coast Identities," 190.

6. Leo F. Goodstadt, *Uneasy Partners: The Conflict between Public Interest and Private Profit in Hong Kong* (Hong Kong: Hong Kong University Press, 2005), 220.

7. So, *Hong Kong's Embattled Democracy*, 215.

8. Frank Ching, "Misreading Hong Kong," *Foreign Affairs* 73(3) (1997): 54.

9. Reprinted in Alan Knight and Yoshiko Nakano, eds., *Reporting Hong Kong: Foreign Media and the Handover* (New York: St. Martin's, 1999), 195–97.

10. Ibid., 197–99.

11. Ibid., 199–200.

12. Quoted in Allan Knight, "Will the Chinese Be Kinder about British Rule? The BBC," in Knight and Nakano, *Reporting Hong Kong*, 120.

13. Reprinted in Knight and Nakano, *Reporting Hong Kong*, 194–95.

14. Quoted in Knight, "Will the Chinese Be Kinder about British Rule?" 122.

15. "Insiders' Insights," in Knight and Nakano, *Reporting Hong Kong*, 60.

16. Yahuda, *Hong Kong*, 17, 94–95.

17. Wu Hung, "The Hong Kong Clock: Public Time-Telling and Political Time/Space," *Public Culture* 9(3) (Spring 1997): 352, 354.

18. Wong Siu-lun, "Deciding to Stay, Deciding to Move, Deciding Not to Decide," in Gary G. Hamilton, ed., *Cosmopolitan Capitalists: Hong Kong and the Chinese Diaspora at the End of the 20th Century* (Seattle: University of Washington Press, 1999), 139–42.

19. So, *Hong Kong's Embattled Democracy*, 252.

20. Goodstadt, *Uneasy Partners*, 4.

Epilogue

Beyond 1997

The burning question surrounding Hong Kong's reversion to Chinese sovereignty has been how this former British colony will survive under the one country, two systems arrangement. "Time of Certainty Begins: Will Beijing Honor Vows?" asked the front page of the *New York Times* on July 1, 1997. Two years later, political scientist James Hsiung noted that most predictions about Hong Kong's future after the handover had been "dismal and downright pessimistic. The worst scenario saw Beijing meddling in Hong Kong's politics and economic life, and trampling upon its freedoms, including freedom of the press, judicial freedom, academic freedom, and free elections. There would be corruption, nepotism, cronyism, and related plagues, brought in by the Mainland Chinese."[1]

As journalist Frank Ching argued in 1999, these doom-and-gloom predictions overlook how People's Republic of China (PRC) policy toward Hong Kong has always been "dictated by self-interest." China could have recovered Hong Kong much earlier if it had wanted to—in 1949 when People's Liberation Army troops stopped at the Hong Kong border, or during the Cultural Revolution when the central government stopped the Red Guards from crossing into Hong Kong—but the PRC government had good reasons for not wanting to bother Hong Kong. The colony served as a window to the outside world and a base for trade with non-Communist countries, provided a supply of smuggled goods during the American and United Nations embargoes in the 1950s, and aided the PRC's economic development in the 1970s. Still, Ching acknowledged concerns that the PRC government might interfere in Hong Kong to protect its monopoly on power: "China's promise not to interfere in Hong Kong's internal affairs is similar to a left-handed person promising only to use his right hand. The promise may very well be sincere but, in the absence of restraints, the left-handed person will sooner or later forget and, without even realizing it, start using his left hand."[2]

The most pressing challenges to the new Hong Kong Special Administrative Region (HKSAR) had little to do with the reversion to Chinese sovereignty. From early 1997 to early 1998, for example, the chicken flu (the H5N1 bird flu virus) killed six people and prompted the HKSAR government to order the slaughter of almost 1.5 million chickens. The Asian financial crisis, caused by currency devaluation in Thailand only one day after the end of British rule in Hong Kong, precipitated a decline in the Hong Kong stock market and property values, unemployment, and a recession from which the HKSAR did not fully recover until 2004. In March 2003, Hong Kong was hit by Severe Acute Respiratory Syndrome (SARS), an extremely contagious and potentially deadly form of pneumonia. When the disease was finally controlled in June, some eighteen hundred people had been diagnosed with SARS, almost three hundred of whom died. Hong Kong's tourist industry suffered, which further harmed the region's economy. The HKSAR government has also faced the problem of keeping Hong Kong economically competitive in a rapidly globalizing world and in the face of increased competition from mainland China, especially since China's entry into the World Trade Organization in 2001 has diminished Hong Kong's traditional position as a doorway to China.

Hong Kong has not only survived the reversion to Chinese sovereignty, but observers also frequently express surprise at how little the region seems to have changed since 1997. Many senior government officials have remained in place. English continues to be the language of success in business and government. Hong Kong's expatriate community still comprises 2–3 percent of Hong Kong's population. Most Western expatriates never learn Chinese, still live in better housing and have higher salaries than most local Chinese, and do not plan to stay in Hong Kong for long. British expatriates, some with family ties to Hong Kong dating back to the late 1800s, continue to make more money than they ever could in Britain. Although in 1996 the British government granted the seven thousand South Asians (mostly Indians) in Hong Kong the right of entry and abode in Britain, there is still a sizable Indian community. The Gurkhas, the Nepalese warriors who once fought so proudly for the British Army, no longer serve their colonial masters, but they are now seen throughout Hong Kong as security guards at apartment complexes, office buildings, and shopping malls. (The majority of expatriates, however, have no historical connections to British colonialism: they are the Filipino and Thai women who work as domestic servants for middle- and upper-class Chinese and expatriate families.) Horse racing, protected under the one country, two systems arrangement, enjoys a fanatical popularity almost inexplicable to visitors. The main leisure activities in Hong Kong are still eating and shopping, with restaurants and shopping malls galore. "Despite the change of guards, and of the emblems," James Hsiung concluded in 1999, "little seemed to have changed for the people in the street."[3]

Even while drawing attention to Hong Kong's uncertain future, the reversion to Chinese sovereignty put the region in the international spotlight in a way that further enhanced its global reputation as a vibrant, cosmopolitan society. In July 2004, a record number of almost two million tourists came to Hong Kong, more than half of them from the mainland. Western tourists also come to Hong Kong in large numbers, although their purpose for coming has changed. Whereas Europeans and Americans used to travel to Hong Kong to catch a glimpse of Communist China across the border, they also came to see traditional China, preserved in the New Territories and seemingly unchanged by the Communist revolution across the border. Now, Western newspapers and magazines brim with articles about Hong Kong, its efforts to promote its heritage, and the dynamic, hybrid flair reflected in its cinema, cuisine, and architecture. The common view of Hong Kong—held mainly by local expatriates—as a cultural desert is not true. Orchestras visit from all over the world (especially during the annual Hong Kong Arts Festival), and Hong Kong has its own orchestra, philharmonic, and dance companies as well as a plethora of new museums. Organizations such as the Hong Kong Branch of the Royal Asiatic Society, founded in 1847 by Governor John Davis, continue to promote interest in Hong Kong's history and culture.

Compared with many other former colonies, Hong Kong's postcolonial experience has been remarkably successful. Still, many people in Hong Kong have been disappointed by the region's brief post-1997 history. Prodemocracy activists and legislators frequently criticize Beijing for slowing Hong Kong's road to democratization. Some scholars fault Chris Patten's last-minute reforms that, however well intentioned, appointed a bureaucratic elite that was committed to promoting democracy but unable to handle Hong Kong's transition from colony to HKSAR. Others blame Hong Kong's colonial legacies for its current problems. All former colonies have suffered from adjustment problems, but Hong Kong's unique status—decolonization without independence—has made it a particularly difficult place to manage. Unlike Hong Kong's colonial administrators, who by the 1960s enjoyed considerable autonomy from the British government and until then generally paid little attention to public opinion, the HKSAR's new rulers have the unenviable challenge of satisfying not only the central government in Beijing but also the powerful business interests and the local population within Hong Kong, which, partly because of the changes in the years leading up to 1997, now expect and demand more of their government.

DISSATISFACTION WITH THE HKSAR GOVERNMENT

In the summer of 2002, the HKSAR celebrated its fifth anniversary. Sponsored by the Leisure and Culture Services Department, the celebrations included the Reunification Cup, a series of soccer matches among teams from Hong Kong,

Scotland, South Africa, and Turkey. The fireworks display over Victoria Harbour was said to be even more expensive than the one in 1997, which had been the most expensive in history. At "The Music of the Dragons," a concert at Hong Kong Coliseum, more than ten thousand young people from Hong Kong, China, Taiwan, and Macau set a Guinness World Record for the largest percussion performance. A rock concert at Queen Elizabeth Stadium featured bands from Hong Kong, mainland China, Taiwan, Japan, and Australia. The visiting military band of the People's Liberation Army provided a dance, musical, and marching performance.

Rather than a celebration, for many Hong Kong people the anniversary of the reversion to Chinese sovereignty has been a yearly occasion to express their dissatisfaction with the HKSAR government. On June 30, 1999, the eve of the second anniversary of the reversion, some two hundred people held a candlelight vigil to commemorate the so-called dark days under the HKSAR. Legislative Council member and union leader Lee Cheuk-yan argued that Hong Kong needed a new chief executive. Members of The Frontier, a prodemocracy party, criticized the "hegemony" of the new administration. On July 1, political groups and the Hong Kong Federation of Students staged a march to government headquarters in Central District. Wearing black armbands that symbolized "the demise of the rule of law" in Hong Kong and bearing pictures of Chief Executive Tung Chee-hwa, Secretary for Justice Elsie Leung, and Security Secretary Regina Ip, the protesters accused the government of "betraying Hong Kong people" and "ruining the rule of law." Lau Ka-yee of Democracy 2000, another prodemocracy group, called the one country, two systems concept "a lie." The protesters ended their march by reading a list of the government's numerous "sins." Democratic Party chairman Martin Lee explained in a press conference that "the honeymoon is over and the 'two systems' are being blurred." Lee accused Elsie Leung of "leading the water of mainland law into the common-law well water" and "assaulting the common-law system and the rule of law." On July 1, 2001, the fourth anniversary of the handover, thousands of prodemocracy activists in several different demonstrations protested against the erosion of democracy since 1997. One group of protesters carried a mock tomb symbolizing "the death of democracy, human rights, and the rule of law" in Hong Kong. Another group demanded direct elections for the chief executive, chanting "one person, one vote."

Some expatriate former colonial officials have been frustrated with the direction that Hong Kong has taken since the late 1990s. Patrick Hase, who started working in Hong Kong in 1972 and retired as assistant director for social welfare in 1996, believes that morale in the civil service is "very poor" and that the ideal of cooperation between government and people "is disappearing or has perhaps already gone." Hase contrasts this with the 1970s and early 1980s, which he considers "by far the best administered period in Hong Kong's history, one where the actions of Government were closer to the real wishes of the people than at any date before or since." The government was "in closer contact with the real public opinion then than either before or after." Morale was high and relations between government and people were "excellent," while among the government "the ideals of dedication to an efficient, honest, intelligent and hardworking service imbued with a genuine commitment to the people of Hong Kong were real and keenly felt."[4] James Hayes, who retired as regional secretary of the New Territories in 1987, laments a "retreat from innocence" that began in the 1970s as government expanded and become more specialized. Hayes is particularly critical of how the interests of the traditional family and lineage in the New Territories have been increasingly under siege since 1997. Whereas the British policy of governing through a few officials meant that many customary practices were recognized and even protected, the Sino-British Joint Agreement and the Basic Law threaten customary law and the rights and privileges of indigenous residents.[5]

Criticizing new postcolonial regimes is a common pattern among former colonial servants (many ex-colonials still insist that India was better off under the British), but some of the same prodemocracy leaders who campaigned for political reforms under the British have also compared the HKSAR government unfavorably with the colonial government. In an interview on July 1, 1999, the second anniversary of the handover, Martin Lee argued that whereas "when the British were here it was a society under the rule of law, now it is the rule of man." Emily Lau of The Frontier noted that many Hong Kong people believed that Governor Patten had done a better job than Tung Chee-hwa. And even if they do not compare it with the colonial government, people from all walks of life have regularly expressed their dissatisfaction with the new government. Surveys in the first few years of the HKSAR showed that many people felt that Tung was more interested in helping big business and ingratiating himself than in providing the medical services, care and housing for the elderly, and better housing for the general population that he had promised. On July 1, 1999, a delegation of senior citizens petitioned Tung to honor the vows he had made during his campaign in 1996 to provide better services for the elderly. An opinion poll conducted to mark the anniversary of the reversion found that even while public perceptions of the PRC government had improved, one-third of respondents felt either "quite negative" or "very negative" about Tung's government. Less than 20 percent were "quite positive" or "very positive," while less than 8 percent felt "positive" about the anniversary.

THE ONE COUNTRY, TWO SYSTEMS CONCEPT AND HONG KONG'S AUTONOMY

Under the one country, two systems arrangement, the PRC government has promised Hong Kong a "high degree of autonomy" for fifty years. Surveys in 1998, a year after the handover, showed that a rising public confidence in the HKSAR's political future, even with the economic recession, was based on satisfaction with Beijing's noninterference in HKSAR affairs. Even observers in the United States and Taiwan, the two countries that had predicted the bleakest future for Hong Kong, conceded that Beijing had stayed out of Hong Kong affairs.

Both PRC and HKSAR leaders understand that mishandling Hong Kong's reintegration with the mainland could have disastrous local and international results. It could lead to mass emigration from the HKSAR, which would hurt international investment. Hong Kong is vital to the PRC's economic development and political stability. Having played up the recovery of Hong Kong into an event of huge national importance, Beijing can hardly afford to ruin it. Not only would a failed Hong Kong be an international embarrassment, but it could even hurt the Chinese Communist Party (CCP) itself (although some scholars have suggested that the end of colonial Hong Kong also threatens the CCP's legitimacy since the party is now no longer a vanguard in the struggle against imperialism and oppression). Botching Hong Kong's reversion would also harm the PRC's relations with Britain, the United States, Japan, and other Asian nations. Considering that the one country, two systems model was originally designed for Taiwan, ensuring a smooth reversion is also crucial for reunification with Taiwan: a failed reversion would both hurt economic relations with Taiwan and lead to stronger demands for independence there.

Many Hong Kong people, however, believe that the PRC government has intervened far too regularly in the HKSAR's political affairs. A major concern is Hong Kong's legal and political autonomy under the one country, two systems arrangement. The Basic Law stipulates that Hong Kong residents of Chinese descent qualify for right of abode (permanent residency) in Hong Kong, provided that at the time of birth at least one parent was a Chinese citizen holding Hong Kong right-of-abode status. In 1997, however, the Provisional Legislative Council passed ordinances restricting the procedures for proving right of abode, which led to court challenges. When the Court of Final Appeal supported the legal challenges in January 1999, the HKSAR government warned that the court's ruling would extend right-of-abode eligibility to some 1.67 million potential new Chinese immigrants and strain Hong Kong's resources. (The government claimed that housing and educating the new immigrants would cost more than HK$710 billion, equivalent to around US$91 billion.) The HKSAR government then took its case to the Standing Committee of the National People's Congress (NPC), prompting an outcry from the Hong Kong legal establishment. Martin Lee accused the government of "giving away" Hong Kong's autonomy. On June 30, the eve of the HKSAR's third anniversary, six hundred lawyers dressed in black held a silent protest against the interpretation.

The NPC Standing Committee, which is empowered to interpret the Basic Law, sided with the HKSAR government. This led to a massive legal challenge on behalf of more than five thousand applicants for right-of-abode status, who argued that the NPC decision deprived them of the benefits of the Court of Final Appeal ruling. Critics accused the HKSAR government of manipulating figures and exaggerating strains on housing, employment, and public health to create a climate of fear and encourage public sentiment against immigrants. Pro-Beijing newspapers supported the Standing Committee's decision, however, insisting that the Court of Final Appeal had made a mistake. The chairman of the pro-Beijing Democratic Alliance for Betterment of Hong Kong, Tsang Yok Sing, argued that the HKSAR government should find the "best possible way" to keep the 1.67 million potential immigrants from coming to Hong Kong. Furthermore, although opinion polls after the Standing Committee's interpretation showed a drop in confidence in the government, they also showed that more than 80 percent of the respondents—concerned about increasing immigration from the mainland—were critical of the court's decision, while 65 percent supported government action to keep immigrants out. The overwhelming majority, it seemed, preferred the overall welfare of society to the preservation of the law. Accepting the ultimate authority of the Standing Committee to interpret the Basic Law, in January 2002 the Court of Final Appeal reversed its earlier decision by ruling against some claimants on the right-of-abode issue.

In another case that appeared to test Hong Kong's legal autonomy, in July 2001 the HKSAR government allowed Li Shaomin, a Chinese American professor at Hong Kong's City University, to return after being detained for five months in China. Although Li insisted that he had only been conducting research, he had been convicted in a secret trial for harming China's national security and spying for Taiwan and had then been expelled from China. Many observers saw Li's case as part of a wider politically motivated crackdown on academics with connections to the United States, especially since a Chinese scholar based in the United States had been similarly detained. Li's father, an advisor to CCP leader Hu Yaobang, had been imprisoned for sympathizing with the students after the Tiananmen Square Massacre in 1989. Although the Hong Kong immigration chief denied having consulted Beijing before making his decision, it was apparent that the HKSAR government had allowed Li to return to Hong Kong because Beijing had let it do so. President George W. Bush and American congressional leaders had urged the Chinese government to release Li, and Secretary of State Colin Powell had just visited Beijing. As Martin Lee put it, "whoever made the decision knew it was important for Hong Kong and that the whole world was watching." While the case suggested proof of the HKSAR's legal autonomy, some critics cited it as yet another example of Beijing's—and Hong Kong's—willingness to use legal decisions as political bargaining chips.

Another concern is the future of freedom of expression in Hong Kong. So far, Hong Kong continues to enjoy relatively wide freedom of expression. In March 1999, the Court of Final Appeal overturned the conviction of two men who had been found guilty of desecrating the Chinese national and HKSAR flags. The court argued that their conviction violated the freedom of expression covered by the International Covenant on Civil and Political Rights, which under the Basic Law applies to Hong Kong. People in Hong Kong have also been relatively free to criticize the PRC government. When demonstrators protested President Jiang Zemin's visit on July 1, 1998, the HKSAR police responded simply by playing classical music to drown out the noise. On July 1, 1999, some sixty prodemocracy activists chanting "Down with Li Peng" and "Democracy for China" interrupted Vice President Hu Jintao's speech at the unveiling ceremony for a monument commemorating Hong Kong's reunification with China. On each anniversary of the Tiananmen Square Massacre, protesters have held peaceful demonstrations and vigils. On June 4, 2004, tens of thousands of people, among them many mainlanders, attended a rally commemorating the fifteenth anniversary of the massacre.

Although freedom of the press is guaranteed by the Basic Law, the PRC government has shown since the years leading up to the handover that it has its own view of what this freedom meant. In May 1996, Lu Ping, director of the Chinese State Council's Hong Kong and Macau Affairs Office, told American news network CNN that news articles supporting "two Chinas" or independence for Hong Kong or Taiwan would "absolutely not" be allowed. In October of the same year, Vice Premier and Foreign Minister Qian Qichen promised that the Hong Kong media would enjoy complete freedom and could publish "criticism," but he warned that the media would not be allowed to publish "rumors or lies" or personal attacks on Chinese leaders. These and earlier warnings appear to have created an atmosphere of self-censorship. In January 1994, local television station TVB decided not to broadcast a BBC documentary of Mao Zedong that the PRC government had criticized as being biased. A 1996 survey by Chinese University Hong Kong's Department of Journalism and Communication found that many journalists were reluctant to criticize the PRC government. In 1997 the Hong Kong Journalists Association predicted that self-censorship, rather than direct government intervention, would be more likely to undermine freedom of expression in Hong Kong.[6]

Still, freedom of the press remains greater in Hong Kong than in many Asian societies, certainly more so than on the mainland. At the NPC annual session in Beijing in spring 1998, Xu Simin, a Hong Kong member of the Chinese People's Political Consultative Conference, criticized government-run broadcaster RTHK for broadcasting programs critical of the Chinese and Hong Kong governments. But Jiang Zemin warned Hong Kong members of the NPC to stay out of Hong Kong government affairs. And even though Tung Chee-hwa said that while freedom of the press was important, the HKSAR government should be presented favorably, Chief Secretary Anson Chan insisted that RTHK should have its editorial freedom and that this was a local affair. Frank Ching concluded in 1999 that "freedom of the press continues to thrive, despite prophesies of gloom and doom from both the Western and local media before 1997, most of which continued to look at China through the lens of 1989 events at Tiananmen Square."[7]

The problem is that no one is sure how long this press freedom will last or how far its boundaries extend. In August 1999, Xu Simin and Wang Rudeng, assistant director of the New China News Agency local branch, criticized RTHK for giving a representative of the Taiwan regime airtime to argue that China and Taiwan were separate states. Two leaders of the pro-Beijing Democratic Alliance for Betterment of Hong Kong criticized RTHK for violating the one-China policy enshrined in the Basic Law. Vice Premier Qian Qichen later insisted that support for interstate relations between Taiwan and China violated the one-China principle. In October 2000, President Jiang chided Hong Kong journalists for asking questions about his support for Tung's reelection in 2002. And after Chen Shui-bian of the proindependence Democratic Progressive Party was elected president of Taiwan in spring 2000, Wang Fengchao, deputy director of the Beijing liaison office in Hong Kong, warned the Hong Kong media not to report on proindependence activities in Taiwan. Although PRC authorities have not specified how they will deal with news groups that violate these prohibitions, there has been a distinct trend toward self-censorship in the local media. (Not all media professionals are as concerned about press freedom: the Hong Kong Federation of Journalists was founded in 1996 by journalists working in the left-wing press to counter the influence of the Hong Kong Journalists Association, which has taken a leading role in defending press freedom.)

A particularly sensitive issue has been the PRC and HKSAR governments' concerns about seditious and subversive activities in Hong Kong. Beijing has insisted that Hong Kong must not become a base for subversive activities against China, and in early 2001 Security Secretary Regina Ip declared that her government was keeping a "close eye" on the Falun Gong (Practice of the Wheel of Law). A quasi-religious organization that combines Buddhist meditation with traditional Chinese *qigong* (breathing and movement exercise) techniques, the Falun Gong has been banned in mainland China since 1999 as an "evil cult." But the Falun Gong is legal in Hong Kong, where it is registered with the Societies Ordinance and its members often hold peaceful demonstrations against the widespread suppression of the movement on the mainland. Over the course of 2001, Tung Chee-hwa shifted from calling the Falun Gong "more or less" to "without a doubt" an "evil cult." Executive Council member Nellie Fong encouraged the government to pass an antisedition law to monitor the Falun Gong. In May 2001, the HKSAR government formally announced its intention to draft an anticult law, the presumed target being the Falun Gong. The announcement provoked a controversy in the local media. In late June, Chief Secretary Donald Tsang (who had recently replaced Anson Chan) abruptly withdrew the anticult proposal, insisting that the HKSAR administration would pursue the matter in "the Hong Kong way."

In March 2002, eight Falun Gong followers were arrested in a March demonstration outside the PRC central government's local liaison office; the eight were later convicted for assaulting and obstructing police. In September, during his second term, Tung Chee-hwa tried to introduce an antisedition and antisubversion bill, at the insistence of Beijing and as stipulated in Article 23 of the Basic Law, which gives the HKSAR government the right to "prohibit any act of treason, secession, sedition, subversion against the Central People's Government" and to prohibit local political organizations from having any contact with foreign political organizations. As the colonial government had in the late 1980s, the HKSAR government published a public consultation paper listing the main provisions of the proposed legislation. One provision allowed the government to ban any organizations that were illegal on the mainland (such as the Falun Gong). After large public demonstrations both for and against the proposed legislation, in early 2003 the HKSAR government announced that the Legislative Council would vote on the bill in July before the current legislative session ended.

In the meantime, in March 2003 Hong Kong was struck by SARS. Even while facing a barrage of criticism for not recognizing the disease earlier and for downplaying reports that the infection was coming from the mainland, the HKSAR government decided to go ahead with the controversial security bill. With confidence in the government plummeting, the timing for reintroducing the bill could not have been worse. On July 1, the sixth anniversary of Hong Kong's transition to Chinese sovereignty, more than five hundred thousand people staged the largest public demonstration in the young HKSAR's history. Even more embarrassing for the government, new premier Wen Jiabao was in town for the anniversary and to witness the signing of a new free trade agreement between China and Hong Kong.

Although Tung agreed to withdraw the provision enabling the HKSAR government to ban organizations that were illegal on the mainland, he stuck to his guns on the rest of the security bill. When critics of the bill called for his resignation, Tung agreed to defer the vote. After a meeting in Beijing with Wen Jiabao, new president and CCP general secretary Hu Jintao, and Vice President Zeng Qinghong in Beijing, in August Tung announced that the government would reintroduce a modified version of the security bill for public consultation. However, after pressure from critics of the bill and even from his own supporters, Tung withdrew the bill in early September. The fallout from the security bill controversy also affected the November 2003 District Council elections. Although the mainland and local pro-Beijing media condemned them as unpatriotic, many prodemocracy candidates won election, and candidates supportive of the security bill were defeated.

In early May 2005, the Court of Final Appeal overturned criminal convictions against the eight Falun Gong followers accused of assaulting and obstructing police in the 2002 protest. In its summary, the court declared that "the freedom to demonstrate peacefully is a constitutional right" and that freedom of expression is "at the heart of Hong Kong's system and the courts should give them a generous interpretation." Still, local human rights advocates worry that Hong Kong's judicial system is being undercut by the PRC government's power to interpret the Basic Law in ways that might preempt decisions by Hong Kong courts (as it did, for example, by blocking rapid democratic reforms and limiting eligibility for right of abode). Law Yuk-kai, director of the Hong Kong Human Rights Monitor, warned after the May 2005 ruling that Hong Kong's courts could be "completely sidelined." And many people worry that the Falung Gong case will cause Beijing to take a tougher stance toward less subversive activities in Hong Kong.

Despite its promise of a "high degree of autonomy," the Beijing government has already taken several measures to limit the growth of democracy in Hong Kong. In late 2003, President Hu Jintao warned Tung Chee-hwa that the issue of electoral reforms could not move ahead without prior consultation with Beijing. On April 6, 2004, the Standing Committee of the NPC ruled that any local attempts to modify election laws would require approval from Beijing, that the Hong Kong chief executive could not introduce any electoral reforms bills without approval from the Standing Committee, and that the Legislative Council could not introduce electoral reform legislation. After local opposition parties condemned the ruling as a violation of the one country, two systems model, on April 26 the Standing Committee declared that direct elections for chief executive or the Legislative Council violated the Basic Law, thus ruling out the possibility of popular elections for chief executive in 2007 and for expanded elections for the legislature in 2008.

Most people in Hong Kong appear to have resigned themselves to the fact that the Chinese government has ultimate authority over Hong Kong's constitutional reform. On July 1, 2004, the seventh anniversary of the transition, hundreds of thousands of people protested the PRC government's decision to prohibit general elections. A survey in the spring of 2004 found that public dissatisfaction with the Hong Kong government's handling of relations with the central authorities in Beijing was at its highest level since the 1997 handover. But it is difficult to tell how much the demand for political reform reflects popular opinion in Hong Kong. In the first posthandover elections for the Legislative Council in September 1998, approximately 53 percent of registered voters turned out. In the second elections in September 2000, only around 44 percent of voters turned out; the

Democratic Party lost quite a bit of support. An opinion poll in May 2004 showed that the support for universal suffrage in the 2007 and 2008 elections had declined steeply since July 2003.

COLONIALISM AND ITS LEGACIES

How did being a British colony for more than 150 years affect Hong Kong's history? What are the legacies of colonialism? Despite its rocky start, Hong Kong's status as a British colony and free port helped make it into a thriving commercial center. The rule of law and political stability encouraged both Chinese and foreign investment, while Hong Kong's colonial status protected it from many of the troubles that plagued China in the nineteenth and twentieth centuries. Although the Hong Kong government had more than its share of corruption, its generally efficient and nonpolitical civil service frequently drew praise from the various regimes on the mainland. Under British rule, Hong Kong also achieved a high standard of living for many of its inhabitants. By the early 1990s, Hong Kong's per capita income had surpassed Britain's. The region enjoys one of the world's lowest infant mortality rates and has extremely high life expectancy rates.

During the countdown to 1997, the Western media depicted Hong Kong as a bastion of democracy, free expression, and prosperity, often ignoring how for so long Hong Kong had been a colony with little democracy or freedom of expression. But any assessment of the British colonial legacy must consider the entire colonial period rather than only the last decade or so of British rule, when the British introduced last-minute political reforms. Although colonial Hong Kong was theoretically based on the rule of law, some jurists and legal scholars argue that common law has never taken root in Hong Kong, mainly because it is so different from the traditional Chinese legal system, while others suggest that most people in colonial Hong Kong had only a superficial knowledge of common law because the language of the law was English (trials are often still held in English, as many judges are expatriates and most counsels received their legal training in English). Furthermore, the government enacted a wave of anti-Chinese legislation from the earliest years, passed various emergency and discriminatory ordinances, and often censored the Chinese press. The 1951 Control of Publications Ordinance, which made it an offense to publish anything that might incite people to commit sedition or treason, was not repealed until 1987. As journalist C. K. Lau argues, Hong Kong's "supposedly high degree of press freedom" should be "better understood as allowing the press great latitude to comment on Chinese politics, but not on the legitimacy of British rule."[8]

Hong Kong's colonial civil service was generally efficient and politically neutral, but until the last years Europeans dominated senior positions on the grounds that Chinese were not qualified or trustworthy enough. Political power, writes Leo Goodstadt, "was controlled by colonial officials, alien in both language and culture who, with the other members of this European minority, enjoyed superior status and influence solely on account of their race." Because they were so isolated from the Chinese community, "expatriates were in no position to identify the frustrations and the aspirations of their constituents, their fears as well as their hopes." Because these expatriates had little knowledge of life in public housing estates, for example, standards of housing and social services "fell well below what Hong Kong could afford even after its prosperity was assured by its export triumphs."[9] Similarly, James Hsiung argues that because they were not problems facing expatriates, the colonial government had little concern about Hong Kong's inordinate income-distribution inequities, "the very problem of abject poverty amidst affluence"; the "scandalous" condition of the elderly living in poverty; and the lack of unemployment insurance, which the government believed would only encourage laziness. "The sad thing," laments Hsiung, "is that this lack of compassion perpetuated by colonial policy as such has rubbed off on the British-educated local elite even into the post-colonial era."[10]

Hong Kong has often been described as a capitalist's paradise and as one of the world's freest and most competitive economies. But this economy historically depended on political patronage and discriminatory monopolies that favored large British firms. Directors of large British firms such as Jardine and Matheson, the Hong Kong and Shanghai Bank, and the Swire Group regularly held seats on the Executive Council and the Legislative Council. Cable and Wireless, a British corporation, had the telephone monopoly until very recently. Well after World War II, the colonial government refrained from encouraging industrialization because it violated official colonial policy of stressing trade and commerce. The overrepresentation of business and professional classes in the colonial power structure also restricted competition in the property market. As historian Ming Chan puts it, free trade and free enterprise "did not always mean fair trade and equal opportunity."[11]

Free-market economists frequently praise Hong Kong's laissez-faire system, but this commitment to laissez-faire enabled the colonial government to shirk many of its responsibilities. Compulsory and free primary education was not guaranteed until 1971, and three years of compulsory and free secondary education was not guaranteed until 1978. Nor did the colonial administration have a shining record in higher education. Until the mid-1980s—the last decade of British rule—less than 5 percent of high school graduates could attend degree-granting institutions. (By 1997 the number had risen to 18 percent after the number of degree-granting institutions increased by four times.) And even though by the 1990s more than 40 percent of Hong Kong's population owned their apartments, at least three hundred thousand people were still living in squatter huts. Although the colonial government frequently justified its low social welfare spending on budgetary grounds, in the postwar period the government faced only a handful of budget deficits. By the end of British rule, writes Goodstadt, "most of the adult population had been reared, educated and spent much of their working lives in an environment disadvantaged and even impoverished by the failure to upgrade the social infrastructure in line with economic growth." The colonial government was so successful in "making laissez faire and minimal economic and social intervention an integral part of the Hong Kong outlook," Goodstadt argues, "that not a single serious political party in Hong Kong sought to challenge the legitimacy of this old-fashioned set of doctrines or their primacy in economic management before 1997."[12]

The British will be remembered for their many contributions to Hong Kong, but they will also be remembered for their many failures. Anna Wu, a lawyer who in 1975 helped found the Hong Kong Observers, a pressure group dedicated to discussing contemporary issues, and who was appointed by Patten to the Legislative Council in 1992, argues that Murray MacLehose's refusal to introduce elections to the Legislation Council during his tenure was "disastrous" for Hong Kong. Such reforms would have given Hong Kong a "much more stable and more mature alternative" to colonial rule and would have prepared Hong Kong much better for the post-1997 HKSAR government. Politics, Wu maintains, would have "been part of our lives and culture, not a new concept." By not introducing democracy until the 1990s, the colonial government actually legitimized the PRC government's opposition to political changes.[13] Thus, it is not only Beijing that is to blame for the HKSAR's problems. Rather, argues Ming Chan, "the inadequate foundation, unhealthy political culture, flawed legal-administrative framework and questionable bureaucratic practices inherited from the British—together with the inability of the Hong Kong people to stand firmly to defend their much cherished freedom, democracy and high degree of autonomy because of their colonial deprivation—ought to be blamed as well."[14]

Colonial officials often blamed Hong Kong's retarded political culture on its Chinese residents, their traditional culture, and their refugee mentality. Historian David Faure disagrees: "Confucianism no more dictates the evolution of the economy or the evolution of politics in Hong Kong or anywhere else in East Asia than Christianity may be said to be the driving force of such in Europe and America." Rather, Faure argues, "the failure to widen the franchise in the late 1940s and early '50s deprived all of Hong Kong of any effective channel of politicking." Realizing that there was no room for them in Hong Kong's administrative structure, Hong Kong people exerted their power in the few arenas where they could, such as business and the professions, thereby creating "the impression that Hong Kong people were apolitical."[15] Similarly, Leo Goodstadt rejects as "blaming the victims" the standard argument that Chinese political apathy was a legitimate reason for not introducing political reforms. "A more accurate explanation of why Hong Kong had no directly-elected members of its legislature until the final decade of British rule was to be found in a colonial culture that combined self-satisfied complacency with mistrust of the local population." Because the British "lacked the confidence to allow the public to participate directly in the political process," Goodstadt argues, Hong Kong "remained a constitutional anachronism whose political arrangements remained virtually unchanged from the previous century until the final decade of the colonial era."[16]

To claim, however, as some observers have, that the interest in politics in the 1980s and 1990s entirely disproves the common image of Hong Kong people as historically being politically apathetic is anachronistic. Demands for reform in the 1980s and 1990s were shaped by Hong Kong's changing social, economic, and political conditions, in particular the rise of a local identity, the Sino-British Joint Declaration, and the local reactions to the Tiananmen Square Massacre. By this time, Hong Kong was a different place, its citizens a different people. Furthermore, if Hong Kong people deserve much of the credit for Hong Kong's economic prosperity and political stability, they must also bear some of the blame for its poor housing conditions and social services, repressive education system, and weak political culture. If the Hong Kong public was indeed as resentful of the colonial administration's poor record in terms of social services and political reform as critics sometimes charge, it could have demanded more from its government. Political and social activists in the 1970s often encountered resentment and resistance from all classes of the Chinese community who, insisting that conditions in Hong Kong were already much better than in China, warned against becoming involved in politics and causing trouble for the government.

The end of British rule did not give Hong Kong a fresh start. On the contrary, Beijing is committed to keeping Hong Kong's political structure in the form it had assumed by the last years of the colonial era, especially the functional constituency model for the new Legislative Council because legislators from these constituencies consistently vote against any measures to promote democratic reforms, civil liberties, or political accountability. In his July 1, 1997, speech celebrating the establishment of the HKSAR, Tung Chee-hwa explained that the Basic Law "reaffirms the implementation of a different system within one country" and "protects the rights and lifestyle of Hong Kong people and delineates our obligations."[17] But some critics argue that the Basic Law prevents the HKSAR from modifying or expanding its welfare and economic policies to fit the needs of changing times and that it has expanded the role of the business elite, especially from the property sector, in Hong Kong's power structure. According to Goodstadt, the Basic Law has made it hard for the HKSAR government to break from the old laissez-faire doctrine, guaranteeing that Hong Kong's economy "should be managed along the most conservative lines."[18]

One considerably less controversial legacy of colonialism in Hong Kong is the English language, which continues to be important in government, business, and the professions and which according to the Basic Law will remain an official language in the HKSAR. Despite controversial and not entirely successful efforts by the government to promote the study of Mandarin (or Putonghua), there is little doubt that English will survive in Hong Kong. Unlike some postcolonial societies, there have been no attempts in Hong Kong to eradicate English for nationalist or political reasons. Far from being condemned as the language of the colonial oppressor, English is widely regarded as crucial for maintaining Hong Kong's status as a regional headquarters to multinational companies (even while many of these companies have opened offices in mainland China) and as the language of success in the business, financial, and professional communities. When the Hong Kong government decreed shortly before the handover that Chinese would be the language of instruction for most schools after 1998, many schools and parents opposed the decree. And while learning Mandarin is becoming increasingly important for doing business with the mainland, a command of English will always be an important asset for another valuable prize: emigrating to English-speaking countries.

While the role of English as the language of the colonial administration helped make Hong Kong an international city, the weak command of English in Hong Kong is also a legacy of colonial rule. Some educators and employers have noted a decline in the quality of English since 1997, but longtime observers realize that the level of English in Hong Kong has always been low. It is not only poorly trained teachers employing ineffective and outdated teaching methods who are to blame; the weak command of English is also a result of Hong Kong's divided colonial social structure. As C. K. Lau argues, "the English-speaking community and the Chinese-speaking community have always lived parallel but largely separate lives." Thus, there are "virtually no opportunities for most Hong Kong Chinese to use the English they learn at school in real life." Unlike in Singapore, where the postcolonial government has promoted the use of English both to strengthen Singapore's status as a shipping and trading center and to achieve racial harmony among that city-state's multiethnic population, "English is not a language that the average Hong Kong Chinese use spontaneously as a means of communication."[19]

THE LEADERSHIP PROBLEM

One of the most serious weaknesses of Hong Kong's post-1997 political system is also a legacy from the colonial period. This weakness, in the words of Lau, is the HKSAR's "failure to produce political leadership."[20] In January 2001, Anson Chan, Hong Kong's highly popular chief secretary, suddenly announced that she would resign in May, a year before her contract expired. Known for disagreeing with Tung Chee-hwa about the pace of democratic reforms and for defending press freedom in Hong Kong, Chan had earlier declared that she would resign before approving policies that would compromise her principles. In July 2003, two of the most unpopular members of Tung's cabinet resigned. On July 16, 2003, Security Secretary Regina Ip resigned after the July 1 demonstration against her proposed National Security Bill. Hours later, Financial Secretary Antony Leung, who was already under fire for failing to reduce Hong Kong's high unemployment rate and to restore consumer confidence in the economy, stepped down. Leung had been criticized for purchasing a luxury Lexus automobile just before delivering the 2003 budget, which included increasing the tax rate on new cars. Although Leung insisted that he had decided to increase the tax, which would have cost him HK$50,000 (US$6,400), only after purchasing his new car, the case embarrassed the HKSAR government and hurt its credibility, especially when the government seemed so unwilling to investigate the case, which became known as "Lexusgate." In July 2004, two top health officials stepped down after a Legislative Council report on the SARS epidemic of 2003 found that the government had been slow in trying to contain the contamination from SARS.

The premature resignation of Tung Chee-hwa, Hong Kong's first postcolonial head of government, is only the most celebrated example of this leadership problem. Although Tung insisted that he was stepping down for health reasons, his resignation in March 2005, during the second half of his second five-year term, was widely seen as proof that he had failed to please the PRC government. Tung had lost his main backer in Beijing, former president Jiang Zemin, while new president Hu Jintao, faced with complaints from Hong Kong's business tycoons about Tung's performance, felt no obligation to retain him. In December 2004, Hu had publicly criticized Tung after legal challenges prevented the HKSAR government from making a major sale of government-owned land. As Hong Kong–based editor Hugo Restall explains, Tung was also losing "even the small semblance of control he once enjoyed over his cabinet." Tung resigned just in time for the Selection Committee, whose term was to expire in mid-July 2005, to pick his successor. Had he waited any later to resign, argues Restall, Beijing would have had to form a new selection committee, drawing unwanted attention to the undemocratic nature of the selection process.[21]

If Tung Chee-hwa had a hard time as chief executive of Hong Kong, his successor, former chief secretary Donald Tsang, also has his work cut out for him. Tsang, who in 1995 had been the first Chinese to become financial secretary, had the greatest public approval of any member of Tung's cabinet. Tsang also enjoys the support of the business magnates who urged Beijing to remove Tung. Like the PRC leaders, these tycoons oppose greater democratic reform in Hong Kong. The PRC leaders fear that democratization in Hong Kong might fuel demands for the same on the mainland, while both PRC leaders and the local business moguls worry that democratization would result in higher taxes and in demands for more government spending. Thus, Tsang will have to perform a very careful balancing act: not alienating his business supporters, proving his loyalty to China after so many years of dedicated service to the British (for which he was knighted in 1997), and satisfying the ordinary people who, writes Restall, "are fed up with government and business elites colluding to determine Hong Kong's future without popular input."[22] If the experience of the Tung administration is any lesson, it is the people of Hong Kong who will be shortchanged in this delicate balancing act.

In November 2005, Tsang announced that he had appointed 153 members of the public, including prodemocracy legislators such as Democratic Party leader Lee Wing-tat, to join the Commission on Strategic Development, the HKSAR advisory group that is studying how to expand democratic reforms in Hong Kong. Only three weeks earlier, Tsang had been criticized and ridiculed by prodemocracy lawmakers for comparing Hong Kong's slow progress toward universal suffrage with the United States, where women did not gain the right to vote until well more than a century after the United States won its independence. Surely, critics such as barrister and legislator Ronny Tong asked, Tsang was not suggesting that it might take Hong Kong another century to achieve universal suffrage. Prodemocracy critics have also rejected any assertions that Hong Kong is not ready for democracy, and Tsang's insistence that democratization in Hong Kong must be a gradual process that cannot take place without the approval of the authorities in Beijing, noting that other former colonies and Communist countries have had democracy for years. Other critics have complained that Tsang, despite his own humble origins and professed interest in democratization, has continued his predecessor's habit of appointing mainly older businessmen and bankers to his cabinet.

HONG KONG AND MAINLAND CHINA

Eclipsed by the concerns and speculations about Hong Kong's new status, a less frequently asked question is what Hong Kong's reversion to Chinese sovereignty has meant for people in China. On the eve of the 1997 reversion, many observers predicted that because the PRC would have to tolerate some autonomy for Hong Kong, this would lead other areas of China to copy what has made Hong Kong so successful. But China itself is changing so quickly that Hong Kong's reversion is unlikely to have much of an effect on the mainland. Although the official mainland media covered the countdown to the handover with special television shows and documentaries about Hong

Kong, it now rarely even comments on the anniversary of Hong Kong's return. Indeed, having reverted to Chinese sovereignty, Hong Kong has lost much of its distinctive quality, a distinctiveness that becomes less prominent every year as mainland cities become more developed. At the same time, Hong Kong remains a foreign place to many mainlanders. Until the signing of the Closer Economic Partnership Agreement between Hong Kong and Guangdong in 2003 and the "individual tourism" scheme introduced in autumn 2003 for mainland visitors from Guangdong, other neighboring provinces, and various major Chinese cities, obtaining an entry permit to Hong Kong could be harder than to many overseas countries. Flights to Hong Kong usually depart from the international section of mainland airports, and Hong Kong companies still enjoy tax breaks and other benefits reserved for foreign investors.

In the past decade, Hong Kong and Guangdong have become more closely integrated than at any time since the 1949 revolution in China, so much so that anthropologist Gregory Guldin has predicted the emergence of a giant "Pearl River megalopolis" that includes Guangzhou, Macau, Hong Kong, and some smaller mainland cities.[23] More people than ever before travel across the border between Hong Kong and Guangdong, especially to Shenzhen, while intermarriage—mainly between Hong Kong men and mainland wives—has helped change the texture of Hong Kong society. Although mainlanders in Hong Kong are still sometimes treated as bumpkins who cut in line at bus stops and fast food restaurants and are often blamed for Hong Kong's rising crime rates, they also comprise the majority of Hong Kong's tourists and are the new big spenders in the region's department stores.

These changes are reflected in how Hong Kong people view mainlanders and themselves. Surveys in the early 1990s found that Hong Kong Chinese considered mainlanders poor, lazy, unfriendly, superstitious, coarse, uncultured, and unintelligent, while mainlanders found Hong Kong people arrogant, hypocritical, and unfriendly. The surveys also found that these negative impressions increased the more often the two groups came into contact with each other. Such feelings appear to have been particularly strong among Hong Kong's youth. Polls in January and May 1996 showed that only one-fifth of the young people surveyed considered mainlanders to be reliable, and more than three-quarters identified themselves first as Hong Kongese rather than Chinese. With China's rising profile in the international arena and the emphasis on patriotic education and propaganda, however, Chinese nationalist and patriotic feelings have become pronounced in Hong Kong.

Even as more and more Hong Kong people are beginning to identify themselves primarily as Chinese rather than as Hong Kong Chinese or Hong Kongers, they often see themselves, and Hong Kong, as being culturally and politically distinct. Unlike people in mainland China (or in the United States), most Hong Kong people have not grown up with various forms of political indoctrination, such as singing national anthems or pledging allegiance to flags. Thus, they sometimes have a hard time identifying politically with

China, especially with its Communist regime. The right-of-abode controversy was ostensibly about the autonomy of the Hong Kong judicial system under a new government, but it was also about who qualified as Hong Kong Chinese: many local residents insisted that the mainlanders had no right to settle in Hong Kong. In May 2005, the HKSAR government announced that it intended to raise public hospital charges to deter mainland women from trying to obtain residency for their children by giving birth there. Mainland women, the government explained, accounted for more than 30 percent of births in public hospitals, and the government was determined not to subsidize medical services for nonresidents at the expense of local residents.

HISTORY IN HONG KONG

Hong Kong's history did not, of course, end with the colonial period any more than it began with the colonial period. History has in fact become a crucial and ongoing theme in how the new government has tried to smooth Hong Kong's reunification with China. But this has opened up a host of complicated questions. How, for example, can reunification with mainland China be reconciled with Hong Kong's status as a place whose history was shaped for more than 150 years by not being politically part of China? How are some of the more turbulent events in PRC history to be treated, especially when they have been viewed with such abhorrence by so many people in Hong Kong, not to mention having caused so many people in the PRC to seek refuge in Hong Kong? The answer has been a curious blend of promoting Chinese nationalism by revising, glossing over, or downplaying much of PRC history while emphasizing Hong Kong's historical distinctiveness.

When school began in September 1997, the Chinese history textbooks in Hong Kong were noticeably thinner than in previous years. In late 1995, Beijing had called for general changes in Hong Kong textbooks, but in early 1997 Vice Premier and Foreign Minister Qian Qichen declared that history textbooks should be rewritten "to suit the changes after 1997." Responding to appeals from Beijing, local publishers deleted or reduced topics that might be offensive or controversial: for example, Taiwan and Tibet history, the famine caused by the Great Leap Forward, and the democracy movements in China during the late 1970s and in 1989. The Tiananmen Square Massacre was rephrased as merely an "incident" rather than a "crackdown." The new textbooks devoted considerably more space to the Opium Wars, which in pre-1997 textbooks had often been described as little more than a trade conflict, and to the Cultural Revolution, which had affected several of China's leaders.

The HKSAR government has tried to put aside turbulent parts of Hong Kong's history that are linked to the PRC. Shortly after the reversion to Chinese sovereignty, Tung Chee-hwa invited several elderly leftists involved in the 1967 riots to a tea reception at Government House, where he commended them for their "outstanding contributions to Hong Kong society." Some of the men had worked for pro-Beijing newspapers in Hong Kong; others had been members of the famous East River Column during World War II. In July 1999, the government awarded Lee Chark-tim, who in 1967 had been president of the pro-Beijing Federation of Trade Unions and a member of the Anti-British Struggle Committee, the HKSAR's top honor: the Grand Bauhinia Medal. One of Lee's comrades, Wong Kin-lap, received the Golden Bauhinia Star. In July 2000, Liu Yat-yuen, who had also been a member of the Anti-British Struggle Committee, was awarded the Silver Bauhinia Star. In July 2001, the Hong Kong Security Bureau rescinded deportation orders against several people who had been deported in the 1950s and 1960s as radical leftists. Lo Tong, then principal at a pro-Beijing, patriotic middle school, had been deported in 1950 for raising the PRC flag and singing the national anthem at his school. Tsang Chiu-for, the highest-ranking Chinese police officer in Hong Kong at the time, had been deported in 1961 on suspicion of being a Communist spy. The government also awarded the Grand Bauhinia Medal to Yeung Kwong who, as chairman of the pro-Beijing Federation of Trade Unions and nominal head of the Anti-British Struggle Committee, had led a group of protesters in chanting anti-British slogans outside Government House. The awards were widely criticized by the public and the press as an attempt to vindicate the riots as a legitimate anti-British movement and appease pro-Beijing forces in Hong Kong. Pro-Beijing newspapers and legislators defended the awards, however, arguing that the radical leftists' role in the 1967 disturbances should not overshadow their subsequent contributions to Hong Kong.

For the historian, perhaps the most interesting way in which history figures in the ongoing process of Hong Kong's reunification with China is the HKSAR government's effort to use history and heritage preservation to promote a sense of Hong Kong localness and belonging within a larger sense of Chinese nationalism. Since 1997, several new museums have been devoted to Hong Kong's history, all run by the government's Leisure and Cultural Services Department. The main exhibit at one of these new museums, "The Hong Kong Story" at the Hong Kong Museum of History, introduces Hong Kong's natural and cultural heritage since prehistoric times with dioramas, reconstructed street scenes, films, and interactive exhibits. Here visitors can learn about Hong Kong's rich history through a variety of exhibits: boarding a fishing boat that rocks gently to the sounds of straining ropes, strolling through a traditional Cantonese village, or witnessing the horror and suffering during the Japanese occupation. Visitors can also help commemorate the reversion to Chinese sovereignty in an exhibit that includes an excerpt from Jiang Zemin's handover speech and ends with the handover fireworks display, with Hong Kong's trademark night skyline in the background. As the last caption in this "Hong Kong Story" notes, even though the museum exhibit ends with the reversion to Chinese sovereignty, "the Hong Kong story will continue to be written."

NOTES

1. James C. Hsiung, "The Paradox Syndrome and Update," in James C. Hsiung, ed., *Hong Kong the Super Paradox: Life after Return to China* (New York: St. Martin's, 2000), 1.

2. Frank Ching, "The Hong Kong Press: A Post-1997 Assessment," in Hsiung, *Hong Kong the Super Paradox*, 163–66.

3. James C. Hsiung, "The Hong Kong SAR: Prisoner of Legacy or History's Bellwether?" in Hsiung, *Hong Kong the Super Paradox*, 308.

4. Patrick Hase, "The District Office," in Elizabeth Sinn, ed., *Hong Kong, British Crown Colony, Revisited* (Hong Kong: Centre of Asian Studies, University of Hong Kong, 2001), 134, 144–45.

5. James Hayes, "Colonial Administration in British Hong Kong and Chinese Customary Law," in Sinn, *Hong Kong*, 71.

6. "Insiders' Insights," in Alan Knight and Yoshiko Nakano, eds., *Reporting Hong Kong: Foreign Media and the Handover* (New York: St. Martin's, 1999), 155–56.

7. Ching, "Hong Kong Press," 154.

8. C. K. Lau, *Hong Kong's Colonial Legacy: A Hong Kong Chinese's View of the British Heritage* (Hong Kong: Chinese University Press, 1997), 158–59.

9. Leo F. Goodstadt, *Uneasy Partners: The Conflict between Public Interest and Private Profit in Hong Kong* (Hong Kong: Hong Kong University Press, 2005), 8, 27, 29.

10. Hsiung, "Hong Kong SAR," 316.

11. Ming K. Chan, "The Legacy of the British Administration of Hong Kong: A View from Hong Kong," *China Quarterly* 151 (September 1997): 576.

12. Goodstadt, *Uneasy Partners*, 7, 122.

13. Anna Wu, "Government by Whom?" in Sally Blyth and Ian Wotherspoon, *Hong Kong Remembers* (Hong Kong: Oxford University Press, 1996), 165.

14. Chan, "Legacy of the British Administration," 582.

15. David Faure, *Colonialism and the Hong Kong Mentality* (Hong Kong: Centre of Asian Studies, University of Hong Kong, 2003), 2, 37.

16. Goodstadt, *Uneasy Partners*, 11, 32.

17. Knight and Nakano, *Reporting Hong Kong*, 202.

18. Goodstadt, *Uneasy Partners*, 134.

19. Lau, *Hong Kong's Colonial Legacy*, 109–12.

20. Ibid., 54.

21. Hugo Restall, "Beijing Takes Control of Hong Kong," *Far East Economic Review* 168(3) (March 2005): 40.

22. Ibid., 42.

23. Gregory Eliyu Guldin, "Toward a Greater Guangdong: Hong Kong's Sociocultural Impact on the Pearl River Delta and Beyond," in Reginald Yin-Wang Kwok and Alvin Y. So, eds., *The Hong Kong-Guangdong Link: Partnership in Flux* (Armonk, NY: Sharpe, 1995), 113–14.

Chronology of Key Events

111 BCE	Southern Yue Kingdom defeated by Emperor Han Wu Di. Gradual migration of Han Chinese to the Hong Kong region.
1200s–1300s	Increased migration to Hong Kong during the Yuan dynasty.
1600s–early 1800s	Hong Kong becomes more closely linked with the rest of China.
Early 1800s	Pirate Zhang Baozai uses Hong Kong Island as a base.
1834	Lord Napier urges Britain to take possession of Hong Kong Island. End of East India Company's monopoly over trade with China.
March 1839	Lin Zexu launches antiopium campaign.
November 1839	First Opium War begins.
January 26, 1841	British claim sovereignty over Hong Kong Island in accordance with disputed Convention of Chuenpi.
February 2, 1841	Charles Elliot proclaims that Hong Kong will be a free port and that all inhabitants will be allowed to retain their religions and customs.
February 1842	British Superintendency of Trade moves to Hong Kong from Macau.
August 29, 1842	Treaty of Nanking cedes Hong Kong Island to Britain "in perpetuity."

June 1843	Treaty of Nanking ratified by Britain and China; Hong Kong declared a British colony.
July 1844	Colonial treasurer Robert Montgomery Martin urges British government to abandon Hong Kong.
1847	Establishment of Man Mo Temple.
1849	Gold discovered in California; first shipload of Chinese laborers comes through Hong Kong.
1850s	Sino-British relations plagued by dispute over British access to Canton. British seek more trading and diplomatic concessions from China.
1851–1864	Taiping Rebellion and rise of Chinese emigration.
October 1856	*Arrow* incident and beginning of Second Opium War.
Early 1857	Five thousand Chinese residents heed Governor-General Ye Mingchen's order to leave Hong Kong.
January 15, 1857	E Sing Bakery poisoning.
December 1857	Anglo-French forces occupy Canton and capture Governor-General Ye Mingchen.
January 1858– October 1861	Chinese residents protest Anglo-French occupation of Canton by leaving Hong Kong in large numbers.
June 1858	Treaty of Tientsin fails to end Second Opium War.
July 1858	Twenty thousand Chinese leave Hong Kong.
October 18, 1860	Convention of Peking ends Second Opium War, giving British increased trading and diplomatic rights in China.
January 1861	British occupy Kowloon in accordance with Convention of Peking.
1862	Founding of the Central School.
1864	Establishment of Hong Kong and Shanghai Bank.
1866	Formation of District Watch Force.
1867	Contagious Diseases Ordinance passed.
1869	Formation of Tung Wah Hospital Committee.
Late 1870s–early 1880s	*Mui-tsai* controversy.
August 1882	Po Leung Kuk officially opened.
September 1884	Dockyard workers protest French aggression in China.

1880	Ng Choy becomes first Chinese appointed to Legislative Council.
1887	Establishment of Hong Kong College of Medicine for Chinese.
1888	Peak Tram opened.
1889	Contagious Diseases Ordinance replaced by Women's and Girl's Protection Ordinance.
1894	Hong Kong stricken with bubonic plague.
1896	Founding of Hong Kong Chinese Chamber of Commerce.
June 1898	Convention of Peking; New Territories leased to Britain for ninety-nine years.
Summer 1898	Chinese reformer Kang Youwei flees to Hong Kong after aborted Hundred Days of Reform.
October 1898	Residents of Kam Tin resist British occupation of New Territories.
April 16, 1899	Britain formally occupies New Territories.
1901	Revolutionary Yang Quyun assassinated by Qing agents in Hong Kong.
1904	Peak reserved for residence by Europeans.
1905–1906	Anti-American Boycott.
1908	Anti-Japanese Boycott.
1908	British government orders closing of opium divans in Hong Kong.
1910	Completion of Kowloon-Canton Railway.
October 1911	Republican revolution in China.
January 1, 1912	Establishment of Chinese Republic.
March 11, 1912	Official opening of University of Hong Kong.
July 1912	Assassination attempt on Governor Francis Henry May.
Late 1912–early 1913	Tram Boycott after colonial government bans use of Chinese currency.
1913	Governor May pushes through Education Bill, requiring all private schools to register with government.
1914–1918	During World War I, Hong Kong provides laborers for Western Front.

1917–late 1920s	Anti-*mui-tsai* campaign.
1918	Peak District Bill prohibits non-Europeans from living on Victoria Peak.
February 1918	Fire at Happy Valley racetrack kills six hundred people and wounds four hundred others.
1918	Outbreak of cerebrospinal meningitis kills more than one thousand people.
1919	Part of Cheung Chau reserved as vacation reserve for British and American missionaries.
1919	Riots over rice prices.
May 1919	May Fourth Movement in China leads to boycotts in Hong Kong.
Spring 1920	Mechanics' strike.
January–March 1922	Seamen's strike.
June 1925–October 1926	General strike-boycott.
May 1926	Chow Shouson becomes first Chinese appointed to Executive Council.
1931	Japanese invasion of Manchuria leads to anti-Japanese riots and hostilities in Hong Kong.
1936	Urban Council established.
July 1937	Japan launches full-scale invasion of China. Hong Kong becomes haven for refugees and important source of arms and relief for China.
September 1938	Hong Kong declared neutral zone. Emergency Powers Ordinance reinstated.
July 1941	Japanese assets in Hong Kong frozen.
December 8, 1941	Japanese forces invade Hong Kong.
December 25, 1941	Governor Mark Young surrenders to Lieutenant General Sakai Takashi.
January 1942	British, American, and Dutch residents arrested.
January 1942	Japanese authorities announce that anyone without residence or employment must leave Hong Kong.
January 1942	Japanese authorities attempt to recruit local community leaders through Chinese Representative Council and Chinese Cooperative Council.

Mid-1942	Chiang Kai-shek's Nationalist government approaches Britain to surrender Hong Kong after the war.
Summer 1944	Hong Kong Planning Unit formed in Britain to coordinate postwar recovery.
Spring 1945	Colonial Office, Hong Kong Planning Unit, and China Association consider proposals for constitutional change in Hong Kong.
August 16, 1945	Rear Admiral Cecil Harcourt accepts Japanese surrender on behalf of Britain and China.
November 1945	Government controls on economy lifted.
July 1946	Residential ordinances for Cheung Chau and the Peak repealed.
August 1946	Mark Young announces plans for constitutional reform in Hong Kong.
July 1947	British government approves Young plan "in principle."
1947–1949	During Chinese civil war, Shanghai firms move operations to Hong Kong.
December 1948	British government declares intention to keep Hong Kong.
April 1949	*Amethyst* incident.
June–July 1949	Local organizations petition Governor Alexander Grantham for constitutional reforms.
August 1949	With Communist victory imminent on the mainland, the Hong Kong government issues emergency public security legislation. British government reaffirms commitment to keeping Hong Kong.
October 1, 1949	Establishment of People's Republic of China (PRC).
December 1949	Tramway strike.
Late 1949–June 1952	China National Aviation Corporation and Central Air Transport Incorporation dispute involving China, Taiwan, Hong Kong, Britain, and United States.
1950–1953	U.S. and UN embargoes during Korean War threaten Hong Kong's economy and encourage shift toward industrialization.
May 1950	Hong Kong government limits immigration from mainland China.

March 1952	Riots in Kowloon after Canton comfort mission is denied entrance to Hong Kong.
September 1952	British cabinet plans for constitutional reform in Hong Kong.
October 1952	Lord Lyttelton tells House of Commons that major constitutional reforms would be inopportune.
December 24, 1953	Squatter fire in Shek Kip Mei leaves more than fifty-eight thousand people homeless.
April 1955	*Kashmir Princess,* airplane transporting PRC officials and foreign journalists, explodes after departing from Kai Tak airport.
October 9, 1956	Violent confrontation between pro-PRC and pro-Taiwan supporters leads to riots in Kowloon.
October 1957	Secret agreement between the United States and Britain: the United States will defend Hong Kong in case of an attack by China.
1963	*People's Daily* declares that PRC will settle Hong Kong problem when "the time is ripe."
April 1966	Star Ferry riots.
May 1967–January 1968	Riots by local leftists lead to violent confrontations between leftists and colonial police force.
March 1972	Huang Hua, China's ambassador to UN, declares that Hong Kong's political status will be resolved by PRC government "when conditions are ripe."
June 1972	Landslides kill more than 250 people.
November 1972	UN General Assembly removes Hong Kong and Macau from list of colonial territories. Britain subsequently changes Hong Kong's status from Crown Colony to Dependent Territory.
1974	Establishment of Independent Commission Against Corruption (ICAC).
1975	Vietnamese refugees arrive in large numbers.
May 1975	Queen Elizabeth II visits Hong Kong.
October 1977	Several thousand police officers march on police commissioner and ICAC headquarters.
March 1979	Governor Murray MacLehose visits Beijing to discuss end of 1997 New Territories lease, assured by PRC

	leader Deng Xiaoping that Hong Kong investors can "put their hearts at ease."
October 1980	MacLehose announces touch base policy whereby illegal immigrants from the mainland will be repatriated.
March 1981	British Parliament passes British Nationality (Hong Kong) Act, excluding more than 2.5 million Hong Kong Chinese from right of abode in Britain.
April 1982	Deng Xiaoping informs former British prime minister Edward Heath that Hong Kong people will be allowed to rule after 1997 and that Hong Kong will become a Special Administrative Region.
September 1982	British prime minister Margaret Thatcher arrives in Beijing to discuss Hong Kong's post-1997 future with Deng Xiaoping.
June 1983	Deng Xiaoping declares that PRC will resume sovereignty over Hong Kong in 1997.
September 1983	Stalled Sino-British negotiations lead to drop in value of Hong Kong dollar, subsequently pegged to American dollar.
October 1983	PRC declares that it will make a unilateral declaration if an agreement on Hong Kong's reversion to Chinese sovereignty is not reached by September 1984.
January 1984	Riots by taxi drivers in Mongkok.
June 1984	PRC government invites senior members of Executive Council to visit Beijing.
July 1984	Legislation on introduction of indirect elections for Legislative Council in 1985. Hong Kong government publishes consultation green paper, *The Further Development of Representative Government in Hong Kong*.
November 1984	Hong Kong government publishes policy white paper, *The Further Development of Representative Government in Hong Kong*, announcing that gradual changes to Legislative Council will begin in 1988.
December 19, 1984	Signing of Sino-British Joint Declaration in Beijing by Margaret Thatcher and Zhao Ziyang.
May 28, 1985	Joint Declaration officially ratified.
July 1985	Establishment of Hong Kong Basic Law Drafting Committee.

September 1985	Establishment of Basic Law Consultative Committee.
September 26, 1985	First indirect elections for Legislative Council.
April 1986	Hong Kong joins General Agreement on Tariffs and Trade (GATT).
October 1986	Queen Elizabeth II visits Beijing, Shanghai, Guangzhou, and Hong Kong.
December 5, 1986	Death of Governor Edward Youde in Beijing.
January 1987	Hong Kong government announces that Kowloon Walled City will be demolished before 1997.
April 1987	David Wilson arrives as governor.
February 1988	Hong Kong government publishes policy white paper, *The Development of Representative Government: The Way Forward,* announcing that direct elections for Legislative Council will be postponed until 1991.
April 1988	First draft of Basic Law published for public consultation.
July 1988	Permanent office of Sino-British Joint Liaison Group opened in Hong Kong.
September 22, 1988	Indirect elections for twenty-six of fifty-seven seats in Legislative Council.
November 1988	Governor Wilson visits Beijing, meets with Li Peng and other senior PRC officials.
February 22, 1989	Second draft of Basic Law published for public consultation.
April 15, 1989	Death of Hu Yaobang leads to prodemocracy demonstrations in Beijing.
May 20, 1989	After PRC government declares martial law in Bejing, a massive demonstration is held in Hong Kong. Prodemocracy activists form the Hong Kong Alliance in Support of the Patriotic Democratic Movement in China.
May 24, 1989	Official members of Executive Council and Legislative Council call for half of legislature to be directly elected by 1997.
June 4–5, 1989	More than one million people in Hong Kong protest against Tiananmen Square Massacre. Two members of Basic Law Drafting Committee resign in protest.

July 11, 1989	Jiang Zemin, new general secretary of Chinese Communist Party, warns Hong Kong people not to interfere in mainland politics.
July 1989	The British government rejects calls by Executive Council and Legislative Council for granting right of abode to 3.25 million Hong Kong holders of British passports.
Fall 1989	The Hong Kong government refuses to repatriate PRC swimmer Yang Yang, who has sought asylum in Hong Kong.
October 1989	Governor Wilson announces controversial Port and Airport Development Strategy.
October 31, 1989	End of second Basic Law draft public-consultation period.
December 1989	The British government announces that fifty thousand families will be granted full British National passports, with right of abode in Britain. The PRC government insists that it will not recognize these passports.
January 1990	Governor Wilson visits Beijing and convinces Li Peng of need to increase number of directly elected Legislative Council members in 1991.
February 1990	British and Chinese officials make secret deal on structure of Legislative Council.
March 1990	Draft version of Bill of Rights published.
March 21, 1990	Hong Kong government announces direct elections for Legislative Council in 1991.
April 1990	Final version of Bill of Rights published.
April 4, 1990	PRC government formally approves Basic Law.
August 1990	Hong Kong government insists that airport project does not require approval from British or Chinese governments.
September 1990	Lord Caithness, British minister for Hong Kong, announces that Hong Kong government must consult PRC government on airport project.
October 1990	Hong Kong government announces that construction of first stage of airport project will proceed with public funds.
December 1990	Beginning of application period for British citizenship under British Nationality (Hong Kong) Act.

January 1991	Governor Wilson discusses airport project with PRC officials in Beijing.
April 1991	British foreign secretary Douglas Hurd discusses airport project with PRC officials in Beijing.
June 8, 1991	Hong Kong Bill of Rights enacted. PRC government maintains right to repeal any laws that violate Basic Law.
June 1991	Governor Wilson discusses airport issue with Prime Minister John Major and other senior officials in London.
June 30, 1991	Percy Cradock, foreign policy advisor to John Major, issues Memorandum of Understanding on airport project with PRC officials in Beijing.
July 4, 1991	Governor Wilson announces Sino-British accord on airport project.
September 3, 1991	John Major signs Memorandum of Understanding with Li Peng in Beijing.
September 1991	First direct elections for Legislative Council.
January 1992	U.S. Congress enacts United States–Hong Kong Policy Act, stipulating that the United States will continue to treat Hong Kong as a separate territory after 1997.
May 1992	Martin Lee and Yeung Sum of United Democrats discuss political reforms with John Major and Governor-designate Chris Patten in London.
June 1992	Governor Wilson meets with Li Peng in Beijing.
July 9, 1992	Governor Patten arrives.
July 10, 1992	Pro-PRC groups form Democratic Alliance for Betterment of Hong Kong.
October 7, 1992	Governor Patten announces proposal for political reform.
June 1994	With support of Legislative Council, Governor Patten decides to proceed with proposed political reforms.
August 1994	PRC government closes down Beijing branch of Giordano, owned by Hong Kong entrepreneur and critic Jimmy Lai.
December 1995	Former Kowloon Walled City, razed in 1994, is officially opened as a classical Chinese garden.

January 1996	PRC government establishes Hong Kong Preparatory Committee.
September 1996	Mission to protest Japan's claims to Diaoyutai (Senkaku) Islands ends disastrously when Hong Kong activist David Chan is drowned.
December 1996	Tung Chee-hwa appointed chief executive of Hong Kong Special Administrative Region (HKSAR). Preparatory Committee chooses provisional Legislative Council.
Midnight, July 1, 1997	Hong Kong reverts to Chinese sovereignty.
July 2, 1997	Beginning of Asian financial crisis caused by currency devaluation in Thailand.
July 1998	Opening of new airport at Chek Lap Kok hampered by severe computer errors.
March 1999	Court of Final Appeal overturns convictions of two men previously found guilty of defacing PRC and HSKAR flags.
May 1999	March by civil servants against HKSAR government's plans to privatize certain departments in civil service.
June 1999	PRC's National People's Congress interprets Basic Law, overturning earlier ruling by Court of Final Appeal on right of abode.
January 2001	Chief Secretary Anson Chan announces that she will resign for "personal reasons."
July 2001	HKSAR government allows Chinese American professor Li Shaomin to return to Hong Kong.
January 2002	Court of Final Appeal reverses earlier ruling on right of abode.
February 2002	In an uncontested election, Tung Chee-hwa wins more than 700 of 800 nominations.
July 2002	50,000 civil servants hold a strike against pay cuts.
September 2002	HKSAR government releases antisedition bill for public consultation.
March 16, 2003	World Health Organization declares HKSAR to be infected by SARS; almost three hundred people killed by SARS in next three months.
June 2003	Signing of Closer Economic Partnership Agreement between Hong Kong and Guangdong.

July 1, 2003	Some 500,000 people march against government's proposed security legislation.
July 16, 2003	Resignations of Security Secretary Regina Ip and Financial Secretary Antony Leung.
September 2003	After much opposition, HKSAR withdraws controversial proposal for public security legislation.
April 6, 2004	Standing Committee of National People's Congress rules that local attempts to modify election laws in Hong Kong require approval from PRC central government.
April 26, 2004	Standing Committee rules out possibility of popular elections for chief executive in 2007 and for expanded elections for legislature in 2008.
July 2004	Resignations of two health officials after publication of critical report on government's handling of SARS contamination.
March 10, 2005	Tung Chee-hwa resigns as chief executive of HKSAR; Chief Secretary Donald Tsang becomes acting chief executive.
May 2005	Court of Final Appeal overturns criminal convictions against eight Falun Gong followers.
June 16, 2005	Donald Tsang wins uncontested election to complete Tung Chee-hwa's second term as chief executive.
September 2005	Hong Kong Disneyland opened.
December 4, 2005	Former chief secretary Anson Chan participates in large pro-democracy rally.
December 18, 2005	Riots against World Trade Organization lead to clash between police and protesters led by South Korean farmers.
November 2006	Former HKSAR health director Margaret Chan elected head of World Health Organization.
December 2006	Protesters try unsuccessfully to block demolition of the historic Star Ferry clock tower in Central District.

Bibliography
and Further Reading

Abbas, Ackbar. *Hong Kong: The Culture of Disappearance*. Minneapolis: University of Minnesota Press, 1997.

Baker, Hugh D. "Social Change in Hong Kong: Hong Kong Man in Search of Majority." In David Shambaugh, ed., *Greater China: The Next Superpower*, 212–25. Oxford: Oxford University Press, 1995.

Banham, Tony. *Not the Slightest Chance: The Defence of Hong Kong, 1941*. Hong Kong: Hong Kong University Press, 2003.

Bard, Solomon. *Traders of Hong Kong: Some Foreign Merchant Houses, 1841–1899*. Hong Kong: Urban Council, 1993.

Benedict, Carol. "Framing Plague in China's Past." In Gail Hershatter, Emily Honig, Jonathan N. Lipman, and Randall Stross, eds., *Remapping China: Fissures in Historical Terrain*, 27–41. Stanford, CA: Stanford University Press, 1996.

Birch, Alan, and Martin Cole. *Captive Years: The Occupation of Hong Kong, 1941–45*. Hong Kong: Heinemann Asia, 1982.

Bird, Isabella L. *The Golden Chersonese and the Way Thither*. London: John Murray, 1883.

Blyth, Sally, and Ian Wotherspoon. *Hong Kong Remembers*. Hong Kong: Oxford University Press, 1996.

Bonavia, David. *Hong Kong 1997*. Bromley, Kent, UK: Columbus Books, 1985.

Brown, Judith M., and Rosemary Foot, eds. *Hong Kong's Transitions, 1842–1997*. London: Macmillan, 1997.

Buckley, Roger. *Hong Kong: The Road to 1997*. Cambridge: Cambridge University Press, 1997.

Cai Rongfang. *Xianggang ren zhi Xianggang shi, 1841–1945* [The Hong Kong People's History of Hong Kong, 1841–1945]. Hong Kong: Oxford University Press, 2001.

Cameron, Nigel. *An Illustrated History of Hong Kong*. Hong Kong: Oxford University Press, 1991.

Carnoy, Martin. *Education As Cultural Imperialism*. New York: Longman, 1974.

Carroll, John M. "Displaying the Past to Serve the Present: Museums and Heritage Preservation in Post-Colonial Hong Kong." *Twentieth-Century China* 31(1) (November 2005): 73–103.

———. *Edge of Empires: Chinese Elites and British Colonials in Hong Kong*. Cambridge: Harvard University Press, 2005.

Chan, Anthony B. *Li Ka-shing: Hong Kong's Elusive Billionaire*. Hong Kong: Oxford University Press, 1996.

Chan, Ming K. "The Legacy of the British Administration of Hong Kong: A View from Hong Kong." *China Quarterly* 151 (September 1997): 567–82.

———, ed. *Precarious Balance: Hong Kong between China and Britain, 1842–1992*. Armonk, NY: Sharpe, 1994.

———. "Stability and Prosperity in Hong Kong: The Twilight of Laissez-faire Colonialism?" *Journal of Asian Studies* 42(3) (May 1983): 589–98.

Chan, Ming K., and David J. Clarke, eds. *The Hong Kong Basic Law: Blueprint for Stability and Prosperity Under Chinese Sovereignty?* Armonk, NY: Sharpe, 1991.

Chan, Ming K., and Gerald A. Postiglione, eds. *The Hong Kong Reader: Passage to Chinese Sovereignty*. Armonk, NY: Sharpe, 1996.

Chan, Wai Kwan. *The Making of Hong Kong Society: Three Studies of Class Formation in Early Hong Kong*. Oxford, UK: Clarendon, 1991.

Chan Lau, Kit-ching. *China, Britain and Hong Kong, 1895–1945*. Hong Kong: Chinese University Press, 1990.

———. *From Nothing to Nothing: The Chinese Communist Movement and Hong Kong, 1921–1936*. New York and Hong Kong: St. Martin's/Hong Kong University Press, 1999.

Chan Lau, Kit-ching, and Peter Cunich, eds. *An Impossible Dream: Hong Kong University from Foundation to Re-Establishment, 1910–1950*. New York: Oxford University Press, 2002.

Chang, David Wen-wei, and Richard Y. Chuang. *The Politics of Hong Kong's Reversion to China*. Basingstoke, UK: Macmillan, 1998.

Cheng, Irene. *Clara Ho Tung: A Hong Kong Lady, Her Family and Her Times*. Hong Kong: Chinese University Press, 1976.

Cheng, Joseph Y. S., ed. *Hong Kong: In Search of a Future*. Hong Kong: Oxford University Press, 1984.

Cheng, Joseph Y. S., and Sonny S. H. Lo, eds. *From Colony to SAR: Hong Kong's Challenges Ahead*. Hong Kong: Chinese University Press, 1995.

Cheung, Fanny M., ed. *EnGendering Hong Kong Society: A Gender Perspective of Women's Status*. Hong Kong: Chinese University Press, 1997.

Ching, Frank. "Misreading Hong Kong." *Foreign Affairs* 73(3) (1997): 53–66.

Chiu, Fred Y. L. "Politics and the Body Social in Colonial Hong Kong." In Tani E. Barlow, ed., *Formation of Colonial Modernity in East Asia*, 295–322. Durham, NC: Duke University Press, 1997.

Chiu, Stephen. *The Politics of Laissez-Faire: Hong Kong's Strategy of Industrialization in Historical Perspective*. Hong Kong: Hong Kong Institute of Asia-Pacific Studies, 1994.

Choa, Gerald H. *The Life and Times of Sir Kai Ho Kai*. Hong Kong: Chinese University Press, 1981.

Chu, Cindy Yik-yi. *The Maryknoll Sisters in Hong Kong, 1921–1969: In Love with the Chinese*. New York: Palgrave Macmillan, 2004.

Chung, Stephanie Po-yin. *Chinese Business Groups in Hong Kong and Political Change in South China, 1900–25.* Basingstoke, UK: Macmillan, 1998.

Chung, Sze-yuen. *Hong Kong's Journey to Reunification: Memoirs of Sze-yuen Chung.* Hong Kong: Chinese University Press, 2001.

Clarke, David. *Hong Kong Art: Culture and Decolonization.* Durham, NC: Duke University Press, 2001.

Coates, Austin. *Myself a Mandarin: Memoirs of a Special Magistrate.* London: Frederick Muller, 1968.

Cohen, Warren I., and Li Zhao, eds. *Hong Kong under Chinese Rule: The Economic and Political Implications of Reversion.* Cambridge: Cambridge University Press, 1997.

Cooper, John. *Colony in Conflict: The Hong Kong Disturbances, May 1967–January 1968.* Hong Kong: Swindon, 1970.

Cottrell, Robert. *The End of Hong Kong: The Secret Diplomacy of Imperial Retreat.* London: John Murray, 1993.

Cradock, Percy. *Experiences of China.* London: John Murray, 1994.

Crisswell, Colin N. *The Taipans: Hong Kong's Merchant Princes.* Hong Kong: Oxford University Press, 1981.

Crisswell, Colin, and Mike Watson. *The Royal Hong Kong Police (1841–1945).* Hong Kong: Macmillan, 1982.

Des Voeux, Sir G. William. *My Colonial Service in British Guiana, St. Lucia, Trinidad, Fiji, Australia, Newfoundland, and Hong Kong with Interludes.* 2 vols. London: John Murray, 1903.

Dimbleby, Jonathan. *The Last Governor: Chris Patten and the Handover of Hong Kong.* London: Little, Brown, 1997.

Ding You. *Xianggang chuqi shihua* [Early Hong Kong]. Beijing: Lianhe chubanshe, 1983.

Eitel, E. J. *Europe in China: The History of Hong Kong from the Beginning to the Year 1882.* Hong Kong: Kelly and Walsh, 1895; reprint, Hong Kong: Oxford University Press, 1983.

Endacott, G. B. *A Biographical Sketch-Book of Early Hong Kong.* Singapore: Eastern Universities Press, 1962; reprint with new introduction by John M. Carroll, Hong Kong: Hong Kong University Press, 2005.

———. *An Eastern Entrepot: A Collection of Documents Illustrating the History of Hong Kong.* London: Her Majesty's Stationery Office, 1964.

———. *Government and People in Hong Kong, 1841–1962: A Constitutional History.* Hong Kong: Hong Kong University Press, 1964.

———. *A History of Hong Kong.* Rev. ed. Hong Kong: Oxford University Press, 1973.

———. *Hong Kong Eclipse.* Edited with new material by Alan Birch. Hong Kong: Oxford University Press, 1978.

England, Joe, and John Rear. *Chinese Labour under British Rule: A Critical Study of Labour Relations and Law in Hong Kong.* Hong Kong: Oxford University Press, 1975.

———. *Industrial Relations and Law in Hong Kong.* Hong Kong: Oxford University Press, 1981.

Evans, Grant, and Maria Tam, eds. *Hong Kong: The Anthropology of a Chinese Metropolis.* Richmond, Surrey, UK: Curzon, 1997.

Faure, David. *Colonialism and the Hong Kong Mentality.* Hong Kong: Centre of Asian Studies, University of Hong Kong, 2003.

————, ed. *A Documentary History of Hong Kong: Society.* Hong Kong: Hong Kong University Press, 1997.

————, ed. *Hong Kong: A Reader in Social History.* Hong Kong: Oxford University Press, 2003.

Faure, David, and Lee Pui-tak, eds. *A Documentary History of Hong Kong: Economy.* Hong Kong: Hong Kong University Press, 2004.

Fay, Peter Ward. *The Opium War, 1840–1842: Barbarians in the Celestial Empire in the Early Part of the Nineteenth Century and the War by Which They Forced Her Gates Ajar.* Chapel Hill: University of North Carolina Press, 1975.

Feldwick, W. *Present Day Impressions of the Far East and Prominent Chinese at Home and Abroad: The History, People, Commerce, Industries and Resources of China, Hongkong, Indo-China, Malaya and Netherlands India.* London: Globe Encyclopaedia, 1917.

Feng Bangyan. *Xianggang Huazi caituan, 1841–1996* [Chinese Financial Organizations in Hong Kong, 1841–1996]. Hong Kong: Sanlian, 1997.

————. *Xianggang Yingzi caituan, 1841–1996* [British Financial Organizations in Hong Kong, 1841–1996]. Hong Kong: Sanlian, 1996.

Fok, K. C. *Lectures on Hong Kong History: Hong Kong's Role in Modern Chinese History.* Hong Kong: Commercial Press, 1990.

Fong Mee-yin (Fang Meixian). *Xianggang zaoqi jiaoyu fazhan shi* [The First Hundred Years of Hong Kong Education]. Hong Kong: Zhongguo xueshe, 1975.

Fortune, Robert. *Three Years' Wanderings in the Northern Provinces of China, Including a Visit to the Tea, Silk, and Cotton Countries: With an Account of Agriculture and Horticulture of the Chinese, New Plants, etc.* London: J. Murray, 1847.

Gao Tianqiang and Tang Zuomin. *Xianggang Rizhan shiqi* [Hong Kong under the Japanese Occupation]. Hong Kong: Sanlian, 1995.

Gillingham, Paul. *At the Peak: Hong Kong between the Wars.* Hong Kong: Macmillan, 1983.

Gold, Thomas B. "Go with Your Feelings: Hong Kong and Taiwan Popular Culture in Greater China." In David Shambaugh, ed., *Greater China: The Next Superpower,* 255–73. Oxford: Oxford University Press, 1995.

Goodstadt, Leo F. *Uneasy Partners: The Conflict between Public Interest and Private Profit in Hong Kong.* Hong Kong: Hong Kong University Press, 2005.

Grantham, Alexander. *Via Ports: From Hong Kong to Hong Kong.* Hong Kong: Hong Kong University Press, 1965.

Guan Lixiong. *Rizhan shiqi de Xianggang* [Hong Kong under the Japanese Occupation]. Hong Kong: Sanlian, 1993.

Hamilton, Gary G., ed. *Cosmopolitan Capitalists: Hong Kong and the Chinese Diaspora at the End of the 20th Century.* Seattle: University of Washington Press, 1999.

Hao, Yen-p'ing. *The Comprador in Nineteenth Century China: Bridge between East and West.* Cambridge: Harvard University Press, 1970.

Harter, Seth. "Hong Kong's Dirty Little Secret: Clearing the Walled City of Kowloon." *Journal of Urban History* 27(1) (November 2000): 92–113.

Hayes, James. *Friends and Teachers: Hong Kong and Its People, 1953–87.* Hong Kong: Hong Kong University Press, 1996.

————. *The Hong Kong Region: Institutions and Leadership in Town and Countryside.* Hamden, CT: Archon, 1977.

——. *Tsuen Wan: Growth of a "New Town" and Its People.* Hong Kong: Oxford University Press, 1993.

He Wenxiang. *Xianggang jiazushi* [History of Hong Kong Families]. Hong Kong: Mingbao chubanshe, 1992.

Heald, Tim. *Beating Retreat: Hong Kong under the Last Governor.* London: Sinclair-Stevenson, 1997.

Heaton, William. "Maoist Revolutionary Strategy and Modern Colonialism: The Cultural Revolution in Hong Kong." *Asia Survey* 10(9) (September 1970): 35–49.

Herschensohn, Bruce, ed. *Hong Kong at the Handover.* Lanham, MD: Lexington, 2000.

Hoe, Susanna. *The Private Life of Old Hong Kong: Western Women in the British Colony.* Hong Kong: Oxford University Press, 1991.

Hoe, Susanna, and Derek Roebuck. *The Taking of Hong Kong: Charles and Clara Elliot in China Waters.* Richmond, Surrey, UK: Curzon, 1999.

Holdsworth, May. *Foreign Devils: Expatriates in Hong Kong.* With additional text by Caroline Courtauld. Hong Kong: Oxford University Press, 2002.

Hook, Brian. "British Views of the Legacy of the Colonial Administration of Hong Kong: A Preliminary Assessment." *China Quarterly* 151 (September 1997): 553–66.

——. "Political Change in Hong Kong." In David Shambaugh, ed., *Greater China: The Next Superpower,* 188–211. Oxford: Oxford University Press, 1995.

Hopkins, Keith. *Hong Kong: The Industrial Colony: A Political, Social and Economic Survey.* Hong Kong: Oxford University Press, 1971.

Hsiung, James C., ed. *Hong Kong the Super Paradox: Life after Return to China.* New York: St. Martin's, 2000.

Hughes, Richard. *Hong Kong: Borrowed Place, Borrowed Time.* London: André Deutsch, 1968.

Hunter, William C. *The "Fan Kwae" at Canton before Treaty Days, 1825–1844.* London: Kegan Paul, Trench, 1882.

Huo Qichang. *Xianggang yu jindai Zhongguo* [Hong Kong and Modern China]. Taipei: Shangwu yinshuguan, 1993.

Hyam, Ronald. *Britain's Imperial Century, 1815–1914.* Basingstoke, UK: Palgrave Macmillan, 2002.

Irish University Press Area Studies Series. *British Parliamentary Papers, China, 24–26: Correspondence, Dispatches, Reports, Ordinances, Memoranda and Other Papers Relating to the Affairs of Hong Kong, 1846–60.* Shannon, Ireland: Irish University Press, 1971.

Jarman, R. L., ed. *Hong Kong Annual Administration Reports, 1841–1941,* Vol. 1, *1841–1886.* Oxford, UK: Archive Editions, 1996.

Jarvie, I. C., and Joseph Agassi, eds. *Hong Kong: Society in Transition.* London: Routledge and Kegan Paul, 1969.

Judd, Denis. *Empire: The British Imperial Experience, from 1765 to the Present.* New York: Basic Books, 1996.

King, Ambrose Y. C., and Rance P. L. Lee, eds. *Social Life and Development in Hong Kong.* Hong Kong: Chinese University Press, 1981.

King, Frank H. H. *The History of the Hongkong and Shanghai Banking Corporation.* 4 vols. Cambridge: Cambridge University Press, 1987–1990.

Knight, Alan, and Yoshiko Nakano, eds. *Reporting Hong Kong: Foreign Media and the Handover.* New York: St. Martin's, 1999.

Kwan, Daniel Y. K. *Marxist Intellectuals and the Chinese Labor Movement: A Study of Deng Zhongxia (1894–1933).* Seattle: University of Washington Press, 1997.

Kwok, Reginald Yin-Wang, and Alvin Y. So, eds. *The Hong Kong-Guangdong Link: Partnership in Flux.* Armonk, NY: Sharpe, 1995.

Lau, C. K. *Hong Kong's Colonial Legacy: A Hong Kong Chinese's View of the British Heritage.* Hong Kong: Chinese University Press, 1997.

Lau, Siu-kai. *Society and Politics in Hong Kong.* Hong Kong: Chinese University Press, 1982.

Lau, Siu-kai, and Kuan Hsin-chi. *The Ethos of the Hong Kong Chinese.* Hong Kong: Chinese University Press, 1988.

Lee, Rance P. L., ed. *Corruption and Its Control in Hong Kong: Situations up to the Late Seventies.* Hong Kong: Chinese University Press, 1981.

Lee, Vicky. *Being Eurasian: Memories across Racial Divides.* Hong Kong: Hong Kong University Press, 2004.

Leeming, Frank. "The Earlier Industrialization of Hong Kong." *Modern Asian Studies* 9(3) (1975): 337–42.

———. *Street Studies in Hong Kong: Localities in a Chinese City.* Hong Kong: Oxford University Press, 1977.

Lethbridge, Henry J. *Hard Graft in Hong Kong: Scandal, Corruption, the ICAC.* Hong Kong: Oxford University Press, 1985.

———. *Hong Kong: Stability and Change; A Collection of Essays.* Hong Kong: Oxford University Press, 1978.

Levine, Philippa. "Modernity, Medicine, and Colonialism: The Contagious Diseases Ordinances in Hong Kong and the Straits Settlements." *positions* 6(3) (Winter 1998): 675–705.

Li Jiayuan. *Xianggang baoye zatan* [On the Hong Kong Press]. Hong Kong: Joint Publishing, 1989.

Liang Shangyuan. *Zhonggong zai Xianggang* [The Chinese Communists in Hong Kong]. Hong Kong: Guangjiaojing, 1989.

Lin Youlan. *Xianggang shihua, zengding ben* [Stories of Hong Kong, Revised Edition]. Hong Kong: Shanghai shudian, 1985.

Liu, Shuyong. "Hong Kong: A Survey of Its Political and Economic Development over the Past 150 Years." *China Quarterly* 151 (September 1997): 583–92.

Liu Shuyong, ed. *Jianming Xianggangshi* [Concise History of Hong Kong]. Hong Kong: Joint Publishing, 1998.

Liu Zesheng. *Xianggang gujin* [Hong Kong Past and Present]. Guangzhou: Guangzhou wenhua chubanshe, 1988.

———. *Xiangjiang yetan* [Evening Chats about Hong Kong]. Hong Kong: Joint Publishing, 1990.

Lo, Hsiang-lin. *Hong Kong and Its External Communications before 1842: The History of Hong Kong Prior to the British Arrival.* Hong Kong: Institute of Chinese Culture, 1963.

———. *The Role of Hong Kong in the Cultural Interchange between East and West.* Tokyo: Centre for East Asian Studies, 1963.

Lo, Shiu-hing. *The Politics of Democratization in Hong Kong.* New York: St. Martin's, 1997.

Louis, Wm. Roger. "Hong Kong: The Critical Phase, 1945–1949." *American Historical Review* 102(4) (October 1997): 1052–1084.

Lu Yan, et al. *Xianggang zhanggu* [Hong Kong Anecdotes]. 12 vols. Hong Kong: Guangjiaojing chubanshe, 1977–1989.

Luk, Bernard Hung-kay. "Chinese Culture in the Hong Kong Curriculum: Heritage and Colonialism." *Comparative Education Review* 35(4) (November 1991): 650–68.

Ma, Eric Kit-wai. "Re-Advertising Hong Kong: Nostalgia Industry and Popular History." *positions* 9(1) (2001): 131–59.

Mark, Chi-kwan. "Defence or Decolonisation? Britain, the United States, and the Hong Kong Question in 1957." *Journal of Imperial and Commonwealth History* 33(1) (January 2005): 51–72.

———. *Hong Kong and the Cold War: Anglo-American Relations, 1949–1957.* Oxford, UK: Clarendon, 2004.

Mathews, Gordon. "Heunggongyahn: On the Past, Present, and Future of Hong Kong Identity." *Bulletin of Concerned Asian Scholars* 29(3) (1997): 3–13.

McGurn, William. *Perfidious Albion: The Abandonment of Hong Kong, 1997.* Washington, DC: Ethics and Public Policy Center, 1992.

Miller, John, and Kirsten Miller, eds. *Chronicles Abroad: Hong Kong.* San Francisco: Chronicle Books, 1994.

Mills, Lennox A. *British Rule in Eastern Asia: A Study of Contemporary Government and Economic Development in British Malaya and Hong Kong.* London: Oxford University Press, 1942.

Miners, Norman J. *The Government and Politics of Hong Kong.* Hong Kong: Oxford University Press, 1991.

———. *Hong Kong under Imperial Rule, 1912–1941.* Hong Kong: Oxford University Press, 1987.

Morris, Jan. *Hong Kong: Epilogue to an Empire.* New York: Vintage, 1997.

Munn, Christopher. *Anglo-China: Chinese People and British Rule in Hong Kong, 1841–1880.* Richmond, Surrey, UK: Curzon, 2001.

———. "The Chusan Episode: Britain's Occupation of a Chinese Island, 1840–46." *Journal of Imperial and Commonwealth History* 25(1) (January 1997): 82–112.

———. "Colonialism in a Chinese Atmosphere: The Caldwell Affair and the Perils of Collaboration in Early Colonial Hong Kong." In Robert Bickers and Christian Henriot, eds., *New Frontiers: Imperialism's New Communities in East Asia, 1842–1953,* 12–37. Manchester, UK: Manchester University Press, 2000.

———. "The Hong Kong Opium Revenue, 1845–1885." In Timothy Brook and Bob Tadashi Wakabayashi, eds., *Opium Regimes: China, Britain, and Japan, 1839–1952,* 105–26. Berkeley: University of California Press, 2000.

Myer, David R. *Hong Kong As a Global Metropolis.* Cambridge: Cambridge University Press, 2000.

Ng, Alice Lun Ngai Ha. *Interactions of East and West: Development of Public Education in Early Hong Kong.* Hong Kong: Chinese University Press, 1984.

Ng, Peter Y. C., and Hugh D. R. Baker. *New Peace County: A Chinese Gazetteer of Hong Kong Region.* Hong Kong: Hong Kong University Press, 1983.

Ngo, Tak-Wing, ed. *Hong Kong's History: State and Society under Colonial Rule.* London: Routledge, 1999.

Norton-Kyshe, James William. *The History of the Laws and Courts of Hong Kong.* Hong Kong: Noronha and Company, 1898.

Patten, Chris. *East and West: The Last Governor of Hong Kong on Power, Freedom and the Future.* London: Macmillan, 1998.

Pearson, Veronica, and Benjamin K. Leung, eds. *Women in Hong Kong.* Hong Kong: Oxford University Press, 1995.

Pedersen, Susan. "The Maternalist Moment in British Colonial Policy: The Controversy over 'Child Slavery' in Hong Kong 1917–1941." *Past and Present* 171 (2001): 161–202.

Picturing Hong Kong: Photography 1855–1910. New York: Asia Society Galleries, 1997.

Pope-Hennessy, James. *Half-Crown Colony: A Hong Kong Notebook.* London: Jonathan Cape, 1969.

Rabushka, Alvin. *Hong Kong: A Study in Economic Freedom.* Chicago: University of Chicago Press, 1979.

Rafferty, Kevin. *City on the Rocks: Hong Kong's Uncertain Future.* London: Viking, 1989.

Roberti, Mark. *The Fall of Hong Kong: Britain's Betrayal and China's Triumph.* New York: Wiley, 1994.

Sayer, Geoffrey Robley. *Hong Kong: Birth, Adolescence, and Coming of Age, 1841–1862.* London: Oxford University Press, 1937.

———. *Hong Kong 1862–1919: Years of Discretion.* Hong Kong: Hong Kong University Press, 1975.

Schenk, Catherine R. *Hong Kong As an International Financial Centre: Emergence and Development, 1945–65.* London: Routledge, 2001.

Scott, Ian. *Political Change and the Crisis of Legitimacy in Hong Kong.* Honolulu: University of Hawaii Press, 1989.

Sinn, Elizabeth, ed. *Between East and West: Aspects of Social and Political Development in Hong Kong.* Hong Kong: Centre of Asian Studies, University of Hong Kong, 1990.

———. "Chinese Patriarchy and the Protection of Women in 19th-century Hong Kong." In Maria Jaschok and Suzanne Miers, eds., *Women and Chinese Patriarchy: Submission, Servitude, and Escape,* 141–70. Hong Kong: Hong Kong University Press, 1994.

———. "Fugitive in Paradise: Wang Tao and Cultural Transformation in Late Nineteenth Century Hong Kong." *Late Imperial China* 19(1) (1998): 56–81.

———. *Growing with Hong Kong: The Bank of East Asia, 1919–1994.* Hong Kong: Bank of East Asia, 1994.

———. *Hong Kong, British Crown Colony, Revisited* (Hong Kong: Centre of Asian Studies, University of Hong Kong, 2001).

———. *Power and Charity: The Early History of the Tung Wah Hospital, Hong Kong.* Hong Kong: Oxford University Press, 1989.

Smart, Alan. *The Shek Kip Mei Myth: Squatters, Fires and Colonial Rule in Hong Kong, 1950–1963.* Hong Kong: Hong Kong University Press, 2006.

Smith, Carl T. *Chinese Christians: Elites, Middlemen, and the Church in Hong Kong.* Hong Kong: Oxford University Press, 1985.

———. "Protected Women in Nineteenth-Century Hong Kong." In Maria Jaschok and Suzanne Miers, eds., *Women and Chinese Patriarchy: Submission, Servitude, and Escape,* 221–37. Hong Kong: Hong Kong University Press, 1994.

————. *A Sense of History: Studies in the Social and Urban History of Hong Kong.* Hong Kong: Hong Kong Educational Publishing, 1995.

Smith, Rev. George. *A Narrative of an Exploratory Visit to Each of the Consular Cities of China and to the Islands of Hong Kong and Chusan, in Behalf of the Church Missionary Society in the Years 1844, 1845, 1846.* London: Seely, Burnside and Seeley, 1847.

Snow, Philip. *The Fall of Hong Kong: Britain, China, and the Japanese Occupation.* New Haven, CT: Yale University Press, 2003.

So, Alvin Y. *Hong Kong's Embattled Democracy: A Societal Analysis.* Baltimore: Johns Hopkins University Press, 1999.

Sung, Yun-wing. *The China-Hong Kong Connection: The Key to China's Open Door Policy.* Cambridge: Cambridge University Press, 1991.

Sweeting, Anthony. *Education in Hong Kong, Pre-1841 to 1941, Fact and Opinion: Materials for a History of Education in Hong Kong.* Hong Kong: Hong Kong University Press, 1990.

————. *A Phoenix Transformed: The Reconstruction of Education in Post-War Hong Kong.* Hong Kong: Oxford University Press, 1993.

Tsai, Jung-fang. *Hong Kong in Chinese History: Community and Social Unrest in the British Colony, 1842–1913.* New York: Columbia University Press, 1993.

Tsang, Steve. *Democracy Shelved: Great Britain, China, and Attempts at Constitutional Reform in Hong Kong, 1945–1952.* Hong Kong: Oxford University Press, 1988.

————, ed. *A Documentary History of Hong Kong: Government and Politics.* Hong Kong: Hong Kong University Press, 1995.

————. *Hong Kong: An Appointment with China.* London: Tauris, 1997.

————. *A Modern History of Hong Kong.* London: Tauris, 2004.

————. "Target Zhou Enlai: The 'Kashmir Princess' Incident of 1955." *China Quarterly* 139 (September 1994): 766–82.

Tu, Elsie. *Colonial Hong Kong in the Eyes of Elsie Tu.* Hong Kong: Hong Kong University Press, 2003.

Tucker, Nancy B. *Taiwan, Hong Kong, and the United States, 1945–1992: Uncertain Friendships.* New York: Twayne and Maxwell Macmillan International, 1994.

Turnbull, C. Mary. "Hong Kong: Fragrant Harbour, City of Sin and Death." In Robin W. Winks and James R. Rush, eds., *Asia in Western Fiction,* 117–36. Honolulu: University of Hawaii Press, 1990.

Vickers, Edward. *In Search of an Identity: The Politics of History As a School Subject in Hong Kong, 1960s–2002.* New York: Routledge, 2003.

Vines, Stephen. *Hong Kong: China's New Colony.* London: Aurum, 1998.

Wang Gengwu, ed. *Xianggangshi xinbian* [Hong Kong History: New Perspectives]. 2 vols. Hong Kong: Sanlian, 1997.

Welsh, Frank. *A Borrowed Place: The History of Hong Kong.* New York: Kodansha, 1993.

Wesley-Smith, Peter. *Unequal Treaty, 1898–1997: China, Great Britain, and Hong Kong's New Territories.* Rev. ed. Hong Kong: Oxford University Press, 1997.

Wesley-Smith, Peter, and Albert H. Y. Chen, eds. *The Basic Law and Hong Kong's Future.* Hong Kong: Butterworths, 1988.

White, Barbara-Sue, ed. *Hong Kong: Somewhere between Heaven and Earth.* Hong Kong: Oxford University Press, 1996.

————. *Turbans and Traders: Hong Kong's Indian Communities.* Hong Kong: Oxford University Press, 1994.

White, Lynn, and Li Cheng. "China Coast Identities: Regional, National, and Global." In Lowell Dittmer and Samuel S. Kim, eds., *China's Quest for National Identity,* 154–93. Ithaca, NY: Cornell University Press, 1993.

Whitfield, Andrew J. *Hong Kong, Empire and the Anglo-American Alliance at War, 1941–1945.* Hong Kong: Hong Kong University Press, 2001.

Wilson, Dick. *Hong Kong! Hong Kong!* London: Unwin Hyman, 1990.

Wong, J. Y. *Anglo-Chinese Relations, 1839–1860: A Calendar of Chinese Documents in the British Foreign Office Records.* Oxford: Oxford University Press for the British Academy, 1983.

————. *Deadly Dreams: Opium, Imperialism, and the* Arrow *War (1856–1860) in China.* Cambridge: Cambridge University Press, 1998.

Wong, Siu-lun. "Deciding to Stay, Deciding to Move, Deciding Not to Decide." In Gary G. Hamilton, ed., *Cosmopolitan Capitalists: Hong Kong and the Chinese Diaspora at the End of the 20th Century,* 13–51. Seattle: University of Washington Press, 1999.

————. *Emigrant Entrepreneurs: Shanghai Industrialists in Hong Kong.* Hong Kong: Oxford University Press, 1988.

Wong Wang-chi (Wang Hongzhi). *Lishi de chenzhong: Cong Xianggang kan Zhongguo de Xianggang shi lunshu* [The Burden of History: A Hong Kong Perspective of the Mainland Discourse of Hong Kong History]. Hong Kong: Oxford University Press, 2000.

Wright, Arnold, and H. A. Cartwright, eds. *Twentieth Century Impressions of Hongkong, Shanghai, and other Treaty Ports of China: Their History, People, Commerce, Industries, and Resources.* London: Lloyds, 1908.

Wu Hao. *Huai jiu Xianggang di* [Longing for Old Hong Kong]. Hong Kong: Boyi, 1988.

Wu, Hung. "The Hong Kong Clock—Public Time-Telling and Political Time/Space." *Public Culture* 9(3) (Spring 1997): 329–54.

Xianggang kangzhan: Dongjiang zongdui gangjiu duli dadui lunwenji [The Defense of Hong Kong: Collected Essays on the Hong Kong-Kowloon Brigade of the East River Column]. Hong Kong: Hong Kong Museum of History, 2004.

Yahuda, Michael. *Hong Kong: China's Challenge.* London: Routledge, 1996.

Yang Sixian. *Xianggang cangsang* [Hong Kong Vicissitudes]. Beijing: Youyi chubanshe, 1986.

Youngson, A. J., ed. *China and Hong Kong: The Economic Nexus.* Hong Kong: Oxford University Press, 1983.

————. *Hong Kong: Economic Growth and Policy.* Hong Kong: Oxford University Press, 1982.

Yu Shengwu and Liu Cunkuan, eds. *Ershi shiji de Xianggang* [Twentieth-Century Hong Kong]. Hong Kong: Qilin shuye, 1995.

————, eds. *Shijiu shiji de Xianggang* [Nineteenth-Century Hong Kong]. Hong Kong: Qilin shuye, 1994.

Yuan Bangjian. *Xianggang shilue* [History of Hong Kong]. Hong Kong: Zhongliu chubanshe, 1993.

Zhang Xiaohui. *Xianggang Huashangshi* [History of Hong Kong Chinese Merchants]. Hong Kong: Mingbao, 1996.

Index